Traditional Magic Spells for Protection & Healing

"*Traditional Magic Spells for Protection and Healing* presents fascinating source material of magical texts, until now, only known by specialists."

BENGT AF KLINTBERG,
SWEDISH FOLKLORIST AND AUTHOR OF
SVENSKA TROLLFORMLER [SWEDISH MAGIC SPELLS]

"Claude Lecouteux's work on the topic of ancient magic spells stands out as a refreshing reminder and example of what real scholarship should be and can be. The book is eminently researched and readable: it features a substantial introduction, chapters organized by topic, several appendices, an index, and a full bibliography. It is a must-read not only for the specialists of ancient magic and medicine but also for the general public."

JACQUES E. MERCERON,
PROFESSOR EMERITUS OF FRENCH
AT INDIANA UNIVERSITY, BLOOMINGTON

Traditional Magic Spells for Protection & Healing

Claude Lecouteux

Translated by Jon E. Graham

Inner Traditions
Rochester, Vermont

Inner Traditions
One Park Street
Rochester, Vermont 05767
www.InnerTraditions.com

Copyright © 2016 by Éditions Imago
English translation copyright © 2017 by Inner Traditions International

Originally published in French under the title *Le livre des guérisons et des protections magiques* by Éditions Imago, 7 rue Suger, 75006 Paris
First U.S. edition published in 2017 by Inner Traditions

All rights reserved. No part of this book may be reproduced or utilized in any form or by any means, electronic or mechanical, including photocopying, recording, or by any information storage and retrieval system, without permission in writing from the publisher. No part of this book may be used or reproduced to train artificial intelligence technologies or systems.

Volume II
of
The Sorceror's Scholar
Collector's Edition Boxed Set

Traditional Magic Spells for Protection and Healing

Printed and bound in India by Nutech Print Services

10 9 8 7 6 5 4 3 2 1

Text design by Debbie Glogover and layout by Virginia Scott Bowman
This book was typeset in Garamond Premier Pro with Gill Sans MT Pro, Futura Std, and Myriad Pro used as display typefaces.

Inner Traditions wishes to express its appreciation for assistance given by the government of France through the National Book Office of the Ministère de la Culture in the preparation of this translation.

Nous tenons à exprimer nos plus vifs remerciements au gouvernement de la France et au ministère de la Culture, Centre National du Livre, pour leur concours dans la préparation de la traduction de cet ouvrage.

CONTENTS

	Acknowledgments	vii
Introduction	The Manner of the Cure	1
1	Diagnoses	27
2	The Illnesses of Humans and Their Cure	33
3	Evil Spells	179
4	Devils and Demons	191
5	Fantastic Beings and Spirits	202
6	Healing of Animals	212
7	Protections	222

∽

Appendix I	Medical Magic in Italy during the Fourteenth–Fifteenth Centuries	272
Appendix II	The Activities of Sorcerers	274
Appendix III	The Use of Encrypted Spells	281
Appendix IV	Superstitious Healing Methods According to Fernel	284

Appendix V	Knotting the Breeches Laces	286
Appendix VI	Several Popular Saints Invoked in France and Belgium for Illnesses and Protection	289
Appendix VII	The Protective Talismans of Balinas (Apollonius de Tyane)	291

Notes	294
Bibliography	299
Index	319

ACKNOWLEDGMENTS

I would like to extend my deepest gratitude to Monika Kropej (Zagreb), Emanuela Timotin (Bucharest), and Daiva Vaitkevičienė (Vilnius), who allowed me to take advantage of their research; Marie Dominique Leclerc and Alain Robert (Troyes), Anne Martineau (Saint-Étienne), and Gian Marco Mondino (Turin), who provided me with otherwise inaccessible documents; and Ronald Grambo (Kongsvinger), Baujke Finet van der Schaaf (Paris), Claude Thomasset (Paris), and Philippe Walter (Grenoble), who helped me solve several linguistic problems.

INTRODUCTION

THE MANNER OF THE CURE

When illness or misfortune strikes unexpectedly, it always inspires two major questions: Why? How? Human beings have responded to these questions in a variety of ways, one of the oldest of which can be found in the work of Hesiod: such woes are a punishment. This is what he writes about the myth of Pandora:

> For ere this the tribes of men lived on earth remote and free from ills and hard toil and heavy sickness which bring the Fates upon men; for in misery men grow old quickly. But the woman took off the great lid of the jar with her hands and scattered all these and her thought caused sorrow and mischief to men.[1]

But this is only one interpretation; others came before it and later coexisted with it. People have seen misfortunes as being driven by hostile powers, gods, demons, and other beings that today we call fantastic but that are reflections of folk belief, or else the result of actions by sorcerers or witches motivated by jealousy, envy, or vengeance.

One of the great figures in the fight against demons of any kind was Solomon, whose name became attached to a form of magic and even to an herb.* The historian Flavius Josephus (first century AD) tells us just what he did:

---

*It is called Solomon's seal (*Polygonatum multiflorum*) and *herbe à la forçure* in the French countryside. A *forçure* is a strain in the back, or a sprain or hernia. [*Herb à la forçure* could be translated as "sprainwort." In English this plant is also known as common Solomon's seal, David's-harp, ladder-to-heaven, Eurasian Solomon's seal, etc. —*Trans.*].

He composed such incantations also by which distempers are alleviated. And he left behind him the manner of using exorcisms; by which they drive away demons; so that they never return: and this method of cure is of great force unto this day. For I have seen a certain man of my own country, whose name was Eleazar, releasing people that were demoniacal in the presence of Vespasian, and his sons, and his Captains, and the whole multitude of his soldiers: the manner of the cure was this: he put a ring that had a root of one of those sorts mentioned by Solomon to the nostrils of the demoniack: after which he drew out the demon through his nostrils: and when the man fell down immediately, he abjured him to return into him no more: making still mention of Solomon, and reciting the incantations which he composed. And when Eleazar would persuade and demonstrate to the spectators that he had such a power, he set a little way off a cup or basin full of water, and commanded the demon, as he went out of the man, to overturn it; and thereby to let the spectators know that he had left the man. And when this was done, the skill and wisdom of Solomon was showed very manifestly. For which reason it is, that all men may know the vastness of Solomon's abilities.[2]

The Testament of Solomon,[3] an apocryphal text, lists thirty-six demons, including Artosael, who causes violent pain in the eyes;

✚ CΦΡΑΓΙC COΛOMONOC ΑΠΟΔΙΟΞΟΝ ΠΑΝ ΚΑΚΟΝ ΑΠΟ ΤΟΥ ΦΟΡΟΥΝΤΟ(ς)
Seal of Solomon, remove all evil from he who wears (you)!

Horopel, who sends boils, inflammations of the muscles, and abscesses; Kourtael, emissary of intestinal lesions; and Mardero, who induces incurable fever chills. But this notion that demons cause illness can be found much earlier among the Babylonians, who possessed all kinds of recipes for expelling them, such as the following:

> Pull up a clod of clay from the seabed
> Make from it a black statue that resembles the person you seek to heal;
> Attach to its head the fur of a white goat;
> Place the figurine on the body of the ill person.
> Recite the famous incantation of Ea.
> Turn the patient's face toward the west.
> Then the evil spirit that has seen it will go away.
> And the demon that took possession of him will disappear.[4]

According to this view of the world, the whole of Creation is inhabited by demons—sometimes planetary—and spirits. Plants and minerals are under their protection, and it is necessary to gain their help through prayers and offerings for their properties to be effective. "Sometimes the plants themselves are considered to be demons or souls of the dead returned to an earthly existence."[5] Over the centuries, Christian elements were incorporated into pagan harvesting rituals and the names of God or the saints replaced those of ancient gods and supernatural entities.

Charms show that people turned toward the pagan gods to obtain healing. In medieval Ireland, the god of medicine, Dian Cecht, was invoked for hemorrhages, burns, coughs, and tumors, and the mythic smith Goibniu appeared at the side of Jesus in a charm intended to remove a thorn.[6] In Estonia, there were the *maro-deives,* the gods of the plague. A lengthy charm found in Scandinavia lists a hodgepodge of deities: Odin, Thor, the Savior, Freyr, Freyja, and Satan![7] Then, in the course of historical development, these figures became the stuff of legend. Among the Transylvanian gypsies, for example, the king of the Loçolico—intermediary demons—and Ana, queen of the Kešalyia, the mountain fairies, had nine children representing various afflictions:

Melalo (the Dirty or Nasty One) takes possession of people and drives them mad;

Lilyi (the Muddy One), wife of Melalo, causes coughs, diarrhea, and catarrh in both animals and humans;

Tçulo (the Fat One) causes pains in the lower half of the body;

Tçaridyi (the Burning One), spouse of Tçulo, carries childbed fever;

Shilalyi (the Cold One) causes cold fevers;

Bitoso (the Faster), husband of Shilalyi, causes headaches, stomach disorders, and loss of appetite;

Lolmisho (Red Mouse) brings skin disorders;

Minceskre (the Vagina), wife of Lolmisho, is a carrier of syphilis and skin ailments;

Poreskoro (the Tailed One) is linked to plague and cholera.

CHRISTIANITY

The notion of ailments as punishment for a transgression was reasserted by the fathers of the Church, citing a passage from the Gospel of John (5:14) in which, after healing a paralytic, Jesus tells him: "Behold, thou art made whole: sin no more, lest a worse thing come unto thee."[8] And the Old Testament says: "Honor a physician with the honor due unto him for the uses which ye may have of him: for the Lord hath created him. For of the most High comes healing. . . . My son, in thy sickness be not negligent: but pray unto the Lord, and he will make thee whole."[9] For its part, the New Testament shows Jesus healing those who are paralyzed, demonic, blind, possessed, leprous, and epileptic.[10]

But the Church was forced to contend with healing practices inherited from paganism. In his book *On Christian Doctrine,* Saint Augustine (354–430) states:

> All the arrangements made by men for the making and worshipping of idols are superstitious. . . . And to this class belong, but with a bolder reach of deception, the books of the haruspices and augurs. In this class we must place also all amulets and cures which the medical art condemns, whether these consist in incantations, or in marks which they call characters, or in hanging or tying on or even dancing in a fashion certain articles, not with

reference to the condition of the body, but to certain signs hidden or manifest; and these remedies they call by the less offensive name of *physica,* so as to appear not to be engaged in superstitious observances, but to be taking advantage of the forces of nature. Examples of these are the earrings on the top of each ear, or the rings of ostrich bone on the fingers, or telling you when you hiccup to hold your left thumb in your right hand.[11]

Martin (d. 580), bishop of Braga, said it was forbidden, when gathering medicinal herbs, to use incantations;[12] in the seventh century, a sermon by the pseudo-Eligius listed the pagan practices and forbade the enchantment of simples (*herbas incantare*) and the leading of livestock over a hole dug in the ground—we recognize here a ritual for the transference of illnesses or protection against them—and the Visigothic Code condemns those who rob graves to obtain remedies.[13] In 743, the *Indiculus superstitionum et paganiarum* (Index of Superstitions and Pagan Practices), for which we have only the table of contents, devoted two chapters (10 and 11) to phylacteries and ligatures. In 813, the Council of Tours commanded priests to warn their congregations that magical arts and incantations, and amulets of bone or herbs, could not offer remedies to the illnesses of men and beasts.[14]

In 741, Saint Boniface noted that "phylacteries were even in use among the clergy," and again in the eighth century, the Homily on Sacrileges mentioned those who incant over figures, and who write and place the *caracteres** of angels or Solomon, or a serpent's tongue, around a man's neck.[15] The "characters" are understood to be secret letters (*litterae secretae*). In its sixteenth chapter, Charlemagne's capitulary known as the *Admonitio Generalis* (issued in 789) forbids using, naming, or writing the names of unknown Christians, for this is not a Christian act.[16] For their part, the church penitentials routinely repeat these prohibitions and they also turn up in the works of the Inquisition, in which it is revealed that priests used magic healing practices.[17]

Christians appealed to God, to the Christus Medicus, and to each and every prophet, apostle, and saint. Over the course of the centuries, saints

---

*The Latin term refers to written characters in the sense of "cabalistic, magical, or astrological signs or symbols" (*Webster's Second*).

became associated with certain cures,[18] which were most often connected with the form their martyrdom had taken. Because Saint Apollonia's teeth had been broken, she was invoked for toothaches, and so forth. But the prayers, or orisons, rather, often possessed only a veneer of Christianity that barely masked their pagan origin, because of the magic spells and words they contained, as well as the signs called "characters." The statement by Claude Lévi-Strauss "There is no religion without magic any more than there is any magic without at least a trace of religion,"[19] is illustrated perfectly by our corpus. It should also be noted that "every saint that is a healing specialist can also a priori send that illness. This is what is called the illness of the saint."[20] In the sixteenth century, for example, to cure all manner of ailments, the arms of the patient would be bound with a woolen cord in the name of God, and so forth, while speaking the names of the saints that healed these diseases. The cord would tighten, a sign that the spell was working, and the patient would be cured.

What remains most striking is the close structural and rhetorical kinship with the charms of classical antiquity. This reveals that we are dealing with a magical way of thinking, which is certainly not something restricted to the so-called primitive peoples. This way of thinking was condemned as superstitious by the Church, as it considered everything that was not orthodox to be pagan. Saint Augustine of Hippo, as seen earlier, associated these healing and protection practices with the worship of idols in his book *On Christian Doctrine*.

Around the year 1010, Burchard, the bishop of Worms, scolded those who used amulets or ligatures—that is to say, remedies attached to a part of the body—and incantations, especially those made over bread or plants.[21]

In his *Summa Theologica* (written between 1269 and 1272), Saint Thomas Aquinas closely examined Christian objects serving as amulets as well as the healing techniques that used ligatures:

> It would seem that it is not unlawful to wear divine words at the neck. Divine words are no less efficacious when written than when uttered. But it is lawful to utter sacred words for the purpose of producing certain effects; (for instance, in order to heal the sick), such as the "Our Father" or the "Hail Mary," or

in any way whatever to call on the Lord's name, according to Mark 16:17–18, "In My name they shall cast out devils, they shall speak with new tongues; they shall take up serpents." Therefore it seems to be lawful to wear sacred words at one's neck, as a remedy for sickness or for any kind of distress.

Further, sacred words are no less efficacious on the human body than on the bodies of serpents and other animals. Now, certain incantations are efficacious in checking serpents, or in healing certain other animals. Wherefore it is written (Psalm 58:4–5): "Their madness is according to the likeness of a serpent, like the deaf asp that stoppeth her ears, which will not hear the voice of charmers, nor of the wizard that charmeth wisely." Therefore it is lawful to wear sacred words as a remedy for men.

In every incantation or wearing of written words, two points demand caution. The first is the thing said or written, because if it is connected with invocation of the demons it is clearly superstitious and unlawful. In like manner it seems that one should beware lest it contain strange words, for fear that they conceal something unlawful. Hence Chrysostom says that "many now after the example of the Pharisees who enlarged their fringes, invent and write Hebrew names of angels, and fasten them to their persons. Such things seem fearsome to those who do not understand them." Again, one should take care lest it contain anything false, because in that case also the effect could not be ascribed to God, Who does not bear witness to a falsehood.

In the second place, one should beware lest besides the sacred words it contain something vain, for instance certain written characters, except the sign of the Cross; or if hope be placed in the manner of writing or fastening, or in any like vanity, having no connection with reverence for God, because this would be pronounced superstitious: otherwise, however, it is lawful. Hence it is written in the Decretals:[22] "In blending together medicinal herbs, it is not lawful to make use of observances or incantations, other than the divine symbol, or the Lord's Prayer, so as to give honor to none but God the Creator of all."[23]

Elsewhere, Saint Thomas states:

> There is nothing superstitious or unlawful in employing natural things simply for the purpose of causing certain effects such as they are thought to have the natural power of producing. But if in addition there be employed certain characters, words, or any other vain observances which clearly have no efficacy by nature, it will be superstitious and unlawful.[24]

Thomas condemns incantations for the reason that they most often they contain illicit practices and obtain their effectiveness from demons.

In 1496, in the *Malleus maleficarum* (Hammer of Witches), the inquisitors Jacob Sprenger and Heinrich Kramer complained that "superstitious men have invented many vain and illicit things, which they use today over the ill, both man and beast, whereas the clergy, in its sloth, no longer uses the licit words when visiting patients," and, citing Saint Augustine, they add: "Smacking of superstition are a thousand magical artifices, amulets (*ligature*), and remedies that medical science condemns, in the form of prayers, inscriptions (*caracteres*) or other things to wear hung around the neck."[25] In 1536, the Italian jurist Paulus Grillandus (born ca. 1490), whom Voltaire described as "the prototype of the Inquisition," condemned those who "manufacture notes, or letters, or amulets containing magical signs and characters, which the bewitched wear around their necks."[26] He emphasizes that "the medical art does not work in spells" (*ars medicine non operat in sortilegia*).[27]

Nor were the Protestants remiss in the criticism of magical healing methods. In 1568 *The Devil Himself* (*Der Teufel selbs*) appeared, a book by Jodocus Hocker (d. 1566), a pastor of Lemgo (Westphalia), and Hermann Hamelmann (1526–1595), a Lutheran theologian. In it they "demonstrated" that the devil can only heal illnesses by using plants whose virtues he knows thanks to his omniscience.[28]

The evidence cited thus far shows that healing and protecting meant resorting to incantations, ligatures, orisons, and signs. It also shows that the word is all-powerful. Does not Psalm 107 (106 in the Vulgate) say: "He sent his word, and healed them?" When Christ was faced with a demonic epileptic, he threatened the unclean spirit and healed the child;[29]

elsewhere he ordered the fever to leave the patient.[30] Incidentally, I would like to point out that even an image of Christ can heal.

MAGIC THERAPY

For a therapy to be magical and therefore eligible for inclusion in this book, it must contain elements that owe nothing to the remedy's chemical composition. Supernatural elements or figures must play a role. There can be a ritual concerning the application of the remedy that involves words, signs, a specific time, the invocation of God and his saints, or of pagan deities. In Christian recipes, reference is made to a past situation; this is rooted in the idea that what once worked will have the same effect today, based on the principle of analogy. Job was infested with worms on his dunghill and healed; if he is invoked while using the requisite words, then one will be healed likewise. To heal cuts, people referred to those that Christ received from the crown of thorns, and so on. In the fifth century AD, the Pseudo-Theodore noted in a charm against an as-yet-unidentified malady: "When Christ was born, all pain vanished."[31]

The role played by the word is primordial, and the Benedictine monk Leonard Vair (1540–1603) notes:

> One can cause worms to perish and stop the blood, though it may be flowing out all over, by saying certain words. . . . In short, by the utterance of any words all illnesses are expelled from the human body, wounds are cured, and the arrows that cling to the bones are removed without any pain.[32]

The clerics were not the last to offer magical treatments. The doctor Johann Weyer (1515–1588) noted that the "pastors of the churches" seduced the common folk and enticed them with "deceitful activities" that drove the ignorant populace to

> seek illicit forms of assistance in time of affliction and in sudden or chronic disease . . . . Here avails the holy water, blessed over and above God's original consecration, whether it be sprinkled on repeatedly or taken in drink. There is also the salt purified by exorcism, the fragment of a Paschal candle similarly consecrated, or a piece of incense from the Paschal candle,

Sectio II. Cap. XIII.   342

Oremus.

Domine Iesu Christe, qui voluisti pro mundi redemptione de Virgine nasci, & in carne tua sanctissima circumcidi, à Iudæis reprobari, à Iuda proditore osculo tradi, vinculis ligari, sicut agnus, innocens ad victimam duci, atq; in cõspectu Annæ, & Cayphæ, Pilati, & Herodis indecenter offerri, à falsis testibus accusari, flagellis, & opprobrijs vexari, & spinis coronari, & sputis conspui, colaphis cædi, palmis, & arundine percuti, flagellis verberari, in Cruce clauis affigi, inter latrones deputari, & lancea vulnerari: tu Domine per has sanctissimas pænas, quas indignus sacerdos recolo, per crucem, & passionem tuam libera populum istum, & nos ab ista peste, & pænis Inferni, à quibus liberasti Latronem tecum crucifixum. Qui cum Patre &c.

26. Quorsum ergo citra superstitionem, seu cum fructu aliquo spirituali, quod idem est, ponitur illa litera Marginalis, quandoquidem, quidquid illa implicite importat, vel innuit, totum id exprimitur in versu illi respondente? Quid gratu Deo directe, vel indirecte inducere, fingi possit? Quid in membrana exaratio? Quid ad brachiũ potius, quam ad colum, quam ad caput, quam ad pectus circumportatio? QuidOrationis, finita potiusMissa, quam ante inchoatam, recitatio, cõtra ea, quæ in simili hac sect.cap 8. n. præsertim 34. obijciebamus? Sola superest Illustrissimorum insinuata authoritas; si forsan propositam hanc cæremoniam modo aliquo, saltem tacite, idest non reprobando, approbarunt, de quo mihi nihil constat. Nihilominus, quia eorum nomina, præ reuerentia debita, sunt ipso pene timenda sono, neque ego interim reprobo, neque approbo.

Manuel do Vale de Moura, *De incantationibus seu ensalmis* (1620): a "superstitious" orison.

or the burning of candles blessed on the Day of Purification again the "cowering" (if you please!) demon. They also use the fumes of fronds and branches consecrated on Palm Sunday, and those of herbs hung outside the house on the feast of St. John the Baptist or sprinkled with holy water on the feast of the Assumption of the Blessed Virgin.[33]

Therapeutic rituals were accompanied by phrases taken from the Holy Scriptures, which makes it easy to see how Christian magic came to substitute for the pagan magic of antiquity. Johann Weyer points out several practices deserving of notice:

For example, there is the hallowed prophecy that Christ's bones are not to be broken by Jews: You will not break a bone of him [Exodus 12:46; John 19:36]. If one pronounces these words while touching his teeth during the Mass, the pain of a toothache is supposedly allayed. Another person washes his hands along with the patient before the access of fever while secretly reciting the Psalm "I will exalt you, my God, my King" [Psalms 145:1 (144:1 Vulgate)] in order to cure the fever. Then there is the man who takes the hand of the person laboring with disease and says: "May this fever be as easy for you to bear as the birth of Christ was for the Virgin Mary" (*Aeque facilis tibi febris haec sit, atque Mariae virginis Christi partus*). . . . For stanching the flow of blood, some persons take a measure of cold water and add three drops of flowing blood, saying the Lord's Prayer and the Hail Mary before each drop. Then they give this mixture to the patient to drink, asking, "Who will help you?" And the response is given, "Holy Mary." Then they add, "Holy Mary, stay this flowing blood" (*Sancta Maria hunc sanguinem firma*).[34]

Weyer adds: "And certain superstitious monks countered fevers by hanging a piece of paper on the person's neck and ordering him to spout forth certain prayers at each onset of the fever, and then—after the third onset—to be of good hope."[35]

By condemning these practices, the Church has provided us with information. Leonard Vair, for example, says this concerning the harvesting of simples:

> Finally, one is deceiving oneself when superstitiously addressing his orison to inanimate things, as do those who gather herbs while saying several Psalms and other prayers, which, if they are addressed to herbs, are said in vain, given that the herbs cannot hear them; and if they direct them toward some celestial intelligence, or to God, or to the Angels, or to some Demon, if it is to God, it therefore follows that they are praying to him to give a greater virtue to natural things than he did at the beginning when he created the world, and that he would thereby be performing miracles needlessly.[36]

Paulus Grillandus, Tractatus de hereticis et sortilegijs *(Lyon, 1541):
various methods used by healers.*

For healing purposes, magicians and even priests used in their conjuration "barbarous names and characters," psalms they read backward, and certain orisons. Paulus Grillandus cites the use at the devil's instigation of shrouds, shirts, eggs, bones, feathers, wolf teeth, eagle beaks, beaver nails, rooster crests, waxen images that are mistreated and stuck with pins, the Ave Maria, the Pater Noster, the Credo, religious Hosts, and so forth.[37]

Johann Weyer likewise reproduces a recipe that he "transcribed from the book of a priest":

> Take three measures of violet-oil, stand facing the East before sunrise, say the name of the stricken man and of his mother, and invoke the angels of glory who stand in the sixth rank. Do this three times daily for seven days. On the seventh day, let the

man stand naked in the sunlight, and let his flesh be anointed all over with the oil. Then in the rays of the sun let him be perfumed with myrrh and frankincense and choice aromas. Then inscribe the names of these angels of honor upon a plate of silver which has been perfumed with aromatic incense, and hang it about the man's neck. If this is done on the twentieth day of the month, the person afflicted by witchcraft will be cured.[38]

"Healers," whether they were sorcerers, mages, or priests, or simply common folk with some knowledge, went by diverse names and worked in a variety of ways. In 1536 Paulus Grillandus called their actions healing spells (*sortilegia sanativa*) and underscored his assertion, as we saw earlier, that "the medical art does not work at all in spells," with *spell* here meaning "all methods that were not recognized by the medical profession and the Church."

The Jesuit priest Martin Delrio (1551–1608) indicates that "all these ecclesiastical remedies do not always have effect no matter their effectiveness, nor are men always delivered from the ambushes and evil spells of the demons by means of them," and he explains the failure of orison-based therapies as follows: "It seems to me that there are two principal causes: one the sins of the bewitched, or of those providing the medicine, primarily when they place superstition within it or because they are lacking in faith and hope; the other, some greater good of the ill or bewitched individual."[39]

But clerics were not the only ones to assume the duties of healer, and Delrio adds "in Spain there are folk called Saviors (*Saludadores*) or Enchanters (*Ensalmadores, Santiguadores*) who heal the ill with certain orisons they recite for them and over them. The Saviors heal them with their saliva and their breath."[40] Italian soldiers healed wounds by touching the shrouds applied to them, which was called the Art of Saint Anselm. In France, it was believed that the seventh son of a duly wed couple, as long as the succession of children was not interrupted by the birth of a daughter, could heal tertian and quartan fevers as well as scrofula, after he had fasted for three or nine days before touching the patient. In the nineteenth century, French healers held a variety of titles, such as "bandagers of secrets," with the specific names varying by region.

The condemnation of heterodox methods of healing has traveled through the centuries into modern legislation. An edict by the French king Louis XIV, recorded in parliament on August 31, 1682, says this:

> The execution of the ordinances of the kings, our predecessors, against those calling themselves fortune-tellers, magicians, or sorcerers, having been neglected for a great while and this laxity having attracted into our realm several of these impostors, it has arrived that, under the pretext of horoscopes and divination, and by means of tricks, spells, so-called magic, and other similar illusions, which these kind of people customarily make use of, these imposters have caught unawares many ignorant and credulous people who unwittingly engaged with them, while passing from vain curiosities to superstitions and from superstitions to impious and sacrilegious acts.

A European Union regulation (no. 1924/2006), that went into effect on December 14, 2012, stipulates that "healers, faith healers, naturopaths . . . and other professions of alternative medicine do not have the authority to claim that their natural products, or treatments, provide relief, benefit, powers, positive properties to health nor make any allusion to a potential cure." The health code defines the illegal exercise of medicine in its article L.4161-1, and the law has regularly convicted sorcerers, healers, and bonesetters.

DIAGNOSIS

Before all else, the healer, whether a doctor or magician, sought to learn if the patient would die or not. One of the clever methods for determining this was called the Circle of Petosiris, which is also known as the Sphere of either Apuleius or Democritus. The diagnoser added together the numerals corresponding to the letters of the alphabet forming the patient's name, then added to the result the day of the moon when the patient fell ill. The sum total would be divided by 29, the average among the various ways of estimating the duration of the lunar orbit; then the diagnoser looked to see in which of the circle's (or sphere's) six compartments the number equivalent to the final result would be found. The upper half of the circle was that of life, and it was divided into three compartments. If the resulting number was in the first compartment, the healing would be quick; if it was in the second, it would be slower; and in the third, even slower. The lower half, that of death, also contained three compartments: death will be quick if the number is in the first compartment, later in the second, and even later in the third.[41]

Folk medicine developed other means of prognosticating with the help of blood, lard, eggs, or urine. I will provide a number of examples in chapter 1.

THE OPINION OF MEDIEVAL AND SIXTEENTH-CENTURY DOCTORS

In his treatments the physician Arnaldus de Villa Nova (1238/1240–1311) was receptive to strange recipes, folk-medicine spells, and empiric remedies. He wrote three treatises on magic. In the treatise on ligatures (*De physicis ligaturis*), he responded to the question: "Can incantations, talismans, and conjurations help the physician?" In his *Exposition of Dreams* (*Tractatus expositionum visionum*), a treatise on oneiromancy explaining how dreams can be useful in medicine, Arnaldus's classification of the different visions was based on the twelve celestial houses; and in *Contra maleficia* (*Opera* III), a text that is most likely apocryphal, the various types of evil spells and their remedies are set out. Astrology, the physiology of the macrocosm, dominates the movements of the human body, and Arnaldus devotes much space to astrological medicine in his *Capitula astrologiae*. He tells us that all the elementary movements, both those of our atmosphere and those of our body, are due to the modifications that the astral fluid receives from planetary activity. By traveling through the signs of the zodiac, the planets assume a special nature. Furthermore, their reciprocal reactions are constantly changing. In the *melothesia* of the zodiac—the view that the signs of the zodiac correspond to the parts of the human body—the rule "consists of stretching, so to speak, the human body over the unfurled circle of the zodiac, by placing the head over Aries and the feet over Pisces."[42] Behind all this lies the extremely ancient belief in man as microcosm.

Also attributed to Arnaldus de Villa Nova is the healing of Pope Boniface VIII's kidney stone by means of seals, and a treatise on the

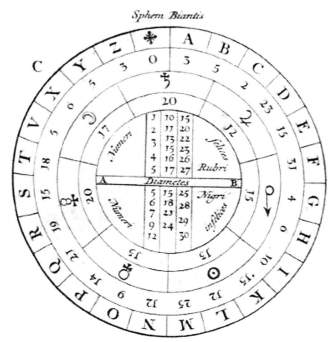

Circle of Petosiris *(top)*; Sphere of Bians *(bottom)*.

latter, *De sigillis,* which presents twelve of them, one for each sign of the zodiac. For example, the seal of Aries is good for demoniacs, manias, anginas, and so forth; that of Libra is good for blood diseases and kidney pains; while that of Taurus is effective against eye afflictions, and pains of the neck and throat. In short, it contains the therapeutic effects deriving from a zodiac-based *melothesia,* combined with astral and religious elements, for example, phrases taken from the Bible.

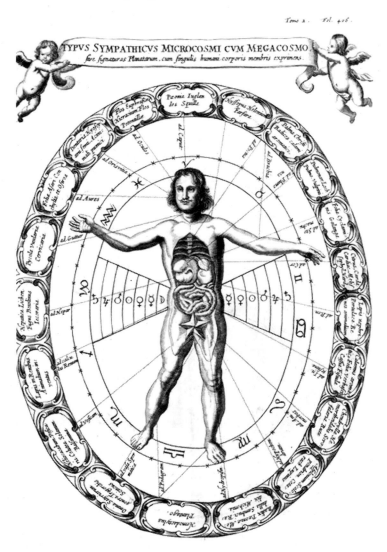

The Zodiacal Man according to Athanasius Kircher (1601/1602–1680).

Agrippa von Nettesheim, *De occulta philosophia,* in *Opera,* vol. 1 (Lyon, n.d.).

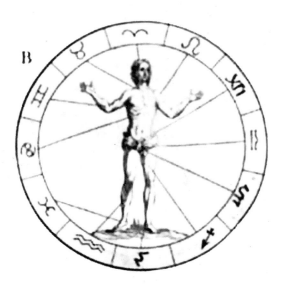

Pierre Lebrun, *Superstitions anciennes et modernes . . .*
(Amsterdam, Jean Frédéric Bernard, 1733).

Arnaldus de Villa Nova, *Opera* (Lyon, 1509):
the beginning of his treatise on seals.

Another physician, Bernard de Gordon (thirteenth–fourteenth century), also established a connection between the human being and the zodiac: Aries rules the neck and head; Taurus the neck and shoulders; Cancer the chest; Gemini the lungs and arms; Leo the heart and stomach; and Virgo the navel and its neighboring parts. Libra, meanwhile, governs the hips, kidneys, and "sensitive natures"; Scorpio rules the womb, penis, testicles, and peritoneum; Sagittarius, the muscles of the thighs; Capricorn, the knees; Aquarius, the legs; and Pisces, the feet.[43]

For Paracelsus (1493–1541), when using plants for remedies, it is necessary to take into consideration their harmony on the one hand with the constellations, and on the other hand with the parts of the body and the diseases, each star attracting, by a kind of magic virtue, the plant with which it shares an affinity and which forms part of its activity in such a way that plants are, strictly speaking, so many sublunary stars.[44] A bleeding should never be performed on just any day, as the astral conjunctions can have a helpful or harmful influence over this operation: "Barbers have almanacs indicating the dates when bleeding is particularly favorable and those when they would expose one to accidents."[45]

In 1583, Leonard Vair noted that "enchanters have gotten accustomed to not only exercising their charms with the help of the imagination, sight, touch, and voice, but also of summoning and involving the sky and heavenly bodies in order to give them greater effectiveness and potency; to do this, they have reduced the number of all the afflictions and disorders of man to seven, so that they respond to and have some sympathy with the seven planets. . . . With this, they divide the human body into twelve parts that necessarily respond and are subject to the twelve signs of the zodiac."[46]

The alchemist and physician Giambattista della Porta (ca. 1535–1615) developed his analogical theory in his *Phytognomonica* (1560).[47] According to this theory, by attributing to each plant one certain shape and way of being instead of another one, the Creator sought to alert human beings that in a given plant, and in accordance with its analogies with the body, resided the properties necessary for healing. In this way, to halt bleeding, one used the red root of the tormentilla, red roses, or bloodstone. For scrofula, people used *Scrophularia nodosa* (figwort), which earned its name because its stem has nodules similar

Goutweed *(Aegopodium podagraria)*.

to those in scrofulous afflictions. The folk names of plants reflect what is known as the "medicine of signatures" and indicates what they are good for: herb for the liver, herb for the spleen (*Asplenium scolopendrium* or *Scolopendrium officinale*), herb for ringworm (*Tussilago petasites*), the herb for gout sufferers (goutweed, *Aegopodium podagraria*), and so on.

CURIOSITIES IN HEALING PRACTICES

Jean Fernel [Johannis Fernelii Ambiani] (1497–1558), one of the most famous doctors of his time, gives us a small panorama of the healing and protection methods used in seventeenth-century France: applying the entrails of a wolf or living duck on the belly to cure colic, fish ossicles for stones, eating the warm heart of a still-living pigeon for intermittent fevers, and so on.⁴⁸ Antoine Mizauld (1510–1578), Marguerite de Valois's doctor and astrologer, also recorded some curious remedies like healing wens by rubbing them with an item of clothing from a hangman who has just performed an execution.⁴⁹ But these kinds of remedies were not new, and Saint Bernardine of Siena (1380–1444) earlier made note of several singular remedies such as touching one's teeth with the tooth of a hanged man or a dead man's bone when hearing the bells of holy Saturday to cure a toothache; to pass children through the roots of hollow oak trees to heal them of certain diseases; and for countering gout cramps (an ancient term for cramps), one should wear a ring made at the moment when the Passion of Our Lord was being recited.⁵⁰ We should note that Jean-Baptiste Thiers (1636–1703), the parish priest of Champrond, similarly collected a good number of strange recipes, several examples of which follow:

> Scarify the gums with one of the teeth of a person who died a violent death to heal toothache. At night drink the water of a fountain in the burnt skull of a dead man, to free oneself from the falling sickness. Make pills from the testes of a hanged man to cure oneself of the bites from a rabid dog. Pierce the roof of the house of a woman in labor with a stone, or an arrow that has been used to kill three animals, to wit, a man, a boar, and a female bear, to make her give birth immediately: this will occur more assuedly when the house has been pierced with the ax or sabre of a soldier that has been torn from a man's body before it hits the ground. . . . With the hands of several people that have died prematurely heal scrofula, the glands that grow around the ears, and sore throats, just by touching them. During the onset of tertian fever, drink three times from a new pot, equal amounts each time, of water from three different wells mixed together, and next throw out the rest. To heal quartan fever, wrap a piece of a nail from the Cross in wool and tie it around the neck.⁵¹

MAGICAL PROTECTION

The sorcerer and witch (*sortiarius, caragius, sortiaria*), enchanter and enchantress (*incarminator, incantator, incantatrix*), hexer (*maleficus*), and deceiver (*praestigiator*), masters of diabolical illusion (*praestigium*), poisoner (*venefica*), and botanist (*herbaria*) all knew the virtues of simples (*herbipotens*). It has always been believed that men and women, in service to demons, could—driven by jealousy or the spirit of vengeance—bring you misfortune by attacking your health or property. The Salic Law (fifth–sixth century) devotes an emendation to evil spells made with herbs and utilizing ligatures.[52] In 650, the Council of Rouen mentioned those who "uttered diabolical charms over bread, herbs, or abominable bandages and hid them in the forks of trees or at the crossroads."[53] Every animal or individual who passed by that way would be bewitched. The Visigothic Code condemns the *malefici* and those who cause storms (*emissores tempestatum*) that will destroy the harvests,[54] and in 858, Agobard, bishop of Lyon, analyzed the actions of the storm bringers in the *Book Against the False Opinions Concerning Hail and Thunder*.[55] Confronted by these multiple threats, people resorted to magic and religion, which commingled in an astonishing syncretism. Protection is essential, as our ancestors believed that sorcerers "harmed and caused the death of others (human beings), not only those of their species, however, by simply their gaze, and others by their breath, and some by their touch."[56]

Once one has discovered the recipes and rituals of protection, one finds oneself more or less in the domain of amulets and phylacteries[57]—in other words, preparations, or more specifically objects, that are reputed to form an obstacle to any attack on one's person or property. They often are spells that one attaches to one's person, hides in one's clothing, or even wears on the skin; and there is a whole group of verbs that describe this.[58] The difference between protection and healing recipes is often negligible. Writing seems to be the preferred medium for the former, whereas the latter are essentially based in speech: the individual speaks or recites charms and orisons, and follows a specific ritual.[59] When plants are involved, the manner in which they are picked, the time they are harvested, and the aspect of the heavens at that moment play a decisive role. For example, the plant should be picked with the thumb and ring finger of the left hand before sunrise, or during the waning moon, while speaking certain phrases aloud. If a stone is used, it should be carved with a specific figure at a precise moment, which is the sole means of causing a magical property to descend into it that is most often connected to the heavenly bodies.[60]

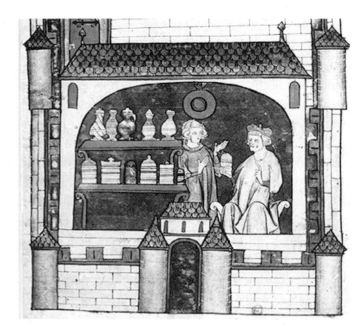

Thirteenth-century apothecary.

Doctors at work, thirteenth century.

THE TRANSMISSION OF HEALING AND PROTECTION PRACTICES

The history of healing and protection recipes is one that has been lost in the depths of time. They were initially passed on by word of mouth, among initiates, before being committed to writing, which is the form in which they have been preserved for us today. The vectors of transmission were medical treatises and pharmaceutical codices,[61] the medicinaries and antidotaries (medieval collections of medicinal recipes), herbals like that of the Pseudo-Apuleius (fourth century),[62] and the lapidaries (treatises dealing with gems).[63] These scholarly works gradually became receptive to the practices of magicians. In the fourth century, the physician Marcellus of Bordeaux[64] noted in this way numerous magical recipes that ranged from the wearing of certain plants as amulets to reducing diagrams: a word is taken and its letters are subtracted one by one, with the idea that the illness will similarly shrink thanks to this process. *The Book of Cyranides* (*Liber Kyranidorum*), a twelfth-century copy of a Greek original that survives only in a version from the fifteenth-century, probably offers the best evidence of the syncretic merger of empirical and magical elements.

Magic remedies are noted almost everywhere, in the margins of manuscripts when white spaces were available, and even in the collections of monastic medicine. Saint Hildegard of Bingen, for example, had no hesitation about transcribing them into her *Physica*. Evidence for their diffusion comes in the form of the *mesnagiers* or *Hausbücher,* domestic books in which the head of the household recorded everything that might prove useful to him.

From the fifteenth century onward, with the proliferation of books due to the printing press, the mass of available information was significantly increased. Information on magical remedies begins to appear in critical treatises on heresies and superstitions. The debate—which had been initiated long before—on the licit or illicit nature of certain therapies hits its full stride, and several major names emerge at this time. These include the inquisitors Jacob Sprenger and Heinrich Kramer with their *Malleus maleficarum* (1496); the Italian jurist Paulus Grillandus with his *Tractatus de hereticis et sortiliegijs* (Treatise on Heretics and Evil Spells, 1536); the Jesuit Martin Delrio with *Les Controverses et*

Recherches magiques (Magical Controversies and Studies, 1611); and Leonard Vair, who became bishop of Pozzuoli, with his treatise on enchantment, *De fascino libri tres* (1583). The list is quite long and it continues with various treatises on superstitions, both anonymous and otherwise.

The value of the texts I have assembled and translated here, and whose study falls into the area of the history of mentalities and cultural anthropology, is to provide us with an abundance of information on the life and fears of human beings, on their most common miseries, and on their vision of the world. They therefore deserve to be known, and not just to a limited circle of specialists. My book covers two thousand years of the history of magical remedies and protection. I have not repeated those that were presented in my *Book of Grimoires*,[65] in order to further expand the perspective and to demonstrate the existence of a form of thought that is still alive and well today, as many recent studies can testify.

NOTE ON THIS EDITION

I have arranged the recipes by subject area, but some of them are multivalent and could fall under several headings. I have therefore classified them in accordance with the dominant theme. Each prescription is accompanied by various pieces of information—language, date, country (for the post-medieval testimonies), source, and further references (full citations are found in the bibliography). A brief commentary (in italics) is provided when deemed necessary.

The Latin texts are often quite inaccurate; cacography and solecisms abound, and many of the terms do not appear in dictionaries. In order to clarify matters, I have had to resort to the lexicons of the Middle Ages.[66] Despite everything, uncertainties remain and they are indicated with a question mark. I have respected the spelling of the more recent texts. Each prescription is followed by its reference.

The symbol 📖 refers to the modern edition of the text and the studies devoted to it.

CHAPTER 1

DIAGNOSES

Before initiating a therapy of any kind, trials are made in order to know if the remedies will be effective. Legends even developed, such as that of the European lark called a calander (caladrius): if the bird is held over a sickbed and turns away from the ailing person, this indicates the patient will die. Here are some examples of these curious experiments that often turned to magic.

1 ◆ An Amulet to Relieve All Pain

According to the Magi, a tick taken from the left ear of a dog and worn as an amulet relieves all pain. They can also take omens from it on matters of life and death. For if the patient answers the individual who brings the tick and who has questioned him about his ailment while standing at the foot of the bed, then there is no fear that he will die; while, if to the contrary, he does not answer, he will be sure to succumb to his disease. They add that the dog with the left ear from which the tick is taken should be entirely black.

📖 Latin, first century. Pliny, *Historia naturalis,* XXX, 82–83.

2 ◆ To Learn If a Man Will Live or Die

If you wish to know if an ill man shall die or not, place some of his urine in a vase and add some drops of the milk of a woman nursing a boy with black hair. If you see that the milk stays at the surface, he will die, but if the milk mixes with the urine, the patient has a chance to get better. If it is a woman who is ill, take the milk of a woman who is nursing a girl.

 📖 France, thirteenth century. Coulon, *Curiosités de l'histoire des remèdes,* 70, no. 80.

3 ◆ To Learn If a Patient Will Be Healed or Not

Take an egg that was laid the same day the illness made its appearance and write on the shell: † *ygo.s ff. x ; g. y. x. g. 9.* Next place the egg outside overnight in the open air. Then break the shell. If blood comes out, the patient will die; if there is not any trace of blood, he will get better.

The manuscripts offer several variants of the spell, such as this one:

+ d + w go |||| d ✠ et go ✠ *s.. pp.. p.. x.. g.. v.. x. 9.*

 📖 Latin, thirteenth century. London, British Library, Sloane 9550, fol. 233v; Paris, Bibliothèque nationale, nouvelle acquisition française 10034, fol. 34.

4 ◆ To Know If a Man Is Going to Die

If you wish to know whether a man is going to die or not when he is sick, place his urine in a container and have a woman nursing a male child pour some of her milk into it. If you see the milk floating, he will die; if it blends with the urine, he will most likely be healed.

From the eleventh to twelfth centuries onward, uroscopy was one of the primary means for detecting illnesses before making a diagnosis, and there are a large number of treatises on this subject. One of them was even inserted in the Garden of Health (Hortus Sanitatus *[Strasbourg: Johann Prüss, 1497]) by Johannes de Cuba.*

 📖 Middle French, thirteenth century. Cambrai, Bibliothèque municipale, MS 351, fol. 174.

 📖 Moulinier, "La science des urines de Maurus de Salerne et les *Sinthomata magistri Mauri* inédits." Also by Moulinier, *L'Uroscopie au Moyen Âge.*

5 ◆ To Know If a Patient Shall Heal or Not

Take lard and rub it on the sole of his feet, then toss the lard to a dog. If he eats it, the patient shall recover; if not, he shall die.

 📖 Latin, circa 1300. London, British Library, Sloane 146, fol. 85v.

6 ◆ To Know If a Patient Will Die

If you wish to know whether a patient will die or not, write these letters

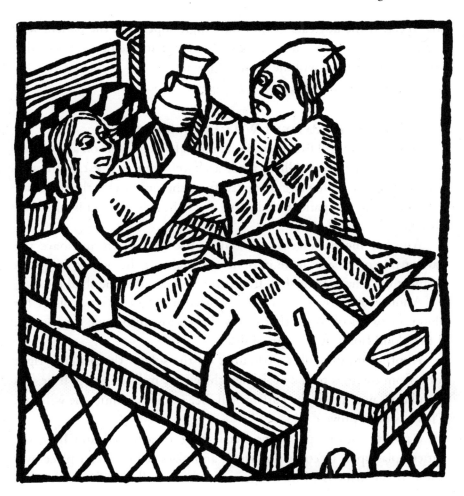

Uroscopy, 1483.

on a laurel leaf and place it on his foot. If the patient speaks, he shall live; if not, he will die.

G b o p o o S D

📖 Provençal, thirteenth century. Cambridge, Trinity College, MS R 14.30, fol. 147v.

7 ◆ To Know If a Patient Will Survive

Some doctors have performed a certain experiment: they take smoked lard and rub it over the soles of the patient's feet; they then give it to a dog to eat. If the dog eats it, they have high hopes that the patient will recover; if the dog does not want it, they come to the opposite conclusion, and the patient will die no matter what.

📖 Germany, 1750. Staricius, *Grimoire*, 387.

8 ◆ To Know If a Patient Will Live or Die

To know if a man will live or die, write the following letters on an egg that was laid the same day the illness made itself known: †. q. p. x. t. g. y. h. and place the egg in a safe place protected from the sun; peel it the next day; if it is healthy the patient shall live, if not he will die. This has been proven.

Another means: place a stalk of nettle in a basin and have the patient piss on it, and leave it alone overnight. If the nettles are green the next day, the patient shall live; if they have wilted, he shall die.

Another means: when a man is bleeding from a vein, collect his blood on an ear of wheat that you will then toss into some clear water; if the blood floats, it is a sign of death.

Another means: rub a little milk on the sole of the patient's right foot, from the toes to the heel, then throw the milk to a dog; if he eats it and does not vomit, the patient will die, and if he vomits, he will live. This has been proven.

Another means: put some nettle root in a urinal and have the patient piss upon it; cover the urinal and place it in a secret place over night. If the urine is white in the morning, he will die; if it is green, he will be healed.

📖 French, beginning of the fourteenth century. Paris, Bibliothèque nationale, MS Lat. 8654 B.

9 ◆ To Know How a Patient Is Feeling

While holding some verbena in your hand, ask the patient how he is feeling. If he answers, "all right," it is a sign that he will remain alive in his bed; if he says, "I do not feel well," there is no hope that he will remain alive.

📖 Middle High German, Speyer, 1456. Berlin, Staatsbibliothek Codex mgf 817, fol. 41r; Floridus, *De viribus herbarum*, vv. 1859–1902; Gubernatis, *La Mythologie des plantes*, vol. 2, 367.

10 ❖ To Know If a Patient Is Promised to Death

Once you have come close to the patient, if you wish to know whether he will die or live, take a drop of his blood and put it in water. If it does not become diluted and if it falls to the bottom, he will get better. In the contrary case, the patient is promised to death.

📖 Low German, 1487. Royal Library of Stockholm, MS X, 114, fol. 63r–v.

11 ❖ To Know If a Wounded Man Will Recover

To learn if a wounded man shall recover, make him drink some chervil juice and wine; if he vomits, he will die; otherwise, he will live.

📖 Middle French, early fourteenth century. Meyer, "Recettes médicales en français," 364.

12 ❖ To Know When a Patient Will Heal

Every patient will heal on a certain day if it corresponds to the day he fasts. You should cook seven small loaves of bread and give each one the name of one of the days of the week. The patient should not know about this. He will choose a loaf of bread: if it is marked with a Tuesday, he should fast that day on bread and water; then Wednesday the following week, Thursday on the third week, and so on until he has fasted seven days. If he has stumbled upon the good small loaf, he will get better or die in the course of these seven weeks. If he stumbles upon the small loaf marked Friday, he should fast for nine Fridays.

📖 Romania, nineteenth century. Schullerus, *Rumänische Volksmärchen*, 45–46.

13 ❖ To Know Whether a Patient Shall Live or Die

Various are the judgments that many make on whether a patient will live or die; but I will publish this present infallible sign, one that can serve each and let him come to a form decision. Take a nettle and place it in the patient's urine, incontinent after the patient has made it, and so that it shall not be contaminated at all, and leave the nettle in said urine for the space of twenty-four hours; and after if the nettle is found dry, it is a sign of death; and if it is found green, it is a sign of life.

This way of proceeding is so close to the one cited above, that it is possible to imagine a scholarly transmission.

📖 France, sixteenth century. *Petit Albert,* from the section of this grimoire called "Wondrous secrets, which should be taken and made up under the influence of the stars in order to cure in a short time the infirmities mentioned above," 255.

📖 Floridus, *De viribus herbarum,* vv. 115–60.

14 ◆ To Know If a Patient Will Die

Place an emerald over the heart of a seriously ill individual; if he is destined to die, the stone will shatter into pieces. This is a proven fact.

📖 Denmark, nineteenth century. Peuckert, "Die Egyptischen Geheimnisse," 85. See also Fühner, "Lithotherapie," and Daems, "Edelsteine in der Medizin, Die Drei." For more on emerald, see Lecouteux, *A Lapidary of Sacred Stones,* 296–300.

15 ◆ Prognosis of Typhoid Fever

Take some large live slugs and have them crawl over the patient's belly; if the slugs die, the patient's death is certain.

📖 France, nineteenth century. Cabanès and Barraud, *Remèdes de bonne femme,* 160.

CHAPTER 2
THE ILLNESSES OF HUMANS AND THEIR CURE

The treatments of illnesses that I am presenting here reflect an unusual blend of folk traditions and scholarly traditions, with the one type ceaselessly crossing over into the other. A profound syncretism marks the recipes whose pagan origins cannot be denied despite their Christian garb. Disorders of the body and external attacks, mainly by means of invisible arrows, illnesses are battled by all means available: plants, minerals, bodily substances, to which are added orisons, conjurations, exorcisms, and spells of banishment and execration. The recipes are interspersed with commands: Leave! Flee! Go away! and so forth, with threats—I am going to . . . —and appeals to God and his saints for their help, or to a pagan deity. In them we find reference to numerous mythical situations or narratives (historiolae) and analogy, introduced by "just as" or "like." Jesus and Mary are ceaselessly featured in the charms based on the theme of meeting: the saints know how to bind illnesses.

In an edifying tale (exemplum) passed down by a fifteenth-century manuscript, God even grants to each plant growing by the foot of a statue of Jesus the power of restoring health to the ill.[1] A miniature from the Chants royaux (Royal Songs) of Rouen (1519–28) depicts Christ as an apothecary prescribing remedies for Adam and Eve.

Diseases do not always correspond to the modern diagnoses because medieval texts make a disproportionate use of terms like gout *or* fever.

Christ the Apothecary, miniature from the *Chants royaux* of Rouen.

📖 Deroux, *Maladie et Maladies dans les textes latines et médiévaux*; Campbell, Hall, and Klausner, eds., *Health, Disease, and Healing in Medieval Culture*.

ABSCESS, TUMOR

16 ◈ Against a Weeping Abscess

Place lettuce or plantain leaves over the abscess; then throw them into running water several hours later, while saying:

> *God and the abscess were fighting*
> *God won, the abscess disappeared.*
> *In the name of . . . , and so forth.*

📖 Transylvanian Saxons, nineteenth century. Schuster, *Siebenbürgisch-sächsische Volkslieder*, 306.

17 ❖ For an Abscess of the Foot
Plunge the afflicted foot into running water and with the healthy foot on the bank say: "Our Lord Jesus Christ passed over the bridge, the malevolent abscess bit his foot. Evil abscess, fall into the river! Jesus, my lord, heal my foot!"

📖 Transylvanian Saxons, nineteenth century. Schuster, *Siebenbürgisch-sächsische Volkslieder,* 306.

18 ❖ A Spell for an Abscess of the Foot
Make the sign of the cross and say: "I am removing you from here and putting you into the earth where you will cook and die. If you do not disappear, I will cut you with a knife and tear you off."

📖 Romania, nineteenth century. Schullerus, *Rumänische Volksmärchen,* 44.

19 ❖ A Spell for an Abscess
Three virgins are approaching my hands. One has red shoes, red stockings, a red cover, a red brooch, red gloves, and a red shawl. The second has a yellow cover, a yellow brooch, a yellow headscarf, yellow gloves, yellow shoes, and a yellow apron. The third has a white cover, a white brooch, a white headscarf, white shoes, and white stockings. Leave! Leave my hands!

The colors mentioned refer to the three stages of coloration in an abscess. The three virgins are supernatural beings who started appearing in the fourth century and were Christianized into the Three Marys.

📖 Latvia, nineteenth century. Bartels, "Über Krankheits-Beschwörungen," 30; Trümpy, "Similia similibus."

20 ❖ To Get Rid of a Tumor
Repeat the following phrase:

> Flee, tumor! Flee, tumor! May all evil flee! Wherever you are coming from, stay there! Here you will be pulled and torn apart, nothing good will befall you here! Over there's your home, sleep there! Perkons will hunt you with his nine sons. Disappear like the waning moon, like an old puffball,* like the dew.

---

*[This refers to a fungus, the common Lycoperdon. —*Trans.*]

This charm makes an appeal to the god of thunder, Perkunas (Perun), who was also invoked against chest pains.

📖 Latvia, nineteenth century. Bartels, "Über Krankheits-Beschwörungen," 22.

AFFLICTION

21 ❖ Against a Dark Mood

If someone is dark of mood and cannot find rest because of his pains and grief, he should place in his bed mandrake that he has soaked in water for one day and night, so that it will reheat from his sweat and he should say: "God who created man from silt without pain, as this silt has now passed to the other side, place next to me this same silt, as you have created it, so that it might bring me peace."

📖 Latin, twelfth century. Hildegard von Bingen, *Physica*, I, 56, "On the Mandrake"; Camus, *L'Opera salernitana "Circa instans" ed il testo primitive del "Grant herbier en francoys,"* no. 299; Platearius, *Livre des simples médecines*, vol. 2, 203, chap. 279; Gubernatis, *La Mythologie des plantes*, vol. 2, 213–17.

ANGINA (SORE THROAT)

22 ❖ Against a Sore Throat

While fasting, one charms the patient, who is also fasting, while holding the spot stricken by the illness with three fingers: the thumb, the middle finger, and the ring finger, while saying: "Disappear, it you were born today, if you were born sooner, it you have emerged this day, if you emerged sooner. This illness and disorder, this pain of the tonsils, this swelling of the abscess in the throat, by this charm I expel them from the throat, I make them leave, by this charm, I eradicate from these limbs, from this marrow."

Oddly enough, the use of these three fingers can be seen again in a nineteenth-century Swedish charm for stopping bleeding. One should keep in mind that the ring finger is called digitus medicinalis.

📖 Latin, fourteenth century. Marcellus, *De medicamentis liber*, 15.11.

23 ❖ Against Angina and Pains of the Throat

Blended with an equal weight of myrrh the ashes of a young swallow burned alive will heal wonderfully if you proceed carefully, which is to say if you first introduce a finger [into the throat] then rub it with a feather; one also blows the powder into the throat with a straw. This should be done three or four times a day as it is quite helpful.

📖 Latin, seventeenth century. Bamberg, Staatsbibliothek, *Codex medicinalis* 1, fol. 25v.

24 ◈ INCANTATION FOR SORE THROATS

"Neptune has anginas on the stone; he stayed there, he had no one to heal them. He healed himself with his trident." Say this three times.

📖 Latin, ninth century. St. Gallen, Stiftsbibliothek, Codex 751. Heim, "Incantamenta magica graeca latina," 557.

25 ◈ TO HEAL A SORE THROAT

Take a branch of a plum tree and attach it to the chimney so it will dry out, to heal a sore throat.

📖 France, eighteenth century. Thiers, *Traité des superstitions* (1777), vol. 4, 325.

ANTHRAX

26 ◈ FOR ANTHRAX, FISTULAS, AND OTHER CONTAGIOUS DISEASES

Take a lead strip as long and wide as the wound, then draw a cross on each corner and another in the center, and while doing this, say: "Lord Jesus Christ who died for us on the cross, restore health to your servant [name]. The five wounds of God are his remedies, may the pious cross and the passion of Christ be his remedy!" Once you have done this, make sure the strip does not touch the ground, for it will lose its power. And know that you should say while drawing the cross [in the middle]: "Lord Jesus Christ," and as done previously. Next, while placing this strip on the ailing part, you should recite this charm accompanied by three benedictions: "Lady Holy Mary, mother of the Savior, for the five days you had conceiving him, without any human intervention, and painlessly gave birth to him, and that you saw him come back from the dead, and by his virtue, ascend into heaven; by the five wounds He suffered on the cross, may He heal this illness!" And each time you say this charm, give the blessing: "In the name of the Father, the Son, and the Holy Ghost, amen. Just as the wounds of our Lord Jesus Christ did not putrefy, did not stink, nor produced worms, but healed perfectly." Make sure that this strip of lead is not removed before three days; then take red cabbage, cook it well in water with root and bark, then crush it with your hands and not with iron. Cook it until half the water has disappeared, wash the wound often as well as the affliction, then place the lead strip back over it and say this orison: "Lord Jesus Christ, you who redeemed our sins with your precious blood on the cross, deign to bless this lead so that the affliction it will touch will heal by the virtue of your most holy passion. By the Christ our Lord, amen."

 Latin and Middle French, circa 1300. London, British Library, Additional 15236, folio 31v–32r; Grabner, "Ein Arzt hat dreirlei Gesicht."

BIRTH

Facilitating birth and reducing its pains has always been a major concern. It was once believed that a long and painful labor was the punishment for adultery or other sins of the mother. A host of methods were developed in folk medicine, such as the following: to facilitate childbirth, one should wear a belt made from the hide of a deer hunted during the canicular days, or the heart of a living hare, or hang a viper around the neck, or smear the belly with an ointment made from ant larvae. Even earlier, Pliny the Elder informs us: "It is said, that if a person takes a stone or other missile which has slain three living creatures, a man, a boar, and a bear, at three blows, and throws it over the roof of a house in which there is a pregnant woman, her delivery, however difficult, will be instantly accelerated thereby" (Historia Naturalis, XXVIII, 6).

27 ◆ FOR A WOMAN WHO IS LATE GIVING BIRTH

Write on virgin parchment dyed with grape (juice): "Befriend him, chaste Lucina; 'tis thine own Apollo reigns"; then attach it to her right thigh, and when the child has emerged, pull it off immediately.

There are two kinds of virgin parchment: one from an animal that

TRACTATVS

cúdant & ter percutientes cimbalum sonum illum crepūt valere ad prosperum partū: quod est superstitiosum & vanū. Nam quod ter campana sonet hoc potius fit vt ex hoc omnes audientes deuote orent pro tali parturiente & fere periclitanti offerentes beatę virgini ter Angelicam salutationem: vt illa quę immunis & libera fuit à tali dolore sicut ab omni peccato. Liberet huiusmodi mulierem à periculo illius hore.

Martinus de Arles, Tractatus de superstitionibus
(Rome: Vincentium Luchinum, 1559): for childbirth.

has not yet reached the age of procreation and the other from one that was stillborn. The magic spell is in fact a verse from Virgil's Bucolics *[or* Eclogues *4.10]! Another one that this time was taken from the* Aeneid *(4.129; 11.1) appears in the following charm.*

📖 Latin, fifth century. Pseudo-Theodore, *Theodori Prisciani Euporiston libri III*, 340: 25ff.

28 ❖ TO COMPEL HER TO GIVE BIRTH

Say three times in her left ear: "Chile, come out, your brothers summon you into the light." Once the woman has given birth, write this on the top of the door: "Meanwhile, emerging Dawn abandoned the Ocean."

📖 Latin, fifth century. Pseudo-Theodore, *Theodori Prisciani Euporiston*, 340: 13ff.

29 ◈ To Accelerate Birth

Carve these characters on a crust of bread and attach it to [the woman's] right thigh:

And once she has given birth, detach it.

📖 Latin, ninth–tenth century. *Archiv der Gesellschaft für ältere deutsche Geschichtskunde* 7 (1839), 1020.

30 ◈ To Deliver a Child

Write this on bread: "† Adam† Adam † Adam, leave! † The Christ is calling you †. Holy Mary, free your servant [name]. Arising from the mouth of babes and sucklings is the praise of Thy name that Thou might destroy the enemies and allow the child to live!² Give her this bread to eat and she will deliver the child.

📖 Latin, twelfth century. Franz, *Die kirchlichen Benediktionen in Mittelalter,* vol. 2, 101; *HDA,* vol. 3, 344ff.

31 ◈ To Give Birth without Danger

Write the Our Father in a marble vase that you will rinse with white wine, which you will then give to the woman to drink. She will then give birth without danger.

📖 Middle French, Cambrésis, thirteenth century. Coulon, *Curiosités de l'histoire,* 65, no. 57.

32 ◈ To Deliver a Child

Write these verses and attach them to the right big toe (of the woman giving birth): "The God of gods, the Lord has spoken and called forth the earth."

📖 Latin, thirteenth century. London, British Library, Sloane 146, fol. 30v.

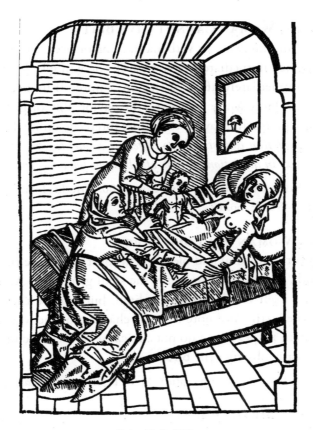

Giving birth, 1483.

33 ◈ To Deliver a Child More Quickly

When a woman is in labor and cannot give birth quickly, and this is posing a threat to her life, one must write a note that is long enough to encircle her body:

> *De viro vir, vincit leo de tribu Juda; Maria peperit Jhesum; Elisabeth sterilis peperit Johannem babtystam; adjuro te, infans, per patrem † et filium † et spiritus † sanctum: sij masculus es aut femina, vt exeas de ista vulva; exanite.*

When the child has been born, remove the note and grate two pfennigs' weight of ivory and give this to the woman to drink in wine; she will expel the placenta if you do not have a midwife near her.

📖 Low German and Latin, 1487, Royal Library of Stockholm, MS X, 114, fol. 55r–v.

34 ◈ When a Woman Cannot Give Birth

Have her drink mugwort or verbena in wine or beer. This herb should also be attached immediately to her navel: she will give birth. Take the herb away immediately after. Write on a note: "Elisabeth conceived the Precursor, Holy Mary conceived the Savior. Boy or girl, come out! Christ calls you forth. May all the saints intercede on my behalf †."

This prescription consists of two different elements, the remedy and an amulet (the text in quotation marks), of which we have numerous examples.

📖 Low Saxon and Latin, shortly before 1400. Utrecht, Library of the Royal University, MS 1355, no. 16.

35 ◈ For a Woman in a Long Labor

Take mugwort and coral and blend them together on the right thigh in a linen cloth, and by their property she shall give birth. And also bind mugwort by itself on the woman's thigh, but remove these things at once after the birth. And note that the chamber of the woman in labor should contain no pears and no nuts. Because of their occult properties, they will greatly obstruct the birth.

📖 France (Troyes), sixteenth century. M.-D. Leclerc, *Les maladies des femmes*, 8.

36 ◈ To Give Birth Quickly

When a woman is ready to give birth, take her belt, go to the church and bind the bell with this belt. Then have it rung three times so that this woman will give birth quickly.

📖 France, seventeenth century. Thiers, *Traité des superstitions* (1679), 320; Traité des superstitions (1777), vol. 4, 325.

37 ◈ To Deliver a Child Immediately

Take some root of henbane, otherwise known as piglet, and place it on the woman's left thigh, and remove it at once, when the child is out, for fear it will disturb her overmuch.

📖 France (Troyes), seventeenth century. M.-D. Leclerc, *Les maladies des femmes*, 8.

38 ◈ For a Difficult Birth

The women of the clan sing the following to the birthing mother and one of the women peels an egg between her thighs:

> *The oak, the oak is so round,*
> *And the belly is full and round;*
> *Child, leave it in good health!*
> *The Lord God is calling you!"*

📖 Gypsies of Transylvania, nineteenth century. Wlislocki, *Volksdichtungen*, 141.

39 ❖ When Pains Are Felt Following the Birth

After the birth, suffumigate the woman with worm-eaten willow wood while humming this song:

> *The smoke flies away, fast and thick,*
> *and the moon is flying, too!*
> *They have found themselves,*
> *You should therefore be healed;*
> *When the smoke has passed,*
> *Be freed of the pain,*
> *Be freed of the pain!*

📖 Gypsies of Transylvania, nineteenth century. Wlislocki, *Volksdichtungen*, 141ff.

BITES

40 ❖ Protection from Snakebites

Anyone who carries the leaves and the root of verbena will be protected from snakebites.

📖 Latin, fourth century. Pseudo-Apuleius, *Herbarius*, 3§7.

41 ❖ Protection from Snakebites

If someone rubs stag suet on himself or carries a piece of untanned deer hide and rewarms it, no snake can approach him.

📖 Germany, sixteenth century. Herr, *Das neue Tier-und Arzneibuch*, chap. 6.

42 ❖ For Dog Bite
Write on virgin parchment: *oscaragi III ego ungues.*

> 📖 Latin, ninth century. St. Gallen, Stiftsbibliothek, Codex 751; Heim, "Incantamenta magica," 564.

43 ❖ Protection from Rabid Dogs
The ash of burnt crayfish (or crab) is an amulet against the bite of rabid dogs.

> 📖 France, sixteenth century. Fernel, *De abditis rerum causis libri dvo*, 243.

44 ❖ Incantation against the Serpent
Say three times, "A multicolored demon but the little skin, the little skin is the flesh, the flesh is the bone, may the bone remain healthy!"

The person undoing the enchantment should remain where the patient welcomed him. And the patient must bring him water and three small hazel branches. And the person undoing the enchantment will take the three branches and dispel the enchantment in this water while saying the words above three times.

> 📖 Romania, 1832. Bucharest, Biblioteca Academiei Române, Romanian MS BAR 5706, fol. 58r: "Descântec de năjit"; Timotin, *Descântecele manuscrise românești*, 257.

45 ❖ Another Incantation against the Serpent

> *Panca pasca cacarat poca poi tocosora panca paca caca panca rata.*

Write these words in a glass and wash them with wine or virgin water and give them to someone who has been bitten to drink and to wash the bite.

> 📖 Romania, eighteenth century. Bucharest, Biblioteca Academiei Române, Romanian MS BAR 1517, fol. 42v.

46 ❖ Against a Snakebite
Say the following verse.

> *Saint Peter put wood on the fire.*
> *A snake then came and hung from Peter's arm.*

> *Peter took the snake and cast it into the fire,*
> *And the snake burned.*
> *I will heal you the same way (name).*
> *††† Amen.*

📖 Sweden (Västergötland), late nineteenth century. Klintberg, *Svenska trollformler*, 67. Bokmål, no. 9, "ormbett." Reichborn-Kjennerud, *Vår gamle trolldomsmedisin*, vol. 2, 134–39.

47 ❖ Talisman against Scorpion Stings

Carve upon a bezoar the image of a scorpion at the hour of the moon when it enters the second decan of Scorpio. The ascendant must be in Leo, Taurus, or Aquarius. The bezoar is then set in a gold ring and one imprints a seal in the incense that has been chewed up by the patient at the said hour, when the moon is in Scorpio, and the victim is given this imprint to drink, then his pains shall vanish.

The author repeats this prescription in the tenth treatise of the second part, which follows.

📖 Arabic magic, mid-eleventh century. *Ghāyat al-hakīm*, II, 10, 32.

48 ❖ Against Scorpions

On the morning of a Monday, on the hour of Scorpio's exultation, carve upon a mahâ (a crystal or white stone) the image of a snake with a scorpion above it; no reptile shall bite the bearer of this stone, and he will be healed of all bites if he places it in a liquid that he next drinks.

📖 Arabic magic, mid-eleventh century. *Ghāyat al-hakīm*, II, 10, 122.

49 ❖ Spell for Driving Ferocious Beasts Away

Say the following verse.

> *Matey, matey, motey, motey a, a, a,*
> *moutef, moutef, mitey, mitey!*
> *May the desert be purified for the unknown one!*

📖 Lexa, *La Magie dans l'Égypte antique*, vol. 2, 4; Maspero, *Recueil de travaux relatifs à la philologie et à l'archéologie égyptiennes et assyriennes*, vols. 4 (1882), and 14 (1892); Kurt Sethe, *Die altägyptischen Pyramiden-Texte*.

50 ❖ To Prevent a Snake from Causing Harm
Say these words: *aussi' osià aussi'*.

📖 Italy, late nineteenth century. *Libro de segretto*, 10

51 ❖ Incantation against Wolf Bite
Say the following prayer:

> Cosmas, Damian, incantation to the Mother of God. A purplish bird is sitting on a whelk, the whelk dries up, just as the whelk's stalk [has been] cut [and] tossed behind the hedge, may the bite of the wolf dry. Amen.

And one takes three young hazel shoots and undoes their enchantment in virgin water and thoroughly washes the wound with this water and gives it to the person to drink, and this will be his remedy.

Another Romanian charm tells us that there are poisonous wolves that cause the death of livestock.

📖 Romania, eighteenth century. Bucharest, Biblioteca Academiei Române, MS BAR 1320, folio 21r; Timotin, *Descântecele manuscrise românești*, 291.

52 ❖ Another Incantation against Wolf Bite

> *Kota tota dota bašalyk, adyk, psyk, cik!*

These words make no sense. Their magical character is based on alliteration.

📖 Lithuania, nineteenth century. Vaitkevičienė, *Lietuvių užkalbėjimai*, no. 1371.

BLEEDING

In The Odyssey *(bk. 19) Homer tells how Odysseus's bleeding, caused by the attack of a wild boar, was halted by a spell.*

53 ❖ Spell against Flowing Blood
One writes the following on a sheet of virgin papyrus and ties it with a thread to a man's waist, or a woman's, whose blood is flowing from a certain place on their body.

> *SICYCVMA CVCVMA VCVMA CVMA VMA MA A*

📖 Latin, fourth century. Marcellus, *De medicamentis liber*, X, 34.

54 ◆ To Stop the Flow of Blood
Repeat the following phrases:

Truncha musa. Daffatana. Quui. Truna. Musa. Daffanata clusa. Sic hicfeda cala feda. Palafeda devulnera.

The soldier Longinus stabbed the Lord with his spear. Nepoecine poluit. Olim fact olio. Amen.

The soldier Longinus stabbed the Lord Jesus Christ with his spear, water and blood poured from his wound.

May the Christ anoint! May he bar the vein. Murmur accessus. Amen Our Father.

Repeat the following three times:

By the Christ, stop, stop, stop as the river Jordan stopped!

📖 Latin, twelfth century. Rationale, Munich, Bayerische Staatsbibliothek, MS Clm 100, fol. 112v; Ohrt, *Die ältesten Segen über Christi Taufe und Christi Tod in religionsgeschichtlichem Lichte;* Edsman, "Folklig sod met rot I heden tid," Arv (1946): 145–76; *HDA*, vol. 5, 1327ff., "Longinussegen."

55 ◆ Against a Gush of Blood
† Caro † cruce † Ysmahelite make that [the wound] of your servant [name] seal back up. Amen. † In the name of the F. † and of the Son

and of the H. † protect, Lord, your servant [name] from this harm and from all debility of body and soul. † Facing this sign, none dies. †††. A. B. G. H. O. Q. 8. 2. F. f. f.

Other spells like this give caruce for cruce, which alters the meaning. Here the Holy Cross is evoked, which confirms that it provides protection against all danger. The series of uppercase letters (characters) seems to be the beginning of the Greek alphabet, and the three "f's" are the abbreviation of a triple fiat, "let it be so."

📖 Latin, twelfth century. Codex Engelbergensis 45, fol. 157; Heim, "Incantamenta magica," 555; Franz, *Die kirchlichen Benediktionen*, 2:175; Thiers, *Traité des superstitions* (1777), 1:357.

56 ◆ To Halt Bleeding of a Vein

If you throw a toad into a new kettle and shred it until it has been reduced to charcoal, its ashes, purified with vinegar, will heal all hemorrhaging of men and women, of the kidneys and uterus, and it will halt the bleeding of a vein or the cut of an artery. If you wish proof, take a knife, rub it with this ash, then stab any quadruped you please, its blood will not flow.

📖 Greek, fourteenth century. *ΚΥΡΑΝΙΣ* I, Φ; Mély, *Les lapidaires grecs*, 77–78.

57 ◆ To Stop Bleeding

Write these letters on parchment in two places and tie them on the two thighs of the man or woman who is bleeding, the blood will stop:

h b c v o x a g

And if you wish to find proof, write them on the knife you are using to kill a pig. No blood will come out.

📖 France, Cambrésis, thirteenth century. Coulon, *Curiosités de l'histoire*, 64, no. 53.

58 ◆ To Stop Blood That Is Flowing

Carve upon an onyx the image of a lion with the characters shown below at the hour of the Lion and in the ascendant of his house, know that it will hold back immediately the blood of the person who holds it and prevent it from flowing.

📖 Arabic magic, mid-eleventh century. *Ghāyat al-hakīm*, II, 10, 130.

59 ◆ For a Hemorrhage

One should write on a limb from which blood is flowing this word: *tetragramaton*, with a cross at the beginning and another at its end.

📖 Latin, ca. 1300, London, British Library, Additional 15236, folio 47v.

60 ◆ Against Blood Loss

> *In Bethlehem the city,*
> *A true child was born,*
> *From a true woman a true child*
> *True veins of this man hold back your blood!*

If the patient is a man, write *Veronix* on his forehead with his own blood; if it is a woman, *Veronia*.

The reference to Bethlehem is quite common in charms against blood loss (ad sanguinem restrigendum; conjuration pro sanguine); it marks a stage in the life of Jesus, followed by his baptism in the Jordan, which then stopped flowing, say the charms. This reference is absent here. As for Veronix, this is Veronica/Beronica, frequently invoked in charms against bleeding.

📖 French and Latin, fifteenth century. *Tractatus de egritudine mulieribus*, Paris, Bibliothèque nationale, MS fr. 7056.

61 ◆ To Stop Bleeding

To stop bleeding, take the moss from a skull and crush it into a powder; this heals, it is proven.

📖 Low German, 1487, Royal Library of Stockholm, MS X, 114, fol. 44v; Ebermann, *Blut- und Wundsegen in ihrer Entwicklung dargestellt.*

62 ❖ To Stop Blood Flow

The stone from a carp skull placed against the fold of the little finger corresponding to the bleeding part stops even the most impetuous blood flow possible.

📖 France, seventeenth century. Laurent Joubert, *La Première et Seconde partie des erreurs populaires,* 171.

63 ❖ For Stopping Bleeding

Repeat the following verse.

> *Blood, blood, be as weary of flowing*
> *As Jesus was of a woman*
> *Who on Sunday did not stop spinning.*
> *Blood, blood, be as sorry to flow*
> *As Jesus was of a woman*
> *Who on Friday brushed her hair*
> *And gave new life to the wounds of Jesus.*
> *Blood, blood, be as weary of flowing*
> *As Jesus is of the gray-haired man*
> *Who goes to the thing,* knows the law*
> *And shares in a wrong.*
> *Blood, blood, be as weary of flowing*
> *As Jesus is of the old graybeard*
> *Who stands at the edge of Hell, a staff in his hand.*

📖 Sweden, 1763, Klintberg, *Svenska trollformler,* 64, no. 2, "Ståmma blod"; Ohrt, *De danske Besvaergelser mod Vrid og Blod.*

64 ❖ For Hemorrhages of the Uterus

Repeat the following verse.

> *Uterus was seated on a marble stone;*
> *An old man approached him.*
> *"Uterus, where do you wish to go?"*

---

*In the Scandinavian countries, the thing is the assembly where legal disputes are settled.

"I am going to [name]'s home,
I wish to see her blood,
I am going to devour her heart,
I wish to take her life."
"Uterus, do not do this thing,
remain on the marble!
May the woman of the wood eat you
As if you never existed!
In the name of the Father, the Son, and the Holy Ghost."

 📖 Saxons of Transylvania, nineteenth century. Von Wlislocki, *Volksglaube und Volksbrauch der Siebenbürger Sachsen*, 86.

65 ◆ To Stop Bleeding

Say: "Blood! Blood! Blood! Stop! Stop! Stop! In the name of God the Father †, the Son †, and the Holy Ghost †" while making the sign of the cross three times. Next, repeat this and the signs of the cross while blowing on the blood.

 📖 Pomerania, nineteenth century. Tettau and Temme, *Die Volkssagen Ostpreussens, Litthauens und Westpreussens*, 242.

66 ◆ To Stop Bleeding

Repeat the following verse:

> *There were three sinful women*
> *Who went to see the blood.*
> *One says: "May it flow;"*
> *The second: "May it stop;"*
> *The third: "Blood, stop flowing,*
> *It is the will of God.*
> *Blood to blood, bone to bone,*
> *Hold as firmly as the rock;*
> *Bleed no more; ooze no more*
> *Until the mother of God gives birth."*

Next the wound was bandaged with the apron of a lady of the night.

 📖 Saxons of Transylvania, nineteenth century. Wlislocki, *Volksglaube*, 85.

67 ❖ **TO STOP BLEEDING**

Repeat the following verse:

> *O wonder of wonders,*
> *The tomb of the Lord is down here!*
> *Three florets are blooming upon it:*
> *The first is called optimism,*
> *The second humility,*
> *The third, blood, stop flowing †.*
> *For it is the will of the Lord.*

📖 Germany (Rugen Island), nineteenth century. Tettau and Temme, *Die Volkssagen,* 342.

68 ❖ **TO STOP BLEEDING**

One writes INRI on a small piece of wood that is then thrown down a well while saying: "Blood, stop, God wishes it. The cross of Christ was made of this wood! Amen!"

INRI, "Iesus Nazarenus Rex Iudaeorum," *[Jesus of Nazareth King of the Jews]*, is Christ's triumphal title. It is regularly used in conjurations of bleeding. It is sometimes associated with the Three Magi.

📖 Saxons of Transylvania, nineteenth century. Wlislocki, *Volksglaube*, 85.

69 ◈ To Stop Bleeding

Say the following words thrice over the place where blood is flowing and make three signs of the cross: *Notre dame ou zimarajne Sa ne lajgne l'atre bouche non sorte giamaj autre goutte,* in the name of the Father and the Son and the Holy Ghost. Amen."

📖 Italy, nineteenth century. *Libro de segretto*, 21.

BLINDNESS

70 ◈ To Heal Those Who Have Been Blind for a Long Time

Dissolved in the milk of a woman who has only engendered once and that only of a male child, the Persian stone placed on the skin as an ointment will heal those who have lost their sight and been blind for a long time.

📖 Latin, eleventh century. Marbode, *De lapidus*, 36.

71 ◈ To Cure Blindness

Three blind men were resting on God's path. Jesus Christ went to them and asked: "Why are you sitting here, poor blind men?" "We are sitting here because we see not our holy God and cannot recognize him." Then Jesus Christ touched them saying: "I bless you, rise and go forth! Know that Jesus Christ has healed you."

Here, the person speaking the charm blows three times into the patient's eyes and says: "In the name of God the Father, and of the Son, and of the Holy Ghost. Amen."

📖 Lithuania, twentieth century. Vaitkevičienė, *Lietuvių užkalbėjimai*, no. 1445; Greeven, *Krankheit und Heilung nach dem Neuen Testament;* Hauck, "Gott als Arzt," in *Text und Bild*, 19–64.

BOILS

72 ◆ To Cure Boils
Repeat the following verse:

> Our Lord Jesus Christ came down from the cross,
> And in his company one hundred thousand angels
> Carrying one hundred thousand lances.
> May they bring them to the harvest
> And may one hundred thousand swords set down foot.
> Mother, Marykind, help!
> Blow, Saint Oufle! Blow Saint Christoufle!
> And I myself blow.

Oufle should be Saint Odulphe (ninth century). The name endings were altered to rhyme with soufle [blow, exhale].

📖 Latin, France, thirteenth century. Vaisbrot, "Édition critique de la *Compilatio singularis exemplorum*," no. 813 (kindly sent to me by Jacques Berlioz).

BURNS

73 ◆ To Heal Burns
Say *Rangarua gauerbat* three times, lick the burn three times, then spit.

📖 Latin, ninth century. Önnerfors, "Iatromagische Beschwörungen,'" no. 34.

74 ◆ For a Burn
Our Holy Father was making his way when he came across a crying child. "Father, what is ailing this child?" "He has grabbed a burning ember. Take some pork fat and three breaths from your body, and the fire will move outside."

Many other healing techniques were employed in the past; here is one of the most singular: "The first snow that falls between Epiphany and the Purification of the Holy Virgin, the Candlemas, is gathered up as precious; once melted it is used to wash the eyes and burns." A. Hock, Croyances et Remèdes populaires *(Liège: Vaillant-Carmane, 1872–74), 164.*

📖 France, eighteenth century. LeBrun, *Superstitions anciennes et modernes, préjugés vulgaires qui ont induit les Peuples à des usages & à des Pratiques contraires à la Religion.*

CANKER

"Canker" covers two types of disease, in fact: the simple canker sore or soft cancer, an ulcerous ailment, and the syphilitic canker. Our texts do not allow this distinction to be made.

In folk beliefs, the word designates certain lesions of the mouth or tongue, primarily thrush and mouth ulcers.

75 ❖ To Cure a Canker

Repeat the following:

> Demon, I conjure you, whatever kind you may be, to leave this Christian, to leave bones and marrow, his blood and flesh! Leave, red-brown canker, watery canker, stinging canker, oozing canker, canker of the bottom!

Canker, I conjure you by the sun and moon, by the river Jordan, by the wind that blows, by the bells that ring, by the saints, by all the saints that God has on heaven and earth—to leave from this Christian and to reside and stay no longer, not in his marrow, not on his blood, not in his flesh! Do not last any longer; do not remain any longer! Just as God placed his foot in the river Jordan and nothing attacked his marrow, his flesh, his blood, and his bones, In the name of the Father, the Son, and the Holy Ghost. Amen.

 📖 Middle Dutch, fourteenth century. Gand, Universiteitsbibliotheek, MS 697, fol. 6v–7r. Ferdinand Ohrt, "Zu den Jordansegen," *Zeitschrift für Volkskunde*, Neue Folge 1 (1930): 269–74.

76 ❖ Against Cankers, Fistulas, Boils, and All Kinds of Pestilences

Repeat the following prayer:

> Blessed be our lord God and the instant he was born. It should be the same for this person [name]. In the name of the Father and the Son and the Holy Ghost. Amen. I believe in the name of the Father and the Son and the Holy Ghost. And in Our Lord Jesus Christ who will truly wish to aid this man [name] against cankers, fistulas, boils, and all kinds of pestilences as

well as all similar ills. In the name of the Father and the Son and the Holy Ghost. Amen.

In medieval texts, *pestilence* means either "contagious disease" or "plague."

📖 Middle Dutch, fifteenth century. London, British Library, Additional 39638, fol. 142v–143r.

📖 Hengel and Hengel, "Die Heilungen Jesu und medizinisches Denken," in *Medicus viator, Festschrift Richard Siebeck*, 331–61.

CATARRH

77 ◈ Against the Catarrhs of Children

Place a cloth smeared with lamb fat on the child's chest every evening. In the morning, tear off a small piece of the cloth and throw it into the house where the chickens roost while saying:

> *There were three midwives*
> *Who were walking in the early morning dew*
> *and speaking about love;*
> *The old man appeared with the illness*
> *and it rendered them mute.*
> *Old man, old man, come!*
> *Carry away the affliction of my child.*
> *In the name of God, and so on.*

📖 Saxons of Transylvania, nineteenth century. Wlislocki, *Volksglaube*, 94.

CHARBON (ANTHRAX)

78 ◈ Orison for Requesting Healing from Charbon and Malignant Pustules

Say the following prayer:

> O Jesus, my Savior, true God and true man, I firmly believe that you spilled your blood for us, I believe that you have suffered for us and spilled your precious blood for us; do not forget me in your holy grace, for the illness about which I implore our holy patron to intercede on our behalf. May it be so.

As medication against charbon, take ivy that is closest to the ground, soap that has not yet been used and beat both together with very fresh cream. This should be applied on the affliction.

 📖 France, nineteenth century. *Le Médecin des pauvres,* 3; Pierre Saintyves, *Les Grimoires à oraisons magiques.*

COLIC

79 ❖ Protection from Colic

According to the magi, if you rub the belly with bat blood, you will be protected from colic for a full year, or, if colic is present, you can be healed by having the courage to swallow the water in which you have washed your feet.

 📖 Latin, first century. Pliny, *Historia naturalis,* XXX, 64.

80 ❖ Charm against Colic

With a cloth or thread, attach around your neck the heart of the crested lark and spread its blood over your belly while saying: "Flee, colic pain, may the crested lark make you flee!" Then eat it.

 The verb "flee" is regularly used in the charms of later antiquity. R. Heim provides numerous examples ("Incantamenta magica," 480ff. and 488).

 📖 Latin, ninth century. Önnerfors, "Iatromagische Beschwörungen," no. 21.

81 ❖ For Stomach Aches and Animal Colic

Write this on whatever you wish and attach it the navel of the man or livestock: *Lolismus, lolistus.*

 📖 Latin, ninth century. Önnerfors, "Iatromagische Beschwörungen," no. 26.

82 ❖ To Be Cured of Colic

You must place your right hand on the abdomen and say: "Mary who was Mary, or colic, passion that is between my liver and my heart, between my spleen and my lungs, stop in the name of the Father, the Son, and the Holy Ghost." You should moreover recite three Paters and three Aves.

 📖 France (Ardennes), nineteenth century. Albert Meyrac, *Traditions, Coutumes, Légendes et Contes des Ardennes,* 175, no. 68; Cabanès and Barraud, *Remèdes de bonne femme,* 283.

83 ◆ Banishment of Colic

One should say: roped colic, cramping colic, red cramping colic, black cramping colic, yellow cramping colic, green cramping colic, blue cramping colic, gray cramping colic, white cramping colic, cramping colic, that has come or been given, I send you back whence you came or whence you were born. Cramping or roped colic, I untie you, cramping colic, I unbuckle you, cramping colic that is in the entrails, I cut you into pieces. Cramping roped colic may God cut you as I cut you.

At this same time in France, colic was also cured this way:

> Find a sorcerer or a person of good will who will touch the affliction and press your navel with a finger while saying: "Mary who was Mary, or colic and poison that is between my liver and my heart, between my spleen and my lungs, stop! In the name of God the Father †, in the name of God the Son †, and in the name of God the Holy Ghost †." Say three Our Fathers and three Hail Marys while naming the patient by his name and saying: "God by his power has healed you. Amen."

📖 France, nineteenth century. *Le Médecin des pauvres,* no. 15.

CONSTIPATION

84 ◆ Cure for Constipation

When a man is constipated and cannot have a bowel movement, take the humerus or tibia of a dead man, and take off their ends so that these bones are hollow, fill them with the excrement of this man you wish to heal, then place this bone in hot water, but it should not be boiling, in this way the patient will have a bowel movement.

📖 Germany, 1750, Staricius, *Grimoire ou la Magie naturelle,* 332ff.

COUGH

85 ◆ Cure for Coughs

For coughs, write on virgin parchment this name: Ialdabrae, and use the fiber of a new sponge to tie it around your neck.

📖 Latin, ninth century. St. Gallen, Stiftsbibliothek, Codex 751; Heim, "Incantamenta magica," 557; Önnerfors, "Iatromagische Beschwörungen," no. 13.

CRAMPS AND SPASMS

86 ❖ Protection from Cramps
† Thebal † Ech † Guth † E Guthany †. Write these names on parchment with the crosses; the one who carries it shall be protected from cramps.

Another Latin manuscript in the British Library (Additional 33996, folio 170v) adds that these names also cure spasms.

📖 England, fourteenth century. London, British Library, Sloane 2584, fol. 31r.

87 ❖ To Cure Spasms
Say this: "Our Lord God and Saint Peter were walking along a road. A cramp seized Peter; he sat on the ground and Our Lord God healed him with his right thumb: "Cramp, you should leave from here! In the name of God, amen."

📖 Middle Dutch, late fifteenth century. London, British Library, Sloane 3002, fol. 31r–v.

88 ❖ Protection from Cramps
A ring of buffalo horn worn on a finger or toe will offer protection from cramps, this is a powerful and proven remedy.

📖 Germany, 1546, Herr, *Das neue Tier-und Arzneibuch,* chap. 10.

89 ❖ Protection from Cramps
I grab you with my right hand, tearing cramp! Cramp, cease! Do not last any longer! You should quickly clear out of here! Like smoke in the wind, like mist in the sun you should leave from here.

📖 Germany (Voigtland), nineteenth century. Bartels, "Über Krankheits-Beschwörungen," 27.

CUTS

90 ❖ Protection from Cuts
On the Isle of Bujan in the great ocean-sea, lies the white Alatyr stone; upon this stone sits a beautiful girl, an expert seamstress who holds a steel needle. She threads it with a thread of red silk and sews up bleeding wounds. I protect God's servant [name] against cuts. Get behind steel, and you, blood, cease flowing!

The Russians place paradise, the land of eternal summer where birds and insects go to spend the winter, on the mythical island of Bujan. Here is how A. N. Afanassiev explains the birth of this myth:

> The sky that shines luminously blue is found beyond the clouds or beyond a sea of rain; to reach the kingdom of the sun [meaning the kingdom where the sun retires for the night], it is necessary to cross through the celestial waters. This heavenly kingdom is depicted this way as being surrounded on all sides by water, in other words, in the form of an island. This metaphor appears in an entirely clear-cut fashion in Russian incantations in which the marvelous island Bujan is featured. . . . "The Isle Bujan" is the name given to the springtime sky.[3]

Placed beneath the sign of beginning, the island played a very important role in Russian folk magic. Charms and incantations should call on it in order to be effective. In fact, it was considered to be the headquarters of all forms of energy; simply invoking its name lent its strength to the magic spell. This compelled A. N. Afanassiev to write that, without it, "incantations have no power."[4]

As for the Alatyr stone, magical texts place it either on this island or at its base. It is white and intense (bel-gorjuč), unknown to all (nikem ne vedomyi), and it was seen as "the father of all stones."

    📖 Russia, nineteenth century. Gruel-Apert, *La Tradition orale russe*, 107.

    📖 Bajburin, "Quelques aspects de la mythologie de l'île," *Cahiers slaves* 7, (2004): 1–9.

DEAFNESS

91 ◈ To Hear Again

Someone who is deaf in one ear must place the heart of a dead widderwalo [golden blackbird] so that it will warm again, and his ear will again hear.

    📖 Twelfth century. Hildegard von Bingen, *Physica*, VI, 62, "Widderwalo."

92 ◈ To Recover Hearing

Take four biles, the first from a trout, the second from an eel, the third from a hare, and the fourth from a crow. Put them into a new pot, pour in the equivalent of nine sous of a good brandy and place the pot over a fire so that it boils for as long as it takes to walk fifty steps, then take it off and let it cool. Next, with a feather, let two or three drops fall into the patient's ear. He should be lying on a bench with the ear that hears poorly turned toward you. He will recover his hearing. If this is ineffective, repeat the operation.

 📖 Germany, 1750, Staricius, *Grimoire ou la Magie naturelle,* 285ff.

DRY PATCH

93 ◆ To Cure Dry Skin

Take a new needle and with its tip trace the contour of the dry patch or eczema while saying: "Dry patch or rash, engendered by nine kinds of roots, you shall vanish as quickly as the dew before the sun of the month of May, from nine to eight, from eight to seven, from seven to six, from six to five, from five to four, from four to three, from three to two, from two to one, from one to zero."

 📖 France, nineteenth century. Cabanès and Barraud, *Remèdes de bonne femme,* 214.

94 ◆ To Cure Dry Patches or Herpes

Open and close the breadbox three times every morning for nine days, and make a draft while opening and closing it, and expose those who have dry patches or herpes on their faces to this draft, in order to cure them.

 📖 France, seventeenth century. Thiers, *Traité des superstitions* (1679), 328; *Traité des superstitions* (1777), 4:335.

95 ◆ To Lose Inflamation

Take the cloth that is used to clean the bakers' oven and vigorously rub the dry patch with it while saying:

> Varpelon, varpelon, you will lose your redness, your width, your hollowness, your inflammation, *in nomine Patris.*

Then one blows on the spot three times.

"Varpelon" is the name of a caterpillar that peasants blame for dry patches, which they still call diarde and guardre.

 📖 France, nineteenth century. Cabanès and Barraud, *Remèdes de bonne femme,* 276.

EPILEPSY

Epilepsy, which was once called "the falling sickness," was regarded by medieval physicians as a brain disease that banished balance and the senses for a period of time due to "congestion of the ventricles of the brain," as Bernard of Gordon (circa 1450–1500) put it. At the same time, it was thought the person was possessed by a demon, hence the use of the word demoniac to describe an epileptic.

96 ◆ To Cure Epilepsy

If you give a lunatic the fruits of the asterion [thought to be cannabis —*Trans.*] to eat during the waning moon, when it is in the sign of Virgo, and you hang some of this plant around his neck, he will be cured.

📖 Latin, fourth century. Pseudo-Apuleius, *Herbarius*, 60§1.

97 ◆ To Stop Epileptic Spasms

For epileptics, in other words demoniacs, and for all those suffering from spasms, do this: take three scruples of mandrake and have them drink it in hot water, and they will be cured.

📖 Latin, fourth century. Pseudo-Apuleius, *Herbarius*, 131.

98 ◆ A Remedy for Epilepsy

Take an equal amount of incense, myrrh, and ivy berries, and blend them all together with water that the patient will be given to drink on a Thursday, while the moon is setting. This is a proven remedy.

📖 Latin, eighth century. Bamberg, Staatstsbibliothek, Codex medicinalis 1, fol. 39r.

99 ◆ To Stop the Spitting Up of Blood

Secretly give the blood of a weasel conserved in vinegar to a person spitting blood, or to an epileptic, and it will cure him.

📖 Latin, ninth century. *Liber Kyranidorum*, 104, 1–2.

100 ◆ For an Epileptic

Have a priest say three Christmas masses. At the start of the first one, the patient should offer three silver coins in honor of the Trinity, and the priest should place them near the corporal* or beneath it so that

---

*[Square white linen cloth on which the chalice and ciborium sit during the mass. —*Trans.*]

the signs of the cross prescribed by the canon [of the mass] extend over them. At the end of the first mass the patient should trade in the three coins for twelve deniers and make a gift of them at the start of the third mass. To finish, he should redeem them for twenty-four deniers and have a ring made from silver coins without any other metal mixed in, and wear it without ever removing it. He will be protected from the disease.

📖 Latin, Germany, late fifteenth century. Hollen, *Preceptorium divinae legis,* 25.

101 ❖ To Help in Memorization

To help in memorization, the recipes were most likely sometimes written in verse, like this one:

> *Again you will say another medicine*
> *Of lovage take the root*
> *Three words write upon it:*
> *Jesus † Christus † dominus †*
> *So long as it is worn hung around the neck,*
> *He shall no longer fall, it is well known.*
> *If he truly believes in God*
> *He will be ever healed, that is sure.*

📖 Middle French, thirteenth century. Cambridge, St. John's College D.4, fol. 88v.

102 ❖ Here Is a True and Proven Medicine against Epilepsy

Write this orison on a parchment of Ascrie(?): *communicantes at memoriam venerantes.*[5] Then the patient should confess all his sins, the priest should chant a mass for the Trinity, and seven tapers or seven candles should be placed on the altar. The first should have Sunday written on it, the second Monday, and so forth, then the patient should take communion. For the duration of the mass and the speaking of its orison, the *bref* [the magic spell on parchment] should remain on the altar.

After the mass, the patient should take as many of the tapers as he wishes. The day inscribed on it guarantees his life and he should conserve it honorably and properly. The priest will tie the *bref* to the patient's neck who should wear it for the rest of his life.

The use of candles in folk cures does not only concern epilepsy. In his

Essai sur l'éducation médicinale des enfants,[6] *N. Brouzet offers the following testimony:*

> When a child suffers from a well-established infestation of worms that has resisted the ordinary aids of Medicine for several days, the women with secrets are in the habit of laying the child out on a table, around whom they light nine candles—nine, no more and no less. Once the candles have been lighted, the main player places herself at the child's feet and says with singular enthusiasm, supported by the most extravagant faces and gestures . . . : "*nau bermis qu'a Job, de nau qu'en a trop, de nau beinguen à ouesit,*" which means: "This little Job has nine worms, he has too many with nine, may they be reduced to eight." All the candles are gradually extinguished while saying the banishing spell (as stated previously) in the same tone and with the same ceremony each time until only the last candle remains and Job only has one worm left. Then, one finishes by saying: "*Qu'aquaes in qu'a je autan de poudé sur Job, couen à part à la Misso lou qui l'enten darré la Carérniessio*": "May this worm that is the lone to remain, have as much power over Job as the one that hears the Mass behind the Servant of the Priest has part of this Sacrifice."

📖 Middle Dutch, 1305, Paris, Bibliothèque nationale, MS Latin 6838 A, fol. 153r and 154r.

103 ❖ AGAINST THE FALLING SICKNESS

Chant a mass of the Holy Spirit and make seven candles of virgin wax. Write Sunday on the 1st, Monday on the 2nd, Tuesday on the 3rd, Wednesday on the 4th, Thursday on the 5th, Friday on the 6th, and Saturday on the 7th. Light them all together at the mass and let them burn until the end. Then arrange things for the patient to select one and, as long as he fasts on bread and water on the day indicated, until the end of his life, or if his mother or father do it for him until he has been cured. Make sure that the patient has confessed and fully fulfilled his penitence, and that he drinks the water of the washbasin after the priest has washed his hands in it. In truth, he shall be healed.

📖 Middle English, fifteenth century. Müller, *Aus mittelenglischen Medizintexten*, 107.

104 ◆ For the Falling Sickness

Take larks from the nest before they have touched the ground and tear off their heads; drain their blood into a copper container, take white incense, shape it, and pour the blood over it, make it into a ball and give it to the patient *in nomine Patris, et Filii, et Spiritus sancti.* Write the verses of the three holy kings:

Caspar, Balthasar, Melchior	Gaspar, Balthasar, Melchior
Hec si quis secum	Whoever wears these names
on portaverit	their person
Solvitur a morbo domini	Will be healed of the falling
pietate caduca	sickness by the grace of God.

These verses must be written on a *bref* to be tied around the neck before sunrise.

📖 Middle High German, fifteenth century. German herbal. CSB 52, "Epilepsie."

105 ◆ To Succor an Epileptic

If you wish to succor an epileptic, take a strap of new buckskin and when the falling sickness strikes him, tie it around his neck, saying: "In the name of the Father, the Son, and the Holy Ghost, I bind this man with this knot!" Take the strap, tie a knot into it and hang it around his neck. The patient should abstain from wine until he happens upon a place where a dead body has just been interred. There you should remove the strap and say: "In the name of the Father, the Son, and the Holy Ghost, I bury this strap in the hope the illness will no longer strike this man until the resurrection of this corpse on Day of the Last Judgment."

📖 Middle High German, mid-thirteenth century. Munich, Bayerische Staatsbibliothek, MS Cgm 92, fol. 14v. On knots, cf. Wolters, "Faden und Knoten als Amulett," *Archiv für Religionswissenschaft* 8 (1905): 1–22.

106 ◆ To Cure and Epileptic

Tie a nail from a crucifix to the arm of an epileptic to cure him.

📖 France, seventeenth century. Thiers, *Traité des superstitions* (1679), 330; *Traité des superstitions* (1777), 4:337.

107 ❖ Mysterious Ring for Healing Falling Sickness

Anneau mystérieux pour guérir du mal caduc.

Vous ferez un anneau de pur argent, dans le châton duquel vous enchasserez un morceau de corne de pied d'élan, puis vous choisiriez un lundi du printemps auquel la lune sera en aspect bénin ou en conjonction avec Jupiter ou Vénus, et à l'heure favorable de la constellation, vous graverez en dedans de l'anneau ce qui suit : † Dabi † Habi † Haber † Habro †, puis l'ayant parfumé trois fois avec le parfum du Lundi, soyez assuré qu'en le portant habituellement au doigt du milieu de la main, il garantit du mal caduc.

You shall make a ring of pure silver in whose bezel you will set a piece of elk hoof; then you will select a Monday in springtime when the moon will be in a benign aspect or in conjunction with Jupiter or Venus, and at the favorable hour of the constellation you will carve the following on the inside of the ring: † Dabi †, Habi †, Haber †, Habro †; then having perfumed it three times with the perfume of Monday, be assured that by wearing it on the hand's middle finger, it will provide surety against the falling sickness.

Monday perfume consists of the head of a green frog, the eyes of a white bull, the seed of the white poppy, incense, and camphor. This is all blended together with the blood of a young goose or dove to form a paste; lastly, this is formed into small seeds that will be used three by three once they are totally dry.

📖 France, eighteenth century. *Petit Albert,* 126.

108 ❖ Orison for Requesting the Healing of Falling Sickness, Saint Vitus' Dance, and Stomachaches

The patient will say, or have said on his behalf, the following prayer: "Like David with his harp healed King Saul, God, cure the brain of this poor man of its affliction; blessed Saint Vitus, intercede for this one who has lost his guide and his freedom of movement.

📖 France, Troyes, eighteenth century. *Le Médecin des Pauvres,* 3.

109 ◈ For Falling Sickness

Blowing into the right ear, speak these words: *"Jasparé, fers migraine, thus, maléchiar, balthazard, ou ronce."* It will still need an hour for the cure, it is necessary to have three nails the length of his little finger, bury them deeply into the spot of his first fall, with each of them name the name of the person. Five Our Fathers, and so forth.

Here we have a fine example of the oral transmission of a charm, the words to be spoken are in fact the spell of the Three Kings: "Gaspar, fert myrrham, thus Melchior, Balthazar aurum," reproduced by hearsay.

 📖 France, nineteenth century. *Le Médecin des pauvres* (1875).

110 ◈ Against Epilepsy

One must tie a living frog between the patient's shoulders with a large strap and say: Frogs, leave my house! You are invited to become a corpse!" Three days later, the strap and the now dead frog should be secretly placed in a dead man's coffin, and while it is being buried, one must say: "In the name of the Father, the Son, and the Holy Ghost I bury this frog and the epilepsy of [full name] so that it remain here until the Last Judgment."

 📖 Saxons of Transylvania, nineteenth century. Wlislocki, *Volksglaube*, 88ff.

ERYSIPELAS
(See also "Saint Anthony's Fire")

111 ◈ Against Erysipelas

Repeat the following verse.

> *In the sky, in the sky, in the sky,*
> *There are three birds.*
> *The first is called swan wave;*
> *the second is called cold wave*
> *and the third tranquil wave.*
> †††

 📖 Sweden (Småland), early nineteenth century. Klintberg, *Svenska trollformler*, 72, no. 20, "ros."

112 ◆ To Treat Erysipelas

One blends in a container the blood of a priest with pounded elder bark, then one places all this in a cloth that is used to treat the afflicted part of the body while saying:

> *I have two eyes,*
> *I have two feet;*
> *Nasal pain*
> *Go down into the feet;*
> *From the feet, go down into the ground;*
> *Go out of the ground*
> *And die!*

📖 Gypsies of Transylvania, nineteenth century. Wlislocki, *Volksdichtungen,* 139.

113 ◆ To Get Rid of Erysipelas

Repeat the following:

> Erysipelas, leave and go to the desert! Erysipelas, whatever you may be, whether you are red or white, black, green yellow, blue-striped, brown, or multicolored (it is necessary to list nine colors). Erysipelas of ninety-six kinds, you must retreat and go to a fallow field. If you do not leave, I will cut you with the knife, I will sweep you with the broom, and burn you. This is to be repeated three times.

📖 Romanians of Transylvania, nineteenth century. Schullerus, *Rumänische Volksmärchen,* 43ff.

ÉTISIE (CONSUMPTION)

114 ◆ To Recover Strength from Étisie

Write the following words on a small piece of bread:

> *Hagios habi, rabi, gabi*

It is then given to eat to the one who is struck by a sudden weakness. If this is written on a crust of bread, the individual will recover his strength.

Étisie, étique, or hectique (*the Swiss German* Fress-Rätticher) *means a fever that causes great weight loss.*

📖 Switzerland (Argovie), nineteenth century. Rochholz, "Aargauer Besegnungen," *Zeitschrift für deutsche Mythologie und Sittenkunde* 4 (1859): 110.

EYE AILMENTS
(See also Leucoma, Ophthalmia, Rheum, Stye)

115 ◆ To Heal the Eyes
When the eyes begin to cause suffering, they can be healed if one knows the patient's name and makes knots in an unbleached cloth while spelling out each letter.

📖 Latin, fifth century. Marcellus, *De medicamentis liber,* VIII, 62.

116 ◆ To Expel Eye Ailments
Mugwort expels the ailments of the eyes from man.

📖 Latin, fourth century. Pseudo-Apuleius, *Herbarius,* 10§1.

117 ◆ To Clean the Eyes
To make dust or other debris come out of the eye, rub it gently with the five fingers of the right hand if it is the right eye, or of the left hand, if it is the left eye, while saying three times: *Te tunc resungo, bregam, gresso.* Spit thrice and do all this three times.

Similarly, while you lightly rub the patient's eye, keep your own eye on the same side closed, and say this charm three times: *In mon dercomarcos axtison.*

📖 Latin, fifth century. Marcellus, *De medicamentis liber,* VIII, 170.

118 ◆ To Remove Pain and White Spots
If you harvest waterlilies before sunrise, it is said they will remove the white spots from the eyes and all ocular pain.

📖 Latin, fourth century. Pseudo-Apuleius, *Herbarius,* 23§1.

119 ◆ For Eye Pain
Write these characters on a virgin parchment and tie it to the forehead:

Obes orbirio

📖 Latin, ninth century. St. Gallen, Siftbibliothek, Codex 751; Heim, "Incantamenta magica," 564.

120 ◆ To Sharpen Sight

The fat of a viper confers sharpened sight and cures all kinds of amblyopia [lazy eye]. Its eyes, when carried in a phylactery, will cure ophthalmia.

📖 Greek, fourteenth century. *KYPANIΣ* II, E.

121 ◆ To Heal Ophthalmia and Headaches

The glaucus is a very large sea fish. Hung around the neck, the stones from its head will heal ophthalmia and headaches.

📖 Greek, fourteenth century. *KYPANIΣ* IV, G.

122 ◆ To Clear White Spots from the Eyes

Three Evangelists were singing as they walked; the apostle Andrew was sitting on a stone. Lord Jesus joined them. "Saint Andrew, what are you doing sitting there?" "I have a cloudy spot over my eyes, I can no longer read or sing, I can no longer devote myself to the Scriptures." The Christ raised his blessed hand and passed it over his face. "Saint Andrew, rise up, take your book, and go straight to church! You will sing and read there, you will zealously devote yourself to the Scriptures, and God shall grant your prayer by the Word and the Holy Blood, and your eyes will be healed, (as sure) as the clear, bright sun climbs through a limpid sky. I command it, by God the Father, and so on. Our Father, the Credo, and so on."

📖 Saxons of Transylvania, nineteenth century. Schuster, *Siebenbürgisch-sächsische Volkslieder*, 310.

123 ◆ To Relieve Eye Pain

Wash the eyes with a blend of saffron and water while saying:

> *Pain of the eyes,*
> *Go into the water;*
> *From the water, go into the saffron;*
> *Leave the saffron and go into the ground,*
> *Go back and join the Phuvush!*

*There is your home,
It's there where you have been invited to celebrate!*

📖 Gypsies of Transylvania, nineteenth century. Wlislocki, *Volksdichtungen,* 138.

FATIGUE

124 ◆ For Travel Fatique
If a traveler carries mugwort in his hand, he will feel no travel fatigue whatsoever.

📖 Latin, fourth century. Pseudo-Apuleius, *Herbarius,* 10§1.

125 ◆ For Fatigue and Imbalance
Hold mugwort in your left hand and say: "I remedy fatigue and imbalance. Carried in the hand, mugwort works wonders."

📖 Latin, ninth century. Önnerfors, "Iatromagische Beschwörungen," no. 42.

FEAR

126 ◆ To Be Safe
If you are scared, write the name of Saint Bernard on paper and swallow it; none will sting you, wound you, or capture you. This is proven.

📖 Germany, ca. 1530, Dresden, Sächsische Landesbibliothek, MS C 326, folio 35r.

127 ◆ To Be Spared from Fear
Mount a bear and perform certain tricks to be spared from fear.

📖 France, seventeenth century. Thiers, *Traité des superstitions* (1679), 330.

FEVER

Fever *was a generic term applied to diseases containing a febrile state that affected the entire body. Martin de Saint-Gille tells us, around 1362–65: "Fever is unnatural heat changed into ardor."*

128 ◆ For a Speedy Cure from Fever
Take the parings of the toenails and fingernails of a sick person, and mix them up with wax, the party saying that he is seeking a remedy

for a tertian, quartan, or quotidian fever, as the case may be; then stick this wax, before sunrise, upon the door of another person—such is the prescription they give for these diseases! What deceitful persons they must be if there is no truth in it! And how highly criminal, if they really do thus transfer diseases from one person to another! Some of them, again, whose practices are of a less guilty nature, recommend that the parings of all the fingernails should be thrown at the entrance of an anthill, taking the first ant that attempts to draw one into the hole; this, they say, must be attached to the neck of the patient, and he will experience a speedy cure.

📖 Latin, first century. *Historia Naturalis,* 28.86.

129 ❖ To Reduce Fever

If the feverish wears a salamander heart by his neck, the fever will fall immediately.

📖 Latin, twelfth century. *Liber Kyranidorum,* 126: 16–17.

130 ❖ For All Fevers

One should begin with the charm below! In the name of the Father, the Son, and the Holy Ghost, amen." Next, both secretly recite the Our Father, then make the sign of the cross on the patient's forehead while saying: "In the name of the Father, and so on." Next, one speaks the charm after drawing with the right thumb a cross on the forehead while saying: "† Christ † vanquishes † Christ rules † Christ † commands † Christ † heals you." Then each should say the Our Father to themselves in silence, then say: "Christ is born † Christ is dead † Christ resurrected from the dead on the third day † May the Father heal you by his power † may the Son heal you by his passion † may the Holy Ghost heal you by his bounty, may the Holy Trinity heal you by its all-powerful glory, whatever their nature, of all illness. Amen. † In the name of the Father, and so on." Each should then silently recite the Our Father and the Credo. With God's permission, he shall be cured. This is proven.

📖 Latin and French, circa 1300, London, British Library, Additional 15236, fol. 42r–43v.

131 ◆ Spell for Repelling Fever

Our Lord Jesus was on a walk with his apostles when he entered into the house of Simon Peter. He found his mother-in-law lying down suffering from fever and exhaustion. Simon Peter said: "My Lord Jesus, have pity on Garbêlêa, daughter of Zoe, and take from her this fever (sent unto her) by the enemy!" [Jesus] grabbed her hand at once, placed it over the fever, and she was healthy, and being healthy got up and served them. Akheletes, Tiometes, Probatios, Sabatios, Eoukenios, Stefanas, Kyriakos! Ananias, Asarlas, Misaël! Setrak, Mnisak, Mnabtinako! Bakak, Thelal, Méal!

Among these names we can recognize those of saints and the three children in the furnace (Deuteronomy 3:52–88).

📖 Lexa, *La Magie dans l'Égypte antique,* 104, from a Coptic magic papyrus.

132 ◆ For all Fevers

Write this on a virgin parchment and place it on the altar near the chalice until three masses have been said over it, then tie the parchment around his neck.

† *on lona onu oni one onus oni one onus*

📖 France, Provençal, thirteenth century. Cambridge, Trinity College, MS R 14.30, fol. 146r.

◆ A Remedy for Fever

Take a leaf of sage and write on it *Christus tonat,* and have the patient eat it on the first day; recite a Pater Noster and an Ave Maria and the Credo. The second day, write *Angelus nunciat* on another leaf and have the patient eat it, then recite two Pater Noster and two Aves Maria and two Credos. The third day, write *Johannes predicat* on the third leaf and have the patient eat it, then recite three Pater Noster and three Ave Maria and three Credos. And when he feels better, he should say three masses: one to the Holy Ghost, one to Saint Michael, and the last to Saint John.

A plant sacred to the Romans, sage should be picked while wearing a white tunic with well-washed bare feet. Its virtues against fever are explained by etymology: its name comes from the verb salvare, *"to save."*

📖 Middle English, fourteenth century. F. Holthausen, "Rezepte, Segen und Zaubersprüches aus zwei Stockholmer Handschriften," *Anglia* 19 (1897): 78ff.

📖 Macer Floridus, *De viribus herbarum*, vv. 870–81; Delatte, *Herbarius: Recherches sur le cérémonial usité chez les anciens pour la cueillette des simples et des plantes magiques*, 3rd ed., Académie Royale de Belgique, Classe des lettres et des sciences morales et politiques, mémoires, vol. 54, fasc. 4.

134 ◈ A Remedy for Fever

Take a crust of bread and write on it

† *O febris, omni laude colenda, o languor sanitatis et gaudy*
† *Ascribendas nox pax max.*

📖 Latin and Middle High German, Tyrol, fifteenth century. Zingerle, "Segen und Heilmittel aus einer Wolfsthurner Handschrift des XV. Jahrhunderts," 175.

135 ◈ For Fever

Good Saint Thomas was crossing through a dark pine forest when he saw before him seventy-seven fevers and jaundices. Good Saint Thomas said: "I shall weave a rope and tie you to it, you, the seventy-seven fevers and jaundices."

📖 Germany, sixteenth century. Heidelberg, Universitätsbibliothek, Cpg 267, fol. 14v.

136 ◈ For Fever and Trembling

If someone is feverish, have three nails forged, like those of Our Lord Jesus Christ, and go to the tree called Ispm (aspen). Bury them in the trunk saying: Just as shivers this Irbrrn (laurel), may the man or woman who has fever and trembling* for as long as the trees are planted in Irbrrn.

We do not understand why the name of the tree was changed, as the analogy between the aspen and the trembling caused by fever is perfectly operational. We should recognize this as an error by the copyist who read one word for another, an easily understood misunderstanding as the names are coded.

📖 Middle High German, early fifteenth century. Marburg, Universitätsbibliothek, MS B 20, fol. 113v.

---

*[In addition to the same meaning as the word holds in English, tremble is the French name for aspen (*Populus tremuloides*). —*Trans.*]

137 ◈ For Fever

Take three sacred hosts and on the first write *Pater pax,* on the second *filus vita,* and on the third *spiritus sanctum est remedium.* On the other side of the first one write *O crux admirabilis,* on the second *euacuacio vvineris,* and on the third *restauracio sanitas.* Have the patient eat the hosts three mornings in a row.

 📖 Latin, fifteenth century. Zingerle, "Segen und Heilmittel," 172–77; Peter Browe, "Die Eucharistie als Zaubermittel."

138 ◈ To Cause a Fever to Vanish

To cause any fever to vanish, write this in a virgin parchment and hang it around the neck of the individual suffering from fever for him to wear for nine days:

> IHC ÷ IHC ÷ IHX ÷ Soter ynos + Adonai O.

 📖 France, Provençal, thirteenth century. Cambridge, Trinity College, MS R 14.30, fol. 145.

139 ◈ To Heal a Fever

To heal fever, write on a virgin parchment: † *on lona, omi, om, one, onus, om one, oni,* then tie it around the patient's neck.

 📖 France, Provençal, thirteenth century. Cambridge, Trinity College, MS R 14.30, fol. 145.

140 ◈ Conjuration of Fevers

Say the following:

> I conjure you, male and female fevers,
> I conjure you by all the saints both men and women,
> I conjure you by the Holy Mass and the Four Gospels,
> I conjure you by the planets and mercy,
> I conjure you by the vij words that God spoke over the
> cross when he knew a bitter death,
> I conjure you by the liiii and the lx wounds inflicted upon
> him by the crown of thorns with the lxxvij prickers,
> I conjure you by the milk that he drank from the breast of
> His mother,

> *I conjure you by His bounty and His innocence,*
> *I conjure you by the Ten Commandments,*
> *I conjure you by the twelve precepts of the Faith,*
> *I conjure you by the sun, by the moon, and by the stars,*
> *I conjure you by the Gospels,*
> *I conjure you to obey under penalty of banishment,*
> *I conjure you by the cross upon which He was nailed,*
> *I conjure you by the blood he spilled on Good Friday and until His death,*
> *I conjure you by all that comes from God and His dear mother, to leave here before an hour has elapsed and to forever remain far from the iiijc 3 ills and the xliij pains that have seized my soul and my body.*

📖 Middle Dutch, late fifteenth century. Bruges, Episcopal Archives, Reckening Kapelnij St. Agnes, 1490–95.

141 ◆ Another Conjuration of Fevers

Repeat the following prayer:

> In the name of the Father and the Son and the Holy Ghost, amen. I conjure you, illnesses and all manner of nocturnal or diurnal demons, by the Father and the Son and the Holy Ghost, by the undivided Trinity, by the intercession of the blessed Mary, by the prayers of the saints, by the merits of the patriarchs, by the suffrage of the angels and archangels, by the intervention of the apostles, by the passion of the martyrs, by the faith of the confessors, by the chastity of virgins, by intercession of all the saints, by the seven sleepers whose names are: Malthus, Maximianus, Dionisius, Johannes, Constantinus, Seraphon, Martinianus, and by the name of God blessed through the centuries: † a † g † l † a—to not harm or cause any evil to this servant of God, [name], neither when he sleeps or wakes. † *Christus vincit* † *Christus regnat* † *Christus imperat* †. May the Christ bless us and protect us from all evil †. Amen.
>
> In the name of the Father and the Son and the Holy Ghost, amen. In my name they expel the demons, they remove the tongues of the talking serpents, and, if they drink poison, it

does nothing to them; they lay hands upon the sick and make them well. † Admirable Cross † elimination of pain, restoration of health † here is the cross of the Lord, flee ill-intentioned parties † the lion of Judah, root of David triumphs, hallelujah † Christ triumphs † Christ rules † Christ commands.

May the Christ protect this servant [name] from all sight and all persecution of the Devil, and from all misfortune, at all times and all places, by the virtue of the holy cross † amen † agios † hyskyros † athanatos † elesyon †.

The incorporation of illnesses into demons is clear from the first sentence of this charm that shares all the features of an exorcism. To fight them, in addition to God, one mobilizes Christianity's most eminent representatives. The references are Mark 16:17–18, the Exaltation of the Holy Cross, and Revelation 5:5.

📖 Latin, fifteenth century. London, British Library, Sloane 962, fol. 9v–10r.

142 ◈ To Cure a Fever
If you find a naked man in a *gagathe* [*jayet*, jet], crowned and proud with a cup in one hand and a sprig of herb in the other, fix the gagathe to a ring made from any metal, and any man stricken by fever will be instantly cured if he wears this ring.

📖 Latin, Italy, 1502, Camillo Leonardi, *Les Pierres talismaniques: Speculum lapidum III,* 3:17, 18.

143 ◈ To Heal Fevers
It is necessary to say nine Our Fathers and nine Hail Marys during nine days in the morning, and tie around the neck of the patient a note on which this orison is written:

> *In nomine Domini Jesu Maria Amen. Deus Abraham* † *Deus Isaac* † *Deus Jacob* † *Deus Moyses* † *Deus Esaie* † *Deus autem:* quartan, tertian, continuous, daily, & and all other fever, I conjure you to leave from atop [full name] and that you have no more power over his body than the Devil has on the priest when he consecrates the mass, and that you have lost your heat, your strength, and your vigor, just as Judas lost his color when he betrayed Our Lord.

📖 France, eighteenth century. Lebrun, *Superstitions anciennes et modernes,* 99.

144 ❖ To Heal Fevers
Roll in the dew of the oats on Saint John's Day before sunrise to heal fevers.

📖 France, eighteenth century. Thiers, *Traité des superstitions* (1777), vol. 3, 262.

145 ❖ Against Fever
You must make your way close to a river where, once there, you will throw nine kinds of things behind you while saying:

> *Fever, fever, go away from me,*
> *I give you water, water!*
> *I am not one of your friends,*
> *So go back then*
> *To where you were nursed,*
> *To where you were cared for,*
> *To where you were loved!*
> *May Mashurdalo help me!*

Mashurdalo, or, to be more precise, Mašmurdalo, "the meal killer" (maš, *"meat," and* murdalo, *"killer"), is a gullible and simple-minded giant with a weakness for human flesh, on the condition it comes from a healthy individual. He haunts the woods and wild places, lying in wait for animals and humans, and has a wife and children. His life is hidden inside an egg guarded by a hen. To kill him, it is necessary to slay the life in the egg. As he is not intelligent, people easily dupe him. He shows gratitude to anyone who lends him their aid when he is in danger. He owns a bridle that when placed around his neck transforms him into an ugly, scrawny horse, but one that is fast as the wind. Whoever drinks his blood acquires incredible strength.*

📖 Gypsies of Transylvania, nineteenth Wlislocki, *Volksdichtungen,* 139.

146 ❖ Prayer for Fever to Christ and the Very Holy Saint Sisinnius
Say the following prayer:

> Eternal God, send away, Lord, the devil from this man, the servant of God George Bratul, from his head and his voice, from his

hair, from the top of his head, his face, his eyes, his ears, his nostrils, his tongue, the top of his tongue, his throat, his chest, his heart, his entire body, his limbs, and the joints of his limbs, from the inside of the member [?] and outside it, from his bones and veins and capillaries, and his whole being [missing]. In the name of the Father, the Son, and the Holy Ghost, and now, and so on.

Carved on a lead sheet, this phylactery bears the name of its recipient, George Bratul. Although the title of the incantation speaks of fever, the text is much closer to an exorcism. Saint Sisinnius (died 708) is often invoked in Greek and Romanian charms, mainly against Gello, a demoness, witch, and child eater.

📖 Slavonic Serbian, Romania (Oltenia), first half of the eighteenth century. Stahl, "L'organisation magique du territoire villageois roumain," 150–162.53.

147 ❖ Against Fevers

Write [these words] on an apple and give them to the patient for him or her to eat: *isvole, io, naculte, iavoleiog, să șezi,* isvoleio, toleja, itrize nevșico, voscrișenia ianco sileschi, iar trisavita procleora, orarbo, boțueo, inumele vreime, otgaisima isfetago duha,† amin.*

Given the length of the magic spell, we have to ask how anyone was able to write it on an apple!

📖 Romania, 1784, Bucharest, Biblioteca Academiei Române din București, MS Romanian BAR 4458, fol. 94r (kindly passed on by Emanuela Timotin).

148 ❖ For Three Types of Fevers

Write these words on a piece of paper and give it to the patient to keep on his person: *arsilisu, arzamisu, pe murat, de dat, faraon*. And he should read these words three times a day, or else these words: *are liea, sadeleia, tracu, leovitu, inelegami, nașegon, isu: islugi, vașah, abaset, blușiaia, nemulea raboja.*

📖 Romania, eighteenth century. Bucharest, Biblioteca Academiei Române, MS Romanian BAR 4743, fol. 184v (kindly passed on by Emanuela Timotin).

---

*"Sit down" in Romanian.
†In Slavonic, *isfetago duha* means "[in the name] of the Holy Ghost."

149 ◈ Against Fever

To lower a fever, write these words on three sheets of paper;

SATAR
APIRA
TITIT
ARIPA
RATAS

The patient will eat one sheet early in the morning, whether with bread or something else. He will eat the second sheet the same way three days later. Three days after this, the third sheet must be cast into running water by the patient's eldest or baby brother without uttering a word and who must return without looking back. This method of healing is called *drugį rišt*.

Drugys is a disease that causes shivering and a high fever that can last several weeks. Drugį rišt, "binding the fever," indicates that the illness must be cured by making knots in a thread. The words of the spell are a corrupted version of the magic square SATOR AREPO TENET OPERA ROTAS. *Spell making with knots has been used since antiquity.*

📖 Lithuania, nineteenth century. Vaitkevičienė, *Lietuvių užkalbėjimai*, no. 1388.

📖 Heim, "Incantamenta magica," 484; Wuttke, *Der deutsche Volksaberglaube der Gegenwart*, 131ff; Descombes, *Les Carrés magiques: Histoire et technique de carré magique, de l'Antiquité aux recherches actuelles.*

150 ◈ Against Fever

The child's mother pricks her left breast with a new needle, drips a drop of blood onto a sacred host, then places it on her daughter's left palm, and pierces the host with the needle, saying: In the name of the Father, the Son, and the Holy Ghost! What was given me by the three Wenken, I give to you, my blood with my blood, in order that milord Satan on the Hoprichberg does you no wrongs.

The three Wenken (Wänjen) are the three goddesses of fate, and the Hoprichberg is a site of the witches' sabbat.

📖 Saxons of Transylvania, nineteenth century; Wlislocki, *Volksglaube*, 81–82.

151 ◈ To Get Rid of Fever
Early in the morning, before sunrise, go into the forest and choose a shrub. When the first ray of sunlight hits it, shake it as hard as you can while saying: "Fever, fever, enter into him, here you should dwell!" The fever will enter the bush and the patient is rid of it. During this procedure, no one should disturb you, meaning speak to you, otherwise the remedy is ineffective.

Here is one of numerous examples of transference of evil or illness (transplantatio morbi) *into a plant. Jean-Baptiste Thiers sites another method: "Tie yourself to certain trees with a rope or other bond, wood or straw, and remain like this for some time, to be cured of fevers."*

📖 Switzerland, 1911, Wittich, "Zauber und Aberglauben der Zigeuner," *Schweizerisches Archiv für Volkskunde* 15 (1911): 151.
📖 *Traité des superstitions* (1679), 322ff.

152 ◈ To Get Rid of Fever
When someone is feverish, one should go to the home of a person of note, or better, the pastor's, then demand a buttered piece of bread, then leave without saying thank you; once the fever has gone, you may return and give thanks.

📖 Germany (Pomerania), nineteenth Tettau and Temme, *Die Volkssagen*, 342.

153 ◈ Treatment of Malaria
In the treatment of quartan fevers (a kind of fever that comes on every three days, after seventy-two hours, that is, on the fourth day) clinical medicine is, so to say, pretty nearly powerless; for which reason we shall insert a considerable number of remedies recommended by professors of the magic art, and, first of all, those prescribed to be worn as amulets: the dust, for instance, in which a hawk has bathed itself, tied up in a linen cloth, with a red string, and attached to the body; the longest tooth of a black dog; or the wasp known by the name of pseudosphex, which is always to be seen flying alone, caught with the left hand and attached beneath the patient's chin. Some use for this purpose the first wasp that a person sees in the current year. Other amulets are a viper's head, severed from the body and wrapped in a linen cloth; a viper's heart, removed from the reptile while still alive.

📖 Latin, first century. Pliny, *Historia naturalis,* XXX, 98.

154 ◆ For Quartan Fever

The evil demon of quartan fever is sent to men and women by the first decan of Capricorn; it is not tamed promptly because being without a head it neither sees nor understands. Take grapes with four seeds, peel them with your nails and not with your mouth, then put them in a piece of rough cloth, hang it around the neck of the patient, and he will heal.

📖 Latin, twelfth century. *Liber Kyranidorum,* 30, 5ff.

155 ◆ For Quartan Fever

Have the patient visit a course of running water while holding in his or her left hand a bref bearing these three written names, and he or she should wash themselves all over. Here are these three names: *Aros, tremos, hely.* Then write on a wax tablet: *Jhesus Christus dominus noster. Alpha et O. Maximilianus, Malchus, Constantius, Dionisius, Johannes, Seraphon, and Maximianus.* Immediately erase the letters with holy water, then blend myrrh with the water and give it to the patient to drink when the fever sets in; she or he will no longer shiver.

📖 Middle High German, fourteenth century. Heidelberg, Universitätsbibliothek, Cpg 265, fol. 12r.

156 ◆ For Quartan Fever

Take three sage leaves and write on the first one † *pater,* on the second ! † *vita,* on the third *filius pax* † *spiritus remedium* † and give them to the patient to eat three mornings in a row.

📖 Latin, fifteenth century. Wroclaw, University Library, MS III, F 10, fol. 271r.

157 ◆ To Heal Quartan Fever

To heal quartan fever, write this on parchment and tie it around the neck of the afflicted individual:

Stephanius, Portarius, Sanbusius, Diontius, Eugenius, Gesilius, and Quiriatius.[7]

Some of the names of the saints are corrupted. We can recognize Porcarius and Quiriacus; Diontius should be Denis (Dionysus), and Gesilus would be

Pople Gelasius I. Enrico Catarino Davila cites a Mons martyr Sanbucuius in his De bello Gallico historiarum *(Rome, 1745, vol. 3, p. 59).*

📖 France (Provence), beginning of the fifteenth century. Cambridge, Trinity College, MS R 14.30, fol. 145.

158 ◆ To Cure Tertian Fever

This is a kind of fever that comes on every two days.

The Magi recommend plucking the leaves of the false anchusa*[8] with the left hand, while saying for whom they are being gathered at the same time. They are to be worn as an amulet, attached to the person, for the cure of tertian fevers.

For tertian fevers, the magi recommend picking parthenion†[9] with the left hand, and saying, without turning around, for whom it is being harvested. Then a leaf is placed under the patient's tongue, which he should then swallow a minute later in a cystile‡ of water.

📖 Latin, first century. Pliny, *Historia naturalis,* XX, 50 and 176.

159 ◆ To Cure Tertian Fever

The theraph [a spider] captured in the name of the patient and thoroughly pulverized in wax will heal tertian fever accompanied by shivering if applied as a plaster to the forehead.

📖 Latin, twelfth century. *Liber Kyranidorum,* 111, 1–2.

160 ◆ To Expel Demi-Tertian Fever

Write *abracadabra* on a sheet of papyrus repeatedly, subtracting one letter each time until all that remains is one letter, which will give this writing the form of a tip. Do not forget to tie the papyrus sheet to the patient's neck with a linen thread.

The cabalistic term abracadabra *was already known in the first century BCE as a magic word. It is used in a reducing diagram against fevers and pain: as the word grows shorter, the problems gradually vanish.*

📖 Latin, second–third century. Quintus Serenas, *Liber medicinalis,* vv. 934–40.

---

*Echium rubrum, L.
†*Parietaria diffusa,* L.
‡0.045 liters

📖 For more on *abracadabra*, cf. Lecouteux, *Dictionary of Ancient Magic Words and Spells*, 8–10.

161 ❖ For Demi-Tertian Fever

Found on roads at the beginning of spring, spider eggs, or those of the tarantula, taken in the name of the patient and wrapped in a black cloth, then hung from the patient's left arm, heals tertian, quartan, and daily fevers. They must be taken during the waning moon, when it is in the sign of Pisces, on the Sabbath day, toward the second hour for demi-tertian fever, around the third hour for tertian fever, and toward the fourth hour for quartan fever, and hung from the patient's neck or arm.

The bite of the tarantula was greatly feared, and to heal it, people danced the tarantella in cemeteries.[8]

📖 Latin, twelfth century. *Liber Kyranidorum*, 135, 15ff.

162 ❖ For Quartan Fever

According to the magi, the patient should knot heliotrope four times for quartan fever, three times for tertian fevers, without ripping it, while promising to untie the knots once health has been restored.

📖 Latin, first century. Pliny, *Historia naturalis*, XX, 61; Wolters, "Faden und Knoten als Amulett," 1–22.

163 ❖ Remedy for Tertian and Quartan Fevers

Magi have attributed powerful effects to these plants [to anemones], instructing that the first plant one sees in the year should be immediately harvested while saying that it is being gathered as a remedy for tertian and quartan fevers; after this the blossoms must be wrapped up in a red rag and kept in the shade, and so be used, should occasion arise, as an amulet.

📖 Latin, first century. Pliny, *Historia naturalis*, XXI, 166.

164 ❖ To Heal Tertian or Quartan Fever

Girded about the waist, germander [*Teucrium chamaedrys*] heals tertian and quartan fevers.

📖 Latin, fourth century. Pseudo-Apuleius, *Herbarius*, 71§2.

165 ◈ To Heal Tertian or Quartan Fever

If you give the head of a bat to someone suffering from tertian or quartan fever, or lethargy, or somnolence, to wear, he will be cured.

📖 Latin, fourteenth century. *KYPANIΣ* I, N; Mély, *Les lapidaires grecs,* 68.

FLUX

166 ◈ To Dissipate Flux and Inflammations

In the vicinity of Ariminous, there is a plant called reseda;* it dissipates fluxes and all inflammations. Those employing it add these words: "Reseda, be the *réséda* [soother] of diseases; Do you know, do you know, who here has bred their young? May the roots have neither head nor feet." These words are repeated three times, the speaker spitting each time.

📖 Latin, first century. Pliny, *Historia naturalis,* XXVII, 131.

GOUT

By gout is meant a joint pain (arthetica), sciatica, chiragra, and podagra. The famous physician Guy de Chauliac notes that gout is caused by "gluttony, drunkenness, indigestion, and lust." But, when combined with other words, "gout" designates other ailments: for example, goutterose is nothing but roseacea and goutte-cramp is merely cramps. . . .

167 ◈ For Gout

If one takes a living frog in someone's name when neither the sun nor moon are above the horizon, then, with scissors cut off this frog's two feet and wrap them in buckskin, and lastly tie them to the feet—the

---

Reseda alba, L.

right one to the right food, and the left one to the left, it is a perfect remedy for gout in the feet.

 📖 Latin, twelfth century. *Liber Kyranidorum*, 104, 1ff.

168 ◆ To Heal Gout

Remove from a living stork its tendons from its feet, legs, and wings, and have them worn by those suffering gout in their hands and feet, limb for limb, and they will by healed.

 📖 Latin, twelfth century. *Liber Kyranidorum*, 166, 11ff.

169 ◆ Conjuration of Gout

Repeat the following:

> I forbid you, gout, by the holy transubstantiation and by the five sacred wounds of Our Lord Jesus Christ and by the blood that flowed from His five wounds, and by the first man that God created or caused to be born; I forbid you, by the three nails that were driven into the hands and feet of God; I forbid you by the four good women who stood there on two feet and said: "Born of the two bodies of woman," and which, with a true love, was granted them all that was possible—this was Mary, the mother of God, and Jesus Christ, and milady Saint Elisabeth and milord John the Baptist; I forbid you, by this judgment that God spoke over me and over the living and the dead; I forbid you by the pious cross of Our Lord Jesus Christ on which he suffered martyrdom for me and for all Christians; I forbid you, by the divine power that is in heaven and earth, from hurting me, me, servant of God, or harming any of my limbs, my head, my brain, my eyes, my teeth, my hands, my feet, my fingers, my ribs, my back, my kidneys, my hops, my bones, my feet, my teeth, my veins, everything! Whatever side I may turn, may the divine power succor me as it did the holy tomb where God rested when all that existed shook. Pilate said: "Have you illnesses or gout?" "No I do not." Any man or woman who bears these words on their person will be assured that gout shall never again paralyze them. I believe that no man and woman

can refute these words because the sinner near the cross was pardoned. Give me, God's servant, health of soul and body like that of Mary when she gave birth to her dear son. Amen.

 📖 Germany, ca. 1370, Grimm, *Deutsche Mythologie*, 3:497; *HDA*, vol. 7, 25ff., "Pilatus."

170 ❖ To Relieve the Pain of Gout

If one cuts the foot off a living rabbit and always carries it on his person, the pains of gout will diminish.

 📖 Germany, sixteenth century. Herr, *Das neue Tier-und Arzneibuch,* chap. 28; Grimm, Deutsche Mythologie, 3 vol., t. 3, p. 497f.

171 ❖ To Provide Relief to the Foot of a Person Suffering from Gout

Write the following names on a band of tin or silver, you attach it to buckskin and bind it to the foot of this person. The buckskin [should have] two streamers.

> *Thembarathem, Nourembrenoutipe, aïokhthou semmarathemmou, naïoou!*

Then say, "Heal [name] to whom [mother's name] gave birth, of all the illnesses that are in his feet and in the soles of his feet!"

 You do this when the moon is in the constellation of the Lion.

 📖 Lexa, *La Magie dans l'Égypte antique,* 93ff.

172 ❖ Against Gout

Say nine times while fasting, *terra pestem tenere salene, salene, salene manete his hire padibus,* then kiss the ground and spit upon it, next rub the afflicted limbs with volatile alkali [ammonia] for seven days, and you will be relieved, for gout cannot be truly healed.

 📖 France, eighteenth century. *Les Œuvres magiques de Henri-Corneille Agrippa,* 94.

173 ❖ Against Gout

Place cow manure mixed with a great deal of salt on the suffering area and say:

"[Full name] I hold you . . . in the name of God the Father, God the Son, and God the Holy Ghost! [Full name] I hold your seventy-seven kinds of gout; I hold the one that pulls you, the one that pinches you, the hot gout, the cold gout, the crying gout, the mute gout, I hold all gouts in my hand of a sinner, I see all the gouts with my eyes of a sinner and I command you, in the name of eternal God, by the [unidentifiable word] crown of thorns of Our Lord Jesus Christ to die in this . . . [only the initial of the word Dr. is given]; may you pulverize the seventy-seven lightning bolts, may seventy-seven winds carry you over the seventy-seven mountains! Amen.

  Saxons of Transylvania, nineteenth century Wlislocki, *Volksglaube*, 91ff.

174 ◈ To Heal a Sufferer of Gout

To heal a sufferer of gout, take his toenail parings and hairs from his legs, and put them in the hole of an oak trunk that has been pierced to the marrow. Plug the hole with a peg made of the same wood and cover the top with cow manure. If the illness does not return in the space of three months, the oak has drawn all the illness into it; if it does not stop, start over.

  France, nineteenth century. Cabanès and Barraud, *Remèdes de bonne femme*, 211; Gaidoz, *Un vieux rite medical*.

175 ◈ To Cure Gout

While Jesus was out walking he met Cananias. "What have you got, Cananias?" "I have gout." "Tie it to a green willow in the name of the Father, the Son, and the Holy Ghost. From twilight Thursday to Friday dawn, go in silence to the willow, take three of its branches, pierce a knot through which the patient will have to breathe.

Cananias is probably a corruption of Ananias, the name offered by other such prescriptions. Two saints have this name. The first, whose feast day is December 16 or 17, is one of the three Hebrews cast into the furnace (Daniel 3:12–30), the second is Ananias of Damascus, celebrated on Januay 25 or October 1, who baptized Saint Paul.

  Germany, nineteenth century. CSB 391, "Gicht" (Gout).

176 ◈ Charm for Relieving Gout

Make a string from elder fibers then wrap it around the afflicted limb while saying:

> Gout, I bind you with this tie,
> Jesus was bound with;
> Jesus was freed and rose up to heaven;
> You, go down into hell,
> In the name of God, and so on.

📖 Saxons of Transylvania, nineteenth century. Wlislocki, *Volksglaube*, 92.

HEADACHE

177 ◈ To Cure a Headache

It is said that if one pours vinegar on the hinges of doors, it will make a mud that, when applied to the forehead, will cure headache; the rope used to hang a man wrapped around the temples will produce the same effect.

📖 Latin, first century. Pliny, *Historia naturalis*, XXVIII, 86.

178 ◈ To Dispell a Headache

Attach plantain root at the throat. It works wonders at dispelling headaches.

📖 Latin, fourth century. Pseudo-Apuleius, *Herbarius*, 1.

179 ◈ For Migraine

If the right side [of the head] is suffering, write *hyof* on the skin, if it is the left side *cela hhhc*. Similarly write on a parchment:

> whti ω σι aa loti poca zonie ho ωaΛΥΡΙΣε.

📖 Latin, fifth century. Pseudo-Theodore, *Theodori Prisciani Euporiston*, 314, 30 ff.

180 ◈ To Heal a Migraine

To heal a migraine, place your hand on the patient's head and say three times: *Hoebae etho oras erbe bo Abraxat boetite.*

📖 Latin, eighth century. Önnerfors, "Iatromagische Beschwörungen," no. 3.

181 ❖ To Heal a Headache

When the sun is in the sign of Aries, if you collect and dry sheep dung, and then apply it with vinegar to the one suffering from headaches, that one will be healed.

 📖 Latin, twelfth century. *Liber Kyranidorum*, 124, 13–14.

182 ❖ To Cure Violent Headaches

If a man is suffering from violent headaches, place a sardonyx on his head while speaking this spell: "Just as God cast the first angel into the abyss, may this ill vanish from [name] and all his awareness be restored."

 📖 Twelfth century. Hildegard von Bingen, *Physica*, IV, 7, "On the Sardonyx." Cf. Lecouteux, *A Lapidary of Sacred Stones*.

183 ❖ To Heal Headaches

Carve the figure of Aries with that of Mars, who is a man armed with a lance, and of Saturn, who is an old man holding a scythe in his hand, both being direct, and Jupiter not being in Aries, nor Mercury in Taurus.

 Or simply mark Aries when the sun is in this sign.

 📖 France, seventeenth century. Dom Jean Albert Belin, *Traité des talismans ou figures astrales*, 109.

184 ❖ To Cure a Headache

Bind your temples with a hangman's rope to no longer feel a headache.

 📖 France, seventeenth century. Thiers, *Traité des superstitions* (1679), 333.

185 ❖ To Find Relief from Head Pain

Our Lord God was sitting at the door of the church when his mother passed by. "Dear Son and Lord, why are you so sad, today?" He answered: "Most dear Mother, I cannot help but be sad: my poor head hurts and has almost made me senseless. Who would have believed that no one would believe me?" She said: "You will be comforted as you have spoken to me of it with your own mouth. What will you give me if I heal you with a benediction?" He answered: "I would give you heaven and earth to find relief and feel better." She blessed him with her hand and his pain quickly vanished.

 📖 Latin, 1416, Kalocsa, Hungary, Föszékeseghyhàzi Könyvatär, MS 629, fol. 25r.

186 ❖ AGAINST HEADACHE
Repeat the following verse:

> *The Virgin Mary and her Virgins*
> *had gone to the beach.*
> *They then saw the brain flowing.*
> *They came out of the water and prayed*
> *and placed it between the brain and the skull.*
> *With God's blessing.*

This charm alludes to the Three Marys who replaced the mythic figures of the Fates.

📖 Sweden (Norrköping), 1617–18, Klintberg, *Svenska trollformler*, 74, no. 25, "huvudvärk."

187 ❖ AGAINST MIGRAINES
The patient should have a third party rub, press, and wet his head with water or vinegar while saying this charm that is meant to exorcise the demon responsible for the affliction:

> *Pain, pain in my head!*
> *With the Father of all ills*
> *You must, cursed pain, vanish!*
> *Go far away, be intelligent,*
> *You have caused me enough suffering!*
> *Your home is by no means here*
> *and I want to expel you from my head*
> *Return back to where you were nursed,*
> *Return there, nasty one!*
> *Go into the head*
> *of the one who is walking on my shadow!*

Confused with the soul in the lexicon of many peoples, the shadow is the tracing of the soul, its double. This is why stepping on someone's shadow is a serious offense in certain cultures.

📖 Gypsies of Transylvania, nineteenth century. Wlislocki, *Volksdichtungen*, 137.
📖 Lecouteux, *Witches, Werewolves, and Fairies*, 137–41.

188 ◆ For Headaches

For headaches, write on a wild beast's hide the following names and attach them around the head: lioness, lion, bull, tiger, bear. While you are attaching them, pronounce these names silently.

> 📖 Latin, ninth century. St. Gallen, Stiftsbibliothek, Codex 751; Heim, "Incantamenta magica," 555ff.

189 ◆ For Headaches

Write the word *Athena* on an olive leaf and bind this leaf to the head with a handful of double parsley.

"Athena" refers to Zeus/Jupiter's migraine when he was giving birth to Athena/Minerva.

> 📖 France, eighteenth century. *Les Œuvres magiques de Henri-Corneille Agrippa*, 83. Morvan, nineteenth century. Cabanès and Barraud, *Remèdes de bonne femme*, 212, although the parsley is no longer mentioned.

HEATSTROKE, SUNSTROKE

190 ◆ To Cure Overheating

To keep your head from overheating in summer, wear pennyroyal, either on your ear or beneath a gold ring.

According to Macer Floridus, pennyroyal (Mentha pulegium) *was also recommended against serpent bites and against the evil eye.*

In nineteenth-century France this was a recommended cure for heatstroke:

> On the stroke of noon, take a glass full of unfiltered water and put in a piece of salt as large as a hazelnut and place the glass on the patient's head while reciting an Our Father and a Hail Mary. Next, Saint Eugenia and the patron saint of the ailing individual should be invoked. These prayers should be repeated three times while keeping the glass of water on the patient's head. Repeat this operation for nine days in a row. On the ninth day, one sees the water boiling and the patient is cured.

> 📖 Latin, fourth century. Pseudo-Apuleius, *Herbarius*, 93.
> 📖 Macer Floridus, *De viribus herbarum*, vv. 626–77; G. Camus, *Circa instans*, no. 391; M. Platearius, *Livre des simples médecines*, 2:233, chap. 343.

191 ❖ Against the Rays of the Sun
Say the following verse:

> *I bless you with my right foot,*
> *You will be protected against two illnesses;*
> *Against the maladies of the lungs,*
> *Against the maladies of the tongue.*

People believed that the rays of the sun were dangerous and imagined them as arrows. The *"sun shot"* (solskott) *designates illnesses that are difficult to diagnose and involves the sudden and unexpected attack of a painful disease. We find this notion in Denmark and southern Sweden. The concept of the healing foot is also familiar. The tongue disease is probably a wound in this organ like a crack or canker sore (Norwegian* munnskåld).

📖 Sweden (Småland), 1870–80, Klintberg, *Svenska trollformler*, 75, no. 30, "solskott."

HEMORRHOIDS

192 ❖ To Cure Hemorrhoids
"By the holy Paschal baptism and by the holy day of Pentecost and by the holy night of Christmas and by the holy words one speaks on these three days, I conjure you, hemorrhoid, to remain tranquil, to not worsen or grow, but to wither. May milady Saint Mary and the most holy Christ succor me, He of whom you have need, amen." A priest should speak this charm.

📖 Alemannic (Alsace), fifteenth century. Birlinger, "Aus einem elsässischen Arzbeibuch des XIV Jahrhunderts."

193 ❖ To Cure Hemorrhoids
Take saliva from your mouth with the middle finger of your left hand, and when touching the hemorrhoids, say: "Pins, go away, God curses you, in the name of the Father, the Son, and the Holy Ghost."

After which, say nine Pater and nine Aves during seven days; on the second day say only eight, and reduce the number by one on each successive day.

Earlier, Pliny the Elder noted the use of saliva in various cases: as an

antidote against snakes, for boils, for eye inflammations. Here is a particularly lovely practice: One heals pains in the neck by applying saliva, while fasting, with the right hand to the right knee and with the left hand to the left knee" (Historia naturalis, XXVIII, 37).

📖 France, seventeenth century. Honorius, *Le livre des conjurations*, 123; *Les Œuvres magiques de Henri-Corneille Agrippa*, 92.

HICCUPS

194 ❖ TO STOP HICCUPS

To make hiccups stop, you must, without breathing, say and repeat this spell:

> *I have the souglot [hiccups]*
> *Barbaro*
> *Please to Gù [God]*
> *I have them no more.*

📖 France (Ardennes), nineteenth century. Meyrac, *Traditions*, 174, no. 58; *HDA*, vol. 7, 1223–24.

HYDROPS OR DROPSY (EDEMA)

195 ◆ To Heal Dropsy

The stone from the head of the hydra heals hydrops; it must be tied to the patient's belly. The stone is procured like this: the snake is hung up and exorcized to make it vomit the stone, and then smoked with laurel wood while saying: "By the God that created you and who you worship rightly with your forked tongue, if you give me the stone I will not harm you but return you to your home." Once he has expelled the stone, keep it in a piece of silk.

📖 Latin, twelfth century. *Liber Kyranidorum,* 200, 12ff.

196 ◆ Prayer for Requesting the Healing of Hydrops and Pale Coloring

Repeat the following prayer:

> My God, command my blood to purify and the water that is too abundant within it to change into blood, as you changed into wine the pitchers of water at the wedding in Cana. My God, do not refuse me this miracle, and if it finally manages to pass, by *Dominum Jesum Christum,* let it be so.

📖 France, nineteenth century. *Le Médecin des pauvres,* 4ff.

HYSTERIA

197 ◆ To Bind the Uterus

> *Here three women are standing*
> *On the southern side of the table.*
> *They are weaving blue thread*
> *And spinning it on a gold loom.*
> *I would bind Pain and Claw*
> *For one hundred years*
> *And then for as long as the world shall exist.*
> *Bite these words and Amen.*

This charm is founded on a notion dating back to antiquity according to which the uterus moves about in the woman's body. When the uterus starts moving, women become hysterical. We should note that in folk beliefs that men are also equipped with a uterus if we take Finnish charms at their word. There are illnesses such as uterine prolapse, digestive disorders, and so on, which are the source of this concept of a uterus that enjoys a certain independence. The three women mentioned in the charm are the Germanic Norns who correspond to the Parcae of classical antiquity.

 📖 Sweden (Småland), 1831, Klintberg, *Svenska trollformler*, 74, no. 27, "Binda barnmodern."

 📖 *HDA*, vol. 2, 438ff., "Dreifrauensegen."

ILLNESSES IN GENERAL

198 ❖ To Banish Fear and Misfortune

In order to banish all fear of disease and misfortune, pluck the Scotch thistle [*Onopordum acanthium*] only if the moon is in Capricorn, as long as you carry it on your person, nothing will happen to you.

 📖 Latin, fourth century. Pseudo-Apuleius, *Herbarius*, 110.

199 ❖ To Make All Illnesses Take Flight

Say this prayer four times over water and give it to the patient to drink: "Here is the sign of the cross †. The cross is the remedy for all things. By this sign of the cross, may all illness immediately take flight! And may by this same sign † be saved whoever wears the cross of the sweet Jesus who triumphs, rules, and commands." Write the Our Father and this benediction nine times.

 📖 Latin and Middle Dutch, mid-fifteenth century. Ghent, Universiteitsbibliotheek, MS 697, fol. 142v.

200 ❖ Against All Illness

Repeat the following phrases:

> I go into the vast plain, beneath the dazzling sun, beneath the clear crescent, beneath the sparkling stars, beneath the floating clouds; I gird myself with clouds, I cover myself with the skies, I place upon my head the dazzling sun, I wrap myself in clear auroras, I scatter countless stars like so many sharp arrows, to protect myself from all harmful illness.

📖 Russia, nineteenth century. Gruel-Apert, *La Tradition orale russe*, 107.

201 ◈ Second Pentacle of Mars
The image below is successfully used against all manner of illness if it is applied over the suffering part.

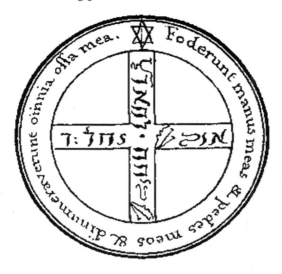

IMPETIGO

Impetigo is a skin disorder characterized by rashes and itching. In the Middle Ages, according to the ancient French translation of Bernard of Gordon's Practica, *it was known as impetigine and serpigine, and was considered to be one of the four forms of leprosy.*

202 ◈ Against Impetigo
Repeat this spell:

> *Impetigo has nine daughters:*
> *The nine have become eight,*
> *The eight have become seven,*
> *The seven have become six,*
> *The six have become five,*
> *The five have become four,*
> *The four have become three,*

The three have become two,
The two have become one,
The one has become none.

A reducing spell of the most common kind found throughout the whole of Europe since late Antiquity.

 📖 Sweden (Småland), 1763, Klintberg, *Svenska trollformler,* 78, no. 40, "revormar"; Tillhagen, *Folklig läkekonst,* 257–59.

INFLAMMATION

203 ❖ CLIP THE INFLAMMATION OF THE JOINTS

The creakings in the limbs are cut with an ax. The diseased limb is placed on a threshold. Then the healer strikes the sensitive sides of the limb while he and the patient exchange these words:

"I strike and strike and strike."
"What are you striking?"
"I am striking the chain of creakings so they leave the limb and enter the vein."

This is for peritendinitis and tendovaginitis. The Swedish knarren involves inflammation, a very painful affliction that makes itself known in the swollen joints, a kind of gout. People who work hard are susceptible to this. The painful joint should be placed on a chopping block and the healer make symbolic chops next to it. Traditionally the healer used an axe to heal the patient, but there are variations.

 📖 Sweden (Angermanland), 1937, Klintberg, *Svenska trollformler,* 73ff., no. 24, "Hugga bort knarren."

INSOMNIA

204 ❖ TO MAKE SOMEONE SLEEP

Unbeknownst to the patient, write in silence on a virgin parchment: "IωIωKONNIAA C. NNOYε to the one who birthed this woman" and place it under his or her head.

 📖 Latin, fifth century. Pseudo-Theodore, *Theodori Prisciani Euporiston,*

307, 23ff.; Franz-Josef Kuhlen, *Zur Geshichte der Schmerz-, Schlaf-, und Betäubungsmittel in Mittelalter und Früher Neuzeit.*

205 ◆ To Sleep
Place a sheet of paper beneath the head of the insomniac with the words below written on it and make him eat lettuce or drink poppy crushed in a mortar and mixed with beer.

> † Ysmael † ysmael † I adjure you by the angel to put this man to sleep.

📖 Middle English, fourteenth century. London, British Library, Sloane 963, fol. 53r. For more on lettuce see Macer Floridus, *De viribus herbarum*, vv. 765–75.

206 ◆ To Fall Asleep
If you hang the beak of a heron with crawfish bile in a donkey skin around the neck of someone who cannot sleep, he will fall asleep.

📖 Greek, fourteenth century. ΚΥΡΑΝΙΣ III, E.

207 ◆ To Induce Sleep
With the blood of a bat that has never alit upon the ground write on a candle: *luculus vennus haben bata biltus*. All will sleep as long as this candle is burning.

📖 Middle Dutch, fourteenth century. Ghent, Universiteitsbibliotheek, MS 697, fol. 35v.

208 ◆ To Return to Sleep
Take a hammer, a broom, and an iron, go out at midnight and shout: "Mother of the forest and of midnight, return to [name] the sleep of lambs, calves, piglets, and, most importantly, all that is small and cute. If you do not return it to him, I will strike you with this hammer, sweep you with this broom, and burn you with this iron."

In north Russia the cause of childhood insomnia is a fantastic female called the Midnight. It comes at night and tickles the soles of the child's feet and makes noise. The most widespread spell for driving out the Midnight is: "You have come from the forest, go back to the forest! You have come from the wind, go back to the wind! You have come with the passersby, go back with the passersby!"

📖 Romania, nineteenth century. Schullerus, *Rumänische Volksmärchen*, 44.

📖 Mazalova, "La médecine populaire dans les villages de la Russie du Nord," *Ethnologie française* 4 (1996): 669.

JAUNDICE

209 ◈ To Cure Jaundice

A person with jaundice should tie this little bird [widderwalo]—feathers and all—when it is dead, over his stomach. The jaundice will pass into it, and he will be cured.

📖 Twelfth century. Hildegard von Bingen, *Physica*, VI, 62, "Widderwalo"; Heinrich Schipperges, *Hildegard von Bingen, Heilkunde: Das Buch von dem Grund und Wesen und der Heilung der Krankheiten*.

210 ◈ To Cure Jaundice

Take an apple, cut it into quarters, throw away the fourth quarter. On the first write "In the name of the Father and the Son Jesus of Nazareth †;" on the second, "† and of the Holy Ghost," and on the third, "king of the Jews. Amen."

📖 Latin, thirteenth century. Oxford, Bodleian Library, Ashmole 1444, fol. 139.

211 ◈ To Cure Jaundice

Jaundice, where do you come from? You are there, whence you came, and you have nothing to do in [name]. Starting today, I forbid you, as true as the clear sun shall rise, to remain in this man.

Leave him, go from his marrow into his bones, from his bones into his flesh, from his flesh into his hand, from his hand into the wind, the gentle son of the holy mother wishes it! In the name of . . . , and so on.

📖 Transylvanian Saxons, nineteenth century. Schuster, *Siebenbürgisch-sächsische Volkslieder*, 309.

212 ◈ To Cure Jaundice

Urinate into a hollowed-out turnip and hang it in the chimney hood. As the urine evaporates the illness will disappear.

In nineteenth-century Belgium, one had the patient urinate on an omelet or round loaf, that was then given to a dog to eat. The dog would die and the person would be healed.

 📖 Saxons of Transylvania, nineteenth century. Wlislocki, Volksglaube, 91; Hock, *Croyances et Remèdes populaires du pays de Liège*, vol. 4, 127.

213 ◆ To Kill Jaundice

Three women took three yellow axes, took them in their yellow hands, rested them on their yellow shoulders, took three yellow paths, reached three yellow forests, chopped down three yellow trees, left by three yellow paths, and arrived at the yellow farm, at the yellow farm they entered the yellow common room, and found themselves facing the yellow [name]. They slew the jaundice with the three yellow trees, they struck it down dead in the name of God.

The three yellow women are fairies or the Three Marys; they countered the illness with its own color.

 📖 Transylvanian Saxons, nineteenth century. Bartels, "Über Krankheits-Beschwörungen," 30.

 📖 D. A. Mackenzie, "Color Symbolism," *FolkLore* 33, no. 2 (1922): 136–69.

LACTATION

214 ◆ To Increase Lactation

If you pierce a galactide* and thread it with the wool thread from a pregnant ewe and hang this stone from the neck of a woman, it will generously fill the breasts with milk when she wears it.

 📖 Latin, ninth century. Marbode, *De lapidus*, 42.

LETHARGY

215 ◆ To Cure Lethargy

Anyone who wears a bat's head wrapped in black cloth tied to his right arm, will not sleep or drowse as long as he carries it; keeping the heart of the bat on his person guarantees the greatest alertness.

 📖 Latin, twelfth century. *Liber Kyranidorum*, 121.

---

*[Stone with a milky appearance. —*Trans.*]

LEUCOMA

A macula or spot over the eye, leucoma was known in Medieval French as maille *or* catharata.

216 ❖ To Cure Leucoma

If one gathers water lilies before sunrise, it is said they will take away the white spots from the eyes and all ocular pain.

    📖 Latin, fourth century. Pseudo-Apuleius, *Herbarius*, 23§1.

217 ❖ To Cure Leucoma

† *Alia* † *nec lia* † *nec gallina* † On the edge of the sea, the macula was sitting †. White † which Christ dispersed † or red, which Christ dissolved † or black, which Christ detached from Your servant † *Agyos* † *agyos* † holy cross. Amen.

This spell was passed on as far north as Denmark, and of course with corruptions. It became † Alia † nec glia † nec alma † *in fifteenth-century Denmark (Ohrt,* Danmarks trylleformler, *no. 1158). Thanks to a tenth-century manuscript from Reims (MS 304, fol. 158) we know that it is the chicken* (gallina) *that heals the patient of his leucoma.*

In France (Burgundy), the following charm was still being used last century:

> *The Three Marys went off*
> *Beyond the mountains*
> *Seeking a cure*
> *For eyespots and buds [cataracts].*
> *They met Our Lord Jesus Christ*
> *Who asked them: "Marys, where are you going?"*
> *"Lord, we are going*
> *Beyond the mountains*
> *In search of a cure*
> *For eyespots and buds."*
> *Our Lord told them: "Mary, Marion,*
> *Go back to your homes*
> *There you will find a cure*
> *For eyespots and buds."*

📖 Latin, ninth–tenth century. Wickersheimer, *La médecine et les médecins en France au temps de la Renaissance*, 154ff.

218 ◈ AGAINST LEUCOMA
Repeat the following prayer:

> Heavenly Father, drive away the spot and cloud from the eyes of this man like you have removed the cloudy spot from the eyes of your servant Jacob. In the name of the Father † and the Son † and the Holy Ghost † amen. *Kirieleison, Kristeleison, Pater Noster.* January, Felix, Philip, Salvan, Alexander, Vital, Martial. These are the seven sons of Saint Felicity, they can help us. Amen.
>
> I conjure you to disappear † spot or pain of the eyes, irritating stain, by the Father † and the Son † and the Holy Ghost † and by His valorous mother, Saint Mary, and by the twenty patriarchs, and by the four Evangelists, and by the twelve apostles †, by all the saints and all the elect. I conjure you by the sign of the holy cross †, by the blessed remedy of the holy body of Our Savior Jesus Christ and His holy blood, by His five wounds, by all the angels of God—to return whence you came, *Kirieleison, Kristeleison, Pater Noster. Nilaria dulcie* (?) *filana Christophorus Abraham divina inclina* (?) *Satripina,* dear saints, help us in this distress, *ayos, ayos, ayos, sanctus, sanctus, sanctus, sominus deus santus, omnipotens,* Lord, take pity on us! I conjure you, eyespot, to vanish from this man, by the power of the holy Trinity. *Kirieleison, Kristeleison, Pater Noster.*
>
> Blow then on his eyes while naming them.
>
> Christ triumphs, Christ rules, Christ commands †. May the blessing of the heavenly Father succor the eyes of His servant as You have healed those of Tobias, and may they expel all that is harmful so that we may celebrate Your compassion and laud You, for all eternity. Amen.

At this moment, touch the ground. Our Lord touches the earth and wets it with His saliva, then smeared it on the eyes of the man born blind while saying: "Wash yourself. Because you believe, you will be enlightened by the sign of the holy cross †.

I command you, eyespot, by God † the Father, by † the Son and by † the Holy Ghost, by the terrible judgment, by the holy name of the holy Trinity, by Saint Mary, by the holy angels Gabri (el) † and Saint Raphael †—to utterly vanish never to return! You are so commanded by the Father, by † the Son and by † the Holy Ghost †. May the blessing of the Trinity touch your eyes, amen."

There where you see a cross, you will make the sign of the cross in contemplation. This blessing is good for the eyes.

📖 Mixture of Latin and Middle High German, fifteenth century. London, British Library, Additional 28170, fol. 113v.

219 ◆ To Cure White Spots on the Eyes

The good Lord and the good Virgin were out walking,
The good Saint John happened by.
God told Saint John:
"Sit down over there!"
"I have too many problems with my eyes."
"Sit down there, I will heal you."
White spot,
I tend to you.
Red spot, I touch you.
Black spot, I heal you.
In the name of the Father, †
The Son, †
The Holy Ghost, †
So shall it be. †

📖 France, twentieth century. Dominique Camus, *La Sorcellerie en France aujourd'hui*, 324ff.

220 ◆ To Cure the Eyes

Repeat this prayer three days in a row and, with the help of the imagination, you will be cured.

Three holy virgins were going
Beyond the mountains
In search of a cure,

The Illnesses of Humans and Their Cure

*For the eyes and the bud
When their road led them to meet
The Baby Jesus who asked them:
"My three virgin ladies, where are you going?"
"Lord, we are going over the mountains
To find a cure*

> *For the eyes and the bud."*
> *Baby Jesus answered them:*
> *"Go back to your homes.*
> *There you will find a cure*
> *For the eyes and the bud."*

The bud is the cataract. This prayer also works for animals.

📖 France, nineteenth century. Cabanès and Barraud, *Remèdes de bonne femme*, 286ff.

221 ❖ Orison for an Eye Problem

Blessed Saint John, passing here, met three Virgins on his path, he asked them: "What are you doing here?" "We are healing spots over the eye." "Heal, Virgins, heal the eye or eyes of [name]." While making the sign of the cross and blowing into the eye, say: "Eye spot, late grief or [what] whether it be nail paring, seed, or spider, God commands you to have no more power over this eye than the Jews did the day of Easter over the body of O.L.J.C." Then make the sign of the cross again while blowing into the person's eyes saying: "God has healed you."

Without forgetting a novena on behalf of the blessed Saint Claire.

📖 France (Troyes), ca. 1840. *Laissez dire et faites le bien: Le Médecin des pauvres,* 8ff.

LOSS OF SPEECH

222 ❖ To Regain Speech

If a man loses the power of speech through an illness, crush alum in water and pour it into his mouth: he will speak.

📖 Old Provençal, early fifteenth century. Cambridge, Trinity College, MS R 14.30, fol. 145.

LUMPS

The following recipe is one of the countless examples of the transfer of ills into something else, in this case into the earth.

223 ❖ Against Lumps

When a child bumps his forehead, press against the bump with a knife blade while saying:

*Soften, soften, soften you
and disappear quickly!
Go into the ground
never to return!
Knife, knife, eradicate it,
send it back into the ground!*

The person then stabs the knife into the ground then pulls it back out.

📖 Gypsies of Transylvania, nineteenth century. Wlislocki, *Volksdichtungen,* 145ff.

LUNACY

It was long believed that a man under the moon's influence was subject to moments of madness and could even act like a beast at these times. The metamorphosis of a man into a werewolf was explained by the stages of the moon in this way.[9]

224 ❖ To Cure Lunacy

If a lunatic wears verbena around his neck during the waning moon and when it is in the first decan of the sign of Taurus or Scorpio, he will be healed.

📖 Latin, fourth century. Pseudo-Apuleius, *Herbarius,* 8§1.

225 ❖ To Cure Lunacy

A pill of felty germander [*Teucrium polium*] and the root of this plant placed in a clean cloth and hung around the neck of a lunatic will cure him. This is proven.

📖 Latin, fourth century. Pseudo-Apuleius, *Herbarius,* 57§1.

226 ❖ To Cure Lunacy

If peony is placed on a sleeping lunatic, he will rise immediately healed, and if he carries it on him, he will never be struck by this evil.

📖 Latin, fourth century. Pseudo-Apuleius, *Herbarius,* 65§1; G. Camus, *Circa instans,* no. 360; Platearius, *Livre des simples médecines,* 2:229, chap. 330.

227 ◆ To Heal Lunatics
A mole's heart in buckskin will heal lunatics.

📖 Latin, twelfth century. *Liber Kyranidorum*, 140, 16.

228 ◆ To Cure Madness
The sting of the scorpion, the tip of the basil holding the seeds, and the heart of a swallow worn hung from the neck or in a buckskin, heals lunatics of their madness. This phylactery also drives away demons who refuse to go away.

📖 Greek, fourteenth century. ΚΥΡΑΝΙΣ IV, Ω.

229 ◆ To Recover the Mind
When someone has lost his reason due to illness, write these words on a piece of bread and give it to him to eat. He will recover his right mind:

† DISTON † GRATON † BORSIBS ††

📖 Germany, sixteenth century. Heidelberg, Universitätsbibliothek, Cpg 268, fol. 24r.

LUXATION (DISLOCATION)

230 ◆ To Heal Dislocation or Fracture
Take a green reed four or five feet long and split it down the middle, and let two men hold it to your hips. Begin to chant: "*motas uaeta daries dardares astataries dissunapiter*" and continue until the two sides of the split reed meet. Brandish a knife over them, and when the reeds meet so that one touches the other, grasp them with the hand and cut them right and left. If the pieces are applied to the dislocation or the fracture, it will heal. However, chant every day, and, in the case of a dislocation, in this manner, if you wish:

Huat hanta huat ista pista sista domiabo, danmaustra.

Or else:

Huat haut haut ista sis tar sis ardannabou dannaustra.

📖 Latin, third century BCE. Cato the Elder, *De agricultura*, 160.

MADNESS

231 ◆ To Cure Delirium
The magi are certain that individuals suffering from delirium will regain their reason if sprinkled with mole's blood.

 Latin, first century. Pliny, *Historia naturalis*, XX, 14.

232 ◆ Against Madness
Take marsh mallow, lupine, paquerette [daisy], polypody, corn-cockle, and elecampane. When night and day divide, sing the Litanies, at church: those of the names of the saints, and Our Father. Leave still stinging, make your way to where the plants are, and circle them three times. When you have gathered them, return to the church singing the same song, and sing twelve masses over them in honor of the twelve apostles, as well as over all the brews indicated for this illness.

 Old English, tenth century. *Leechbok*, in Cockayne, *Leechdoms*, vol. I, 138.

233 ◆ For Someone of Vacillating Mind
Write these letters and hang them about his neck:

> Illness has vanquished you, Jesus treats you, the Virgin saves you,
> *m m a. τ vos.*

 Provence, early fifteenth century. Cambridge, Trinity College, MS R 14.30, fol. 145.

234 ◆ For the Insane
A man devoid of his senses should wear agrimony tied to his right arm, a woman to her left arm: this will restore their good sense and intelligence.

 Middle High German, Speyer, 1456. Berlin, Staatsbibliothek Preussischer Besitz, Codex mgf 817, fol. 6r.

MALEMORT (TRAGIC OR SUDDEN DEATH)

235 ◆ A Charm against Sudden Death
In a collection of exempla, the Compilatio singularis exemplorum *(fifteenth century), we find a sharp critique against charms; it takes the form of this narrative:*

A priest had made a charm against the malemort [or mallemen] and had great success. One of his companions asked the priest to teach it to him. He taught it to him after much beseeching on condition that as long as he lived he would not use it or teach it to anyone else unless he collected two denars from each person. Here is the charm:

> *Belly, belly may God*
> *Let you fart as you are accustomed.*
> *Branchy thistle, horned beetle,*
> *All the shit of the belly sprints to the ass.*

He says nothing more, nothing less, and he obtains healing. What trickery!

📖 Vaisbrot, "Édition critique," ex. 810 (kindly sent to me by Jacques Berlioz).

MULTIPLE-PURPOSE RECIPES

236 ◆ To Expel Illness

You and the patient both fasting, while holding the affliction at fault with three fingers, the thumb, the middle finger, and the ring finger, and while raising the other two, say: "If you were born today or earlier, if you were created today or before, get out!" With this charm and consecration. I expel this illness, this tumor, large or small, this skin rash, this swelling, this scrofula, large or small.

📖 Latin, fourth century. Marcellus, *De medicamentis liber,* VIII, 62.

237 ◆ To Expel Pain

Decomal titianos npocyanteos, which in Latin means "for all pains inside and out," even for those stricken by quartan fever or who have begun to feel feverish. Write these names in ink on virgin parchment. dilute them in three measures of warm water that you will give the patient to drink. This is a proven remedy.

> *acko MENEIBOS cvpω aαopNe avtvRa. dekeviωik.*

📖 Latin, sixth century. *Antidotarium Bruxellense,* 368.

238 ◆ To Deliver from Torment

† Before the front door of the lord centurion, the paralytic is tormented.
† Before the front door of the lord centurion, the paralytic is tormented.
† Before the front door of the lord centurion, the paralytic is tormented.
† You, lord centurion, deliver so-and-so from the power of paralysis, from the power of languor, from the power of fever, from the power of the dropping temperature, from the onset of quartan fever, from the onset of tertian fever, from the onset of daily fever!

📖 Latin, eighth century. Paris, Bibliothèque nationale, Lat. MS 13246, fol. 253v.

239 ◆ A Charm against Vermin

Here is a charm for charming Christians against vermin and all kinds of gout, fistulas, and fevers.

The patient should not eat any meat or ingest any drink.

† In the name of the Father, the Son, and the Holy Ghost. Amen. As true that God was and is, as true as that he was well formed, as true that what he said was well said, as true that he incarnated through the Virgin, as true that he was crucified, as true that he received five wounds in his body, as true that two thieves were hung on either side of Him, as true that His holy feet and hands were pierced by nails, as true that His glorious head was crowned with thorns, as true that He spilled His blood upon the cross, through which the devil was bound and vanquished, as true that on the cross he humbly suffered death, thanks to which we have received the baptism, as true that His holy body rested in the tomb and resurrected on the third day, as true that he rose to heaven when He wished and rested at the right of His father, and that He will come on the day of judgment and that each and all will rise again in flesh and blood, and that Our Lord his five wounds will show and as he wishes will judge, as true as it is true, that healed be [name] of gout, abscess, canker, vermin, and all manner of fever and gout.

Then say three Our Fathers in the name of the Father, the Son, and the Holy Ghost, then have read the Four Gospels: *Rogobat Jesusm quidam Phariseus; Cum natus esset Jesus in Bethleem; Recumbentibus undecim disciple; In principio erat verbum.*

📖 Latin, thirteenth century. London, British Library, Sloane 146, fol. 67rv–68r.

240 ◆ To Heal Conjunctivtis

The quail is known to all. Its eyes, when worn around the neck, will heal conjunctivitis, tertian fever, and quartan fever.

Hung from the right arm, the stones found in the swallow's stomach heal hepatics; they protect from coughs, head colds, inflammation of the uvula and tonsils, and all forms of conjunctivitis.

📖 Greek, fourteenth century. *ΚΥΡΑΝΙΣ* III, O.
📖 Greek, fourteenth century. *ΚΥΡΑΝΙΣ* III, C.

241 ◆ Prayer for Healing Toothaches, Headaches, or Earaches

Saint Apollonia was sitting on a stone of marble, when Our Savior, passing by, asked her: "What is tormenting you?"

"I am here, divine teacher because of the pain, because of my toothache,"

"Apollonia, turn around, if it is a drop of blood, it will fall; if it is a worm, it will die.

📖 France, eighteenth century. *Le Médecin des pauvres,* 7.

242 ◆ Against All Manner of Fevers

When Jesus saw the cross on which his body had been placed, his body shivered, his blood shot through him. He happened upon a Jew named Marquantin, who said to him: "I believe your are scared or in the grip of fever."

"No," Jesus answered, "I have neither fear nor fever at all; but whoever this orison will say, wear on his right arm, never will fever and trembling take hold of him."

> Tertian fever, semi-tertian fever, quartan fever, semi-quartan fever, slow fever, daily fever, intermittent fever, malignant fever,

purplish fever, fever of whatever nature you may be, I conjure you to leave [name]'s body in the name of the Father † the Son † and the Holy Ghost † and of Milord Saint Peter and Milady his Mother, who will cure him of fever, if it is a man, or who will heal her, if it is a woman.

You fold this note while speaking in the name of the Father, and so on, then tie it on to the right arm of the fever sufferer with five needles of crimson thread; also while speaking in the name of the Father, and so on. It should be worn for nine days; when it is put on, one should be fasting.

 📖 France, eighteenth century. *Les Œuvres magiques de Henri-Corneille Agrippa,* 93–94.

243 ◈ A Prayer Against Injury
Say the following prayer:

> In the name of the Father and the Son and the Holy Ghost. Milady Saint Anne who gave birth to the Virgin Mary, the Virgin Mary who gave birth to Jesus Christ, God bless you and heal poor creature [name] of a leg-breaking wound, fracture, and annoyance, and all other kinds of injury of any kind in the honor of God and of the Virgin Mary and of Milords Saint Cosmas and Saint Damina. Amen.

Then say three Pater[s] and three Ave[s].

 📖 France, eighteenth century. Lebrun, *Superstitions anciennes et modernes,* 97.

244 ◈ Orison in Case of Cholera, Typhus, Sweating Sickness, Scarlet Fever, Pox, and So Forth

> Only God, All-powerful God, source of life and health, we fall upon our knees to beg you for your mercy; it is within you, God of clemency, that we come to repent in the soul, and with spirit filled with good intentions, to seek a haven against the afflictions that ravage us. We flee to you, O God, Father of all salvation, to ask you to tame your wrath that we have overly encouraged with our wickedness. Lord, may your exterminating angel no

longer strike with his sword; we confess our sins and transgressions, we proclaim to the heavens our redemption; Lord, grace and pity for our offenses; God give us the time to expiate and atone, as you did for holy King David. May your virtue, Our Father, may your grace, be spread over us like a blanket of protection. O Lord, purify us! O Lord, pour upon us the balm of your *sanite* [health]! O blessed Saint Francis of Sales, intercede for we poor sinners. *Magnificamus te,* we say to you great above all. *Laudamus te,* we praise you. *Glorificamus te,* we glorify you forever. Amen.

Oddly enough we find in this orison the medieval notion of illnesses as punishment for sins, and divine protection like a breastplate (lorica). *The Latin is borrowed from the* Gloria.

We find this significant passage in Johann Weyer's book:

Put on the whole armor of God, that you may be able to stand against the wiles of the Devil. . . . Stand therefore, having girded your loins with truth, and having put on the breastplate of righteousness, and having shod your feet with the equipment of the Gospel of Peace, above all taking the shield of faith with which you can quench all the flaming darts of the evil one. And take the helmet of salvation, and the sword of the spirit—which is the word of God. . . ." (*De praestigiis daemonum*, 5.1, 361–62).

📖 France, eighteenth century. *Le Médecin des pauvres,* 6ff.

NEVUS

245 ❖ TO CURE A BIRTHMARK

For a nevus: while touching the wall and putting your finger in the back, say three times: "Pu pu pu, may I never see you again through the wall."

The nevus is a mole children can have at birth. This ordinarily congenital skin lesion is also called strawberry mark or birthmark.

📖 Latin, fourth century. Marcellus, *De medicamentis liber,* XVIII, 30.

NIGHTMARE

246 ◈ To Cure the Affliction of Nightmares

If someone is afflicted by nightmares, place some betony in his bed.

📖 Greek, fourteenth century. *ΚΥΡΑΝΙΣ* III, O.

📖 Twelfth century. Hildegard von Bingen, *Physica*, I, 56, "On Betony"; G. Camus, *Circa instans*, no. 70; Platearius, *Livre des simples médecines*, 2:90, chap. 59.

247 ◈ For Protection from Insomnia and Nightmares

This sign must be carved on a piece of brown coal with a magnet for protection from insomnia and nightmares.

📖 Iceland, seventeenth century. Ólafur Davidsson, "Isländische Zauberzeichen und Zauberbücher," *Zeitschrift des Vereins für Volkskunde* 13 (1903): 277.

248 ◈ Protection from Nightmare Demons

Repeat the following:

> Witch and all evil spirits, in the name of the Holy Trinity, I forbid you, my belongings, my flesh, my blood, I forbid you all pinholes in my house and farm until you have scaled every mountain, crossed all waters, counted all the leaves of the trees and all the stars of the sky before sunrise, when the mother of God gave birth to her son. †††

It was believed that the nightmare was a demon named Ephialtes (William of Auvergne, De Universo, 2.2, 833 C; 945 B; 2.3, 1069 C) or the double of a witch that would come lie atop the sleeper, or a spirit called the mahr, a term we find in the French word for nightmare, cauchemar. This double could gain entry through the smallest gap—like a keyhole, for example. By obliging it to complete an impossible task, one could find shelter from its nocturnal attacks.

📖 Switzerland, nineteenth century. Rochholz, "Aargauer Besegnungen," 114.

 📖 Lecouteux, "Mara-Ephialtes-Incubus: Le cauchemar," *Études germaniques* 42 (1987): 1–24; "Le double, le cauchemar, la sorcière," *Études germaniques* 43 (1988): 395–405. Bridier, *Le Cauchemar: Étude d'une figure mythique;* Carl-Herman Tillhagen, *The Conception of the Nightmare in Sweden;* Bernard Terramorsi, ed., *Le Cauchemar: Mythologie, folklore, arts et littérature.*

NOSEBLEED (EPISTAXIS)

249 ◈ To Stop Nosebleed

Using the patient's blood write on three laurel leaves: *Tantale pie, pie Tantale, Tantale pie.* Wash them next with pure leek juice, and make the patient drink it.

 📖 Latin, fifth century. Pseudo-Theodore, *Theodori Prisciani Euporiston,* 276, 10ff; Macer Floridus, *De viribus herbarum,* vv. 507–48.

250 ◈ To Stop the Flow of Blood from the Nose or Vein

One must write these letters on the patient's forehead with his own blood: a † g † l † a and speak this charm: "Our Lady was sitting on a bench holding her son in her lap. True mother, true child, true vein hold your blood! In the name of Jesus I command you to not let even one more drop escape!" The patient should then say three Pater Nosters and three Ave Marias with the person who spoke the charm, which he must say three times. Never has this failed.

 📖 Latin and French, ca. 1300, London, British Library, Sloane 146, folio 48v–49r; Lecouteux, "Agla: Remarques sur un mot magique," in *Le Secret d'Odin: Mélanges pour Régis Boyer,* 19–34.

251 ◈ Protection against Blood Flowing from the Nose

Against blood flowing out of the nose, make this sign on the forehead, XX. Next take a wisp of straw with two knots and cut the knots, then write this sign on his forehead with his blood.

 📖 Middle French. Cambridge, Trinity College, MS O 1.20, fol. 43v–44r.

252 ◈ To Stop Bleeding

When a person is bleeding from the nose or elsewhere, you should write

upon him a Greek name O. P. E. W. E. N. with his own blood, it's true, and say into his ear: "I conjure you, blood, by the Father, the Son, and the Holy Ghost, to cease flowing like the Jordan stopped flowing when Jesus was baptized."

 📖 Middle High German, Tyrol, fifteenth century. Zingerle, "Segen und Heilmittel," 315.

253 ❖ Against Epistaxis
Cover the blood with dirt while saying:

> *Phuvush, I give it to you,*
> *Phuvush, take it from me,*
> *Give it to your child,*
> *Carry it off quickly!*

For the gypsies, the Phuvush (Pçvuš, *fem.* pçuvuši) *is a small, ugly, hairy chthonian spirit who lives under the ground. He is sometimes described as resembling a mole with a human head. His name is formed from* pçuv, *"earth," and* "manuš, *"man." he is generally kind but will abduct women.*

📖 Gypsies of Transylvania, nineteenth century. Wlislocki, *Volksdichtungen,* 146.

PAIN, BLADDER

254 ◆ FOR BLADDER PAIN

Write this on pigskin for a man, and on the skin of a sow for a woman, and tie it by the navel:

Abara barbarica borbon cabradu brabaarasaba

📖 Latin, fourth century. Marcellus, *De medicamentis liber,* XXVI, 43.

PAIN, GROIN

255 ◆ TO HEAL TUMORS OF THE GROIN

Some, to heal tumors of the groin, tie nine or seven knots, naming each knot after some widow, on a thread taken from a web that is then attached to the groin as an amulet. To prevent such a wound from being painful, they tie a nail or some other object that patient has walked on to the person with thread.

📖 Latin, first century. Pliny, *Historia naturalis,* XXVIII, 86.

256 ◆ TO HEAL PAINS OF THE GROIN

To heal pains of the groin and excoriations, wear the tip of a sucker of wormwood on the belt.

📖 Latin, fourth century. Pseudo-Apuleius, *Herbarius,* 101§4.

257 ◆ TO MAKE PAIN DISAPPEAR

The root of henbane attached to the thigh and over the pain will cause it to disappear.

📖 Latin, fourth century. Marcellus, *De medicamentis liber,* VIII, 130; Floridus, *De viribus herbarum,* vv. 1933–61.

PAIN, JOINTS

258 ◆ TO EASE JOINT PAIN

To counter joint pains, chant this song nine times over the painful area and spit on it:

The Evil One has bound, the angel has healed, the Lord has saved."

The patient will soon feel better.

📖 Old English and Latin, tenth century. *Læce boc*, in Cockayne, *Leechdoms*, vol. 2, 312.

PAIN, KIDNEY

259 ◆ To Ease Kidney Pain
May someone whose kidneys are suffering write on a virgin parchment the characters below and seal them in gold or copper, and attach them around the kidneys. It is a marvelous remedy:

χαραβραως

📖 Latin, fourth century. Marcellus, *De medicamentis liber*, XXVI, 43.

260 ◆ To Ease Kidney Pain
When you undress to bathe, before getting into the water, take some oil with your left hand and say this name: *Φαρμαχους*. Say this three times while rubbing your hands with the oil; wash them nine times.

📖 Latin, ninth century. Önnerfors, "Iatromagische Beschwörungen," no. 18.

261 ◆ For Kidney Affliction
Say "Lady Moon, daughter of Jupiter, just as the wolf cannot touch you, may the pain not touch my kidneys; if you eat my kidneys, I will hit you."

📖 Latin, ninth century. Önnerfors, "Iatromagische Beschwörungen," no. 19.

262 ◆ Against Kidney Pain
Tie hairs from a virgin to the painful part while saying: "Pain of the kidneys, I bind you with this virgin's hair, not nine times, eight times; not eight times, seven times; not seven times, six times; not six times, five times; not five times, four times; not four times, three times; not three times, two times; not two times but one time; jump ninety-nine times over the hair and stamp your feet one hundred times."

This charm uses the counting-down techniques that is a version of the decreasing or reducing spell: to force the withdrawal of an illness of misfortune, one takes a magic word and subtracts from it a letter one by one until only one remains.

📖 Saxons of Transylvania, nineteenth century. Wlislocki, *Volksglaube*, 91.

263 ◈ A Talisman against Stones

Carve upon a strip of gold the image of a lion who has some gravel in front of him, as if he was playing with it, the hour is that of the sun and under the the middle decan of Leo and the sun is in this degree. He who is suffering from stones should take this strip onto his person and his pains shall disappear. This has been proven.

📖 Arabic magic, mid-eleventh century. *Ghāyat al-hakīm*, I, 5, 34.

PAINS, MULTIPLE

264 ◈ Against Pain

Say the following verse.

> *Our Lord Jesus Christ was pursuing his path,*
> *Blessed be his name!*
> *He met an ill man.*
> *"What is your illness?"*
> *"Erysipelas has settled in and rheumatism is flowing*
> *And I am suffering from migraine, erysipelas, and gout,*
> *Rheumatism, pain when I strike my fist, volatile pain,*
> *Burn, pain in my limbs, explosive pain,*
> *Colic, reed pain, pain when I make a fist,*
> *Fleeting pain, headache, sore throat,*
> *Pain in the heel, pain in the arm, pain in the side,*
> *Pain in the back, pain in the chest, pain in the belly,*
> *Pain in the hip, pain in the thigh, pain in the knee,*
> *Pain in the leg, sharp pain, stabbing pain,*
> *And all the kinds of pains that strike the body."*
> *"All these pains I will confine them*
> *On the crag where no one dwells*

And in the lake where no one paddles;*
This pain shall do you no more wrong
Than the sand beneath a rock stuck in the ground."
 †††

 📖 Sweden (Småland), 1831, Klintberg, *Svenska trollformler*, 72ff., no. 22, "värk."

265 ❖ To Remove Pain

If you find a pain in your body or that of somebody else, get rid of it with a talismanic procedure from the Prophet (*ruqîya rasûl Allah*). When someone complained of an ulcer or a wound, the Prophet would place his finger on the ground then stand up and say: "*Bismillah* the dirt of our home mixed with the saliva of one among us, heals our disease, by the will of our master."

 📖 Arabic magic, twelfth century. From the *Ihyâ'* of al-Ghazali, in Hamès, "Entre recette magique d'Al-Bûnî et prière islamique d'al-Ghazali,", no. 86.

266 ❖ To Heal Several Disorders

If you wish to eliminate the different disorders or diseases that are implicit of disposition, as the doctors say, and prevent evil spells or poison from causing harm, make an image from very pure silver during the hour of Venus in the fourth, seventh, or tenth house and when Venus is well aspected and when the lord of the tenth is looking at fortune in a trine or sextile aspect, and when the lord of the fourth will be in Mercury's quadrant aspect. Make certain that Mercury is not in retrograde or burnt by the sun and is not being injured by the evil rays of the bad aspect of Saturn. This image must be made in the last hour of the day of the Sun, when the lord of the hour will be in the tenth house on the side of the ascendant. This image will therefore infallibly cure the disorders of disposition.

 📖 French translation of the Picatrix [the *Ghāyat al-hakīm*], eighteenth century. Paris, Bibliothèque nationale, Fr. MS 14788.

---

*Ills or evil spells are always banished to the wilderness and solitary places where men do not go.

PAIN, NECK

267 ◈ For Neck Pain

For neck pains you should write on a gold blade in gold letters the characters below on the twentieth day of the first moon, then place the blade in a gold tube or wrap it in a goat hide attached with a strip of goat skin to the right foot, if it is the right side of the throat that hurts, or to the left foot if it is the left that is causing the pain; this is how you should wear it. For as long as one uses this amulet, it is necessary to abstain from the games of Venus, and for the woman to not enter a tomb; all this must be respected. For this neck pain, one must avoid ever putting the shoe on the left foot first.

LYMΘKIA
LYMΘKIA
LYMΘKIA

📖 Latin, fourth century. Marcellus, *De medicamentis liber,* XXVIII, 26.

PALPITATIONS

268 ◈ To Cure Palpitations

For the beatings of the heart, write on virgin parchment: "† Just as the wolf touches not the egg," wrap it in an unbleached fabric that you will tie to your knee. On the fifteenth day of the moon, pluck some celandine and give it to the patient with salt.

📖 Latin, ninth century. St. Gallen, Stiftsbibliothek, Codex 751; Heim, "Incanta magica graeca latina," 564.

PAROTIDES

This is swelling of the parotid glands in the ears.

269 ◈ To Cure Parotides

To calm the parotides, the root of asphodel wrapped in black wool and tied around the neck is a remedy.

📖 Latin, fourth century. Marcellus, *De medicamentis liber,* XV, 35.

270 ◆ Against the Skin Disease called Paishe

I conjure you, angel that brings grace into every illness, which befalls man, and especially in this illness, which attacks man in his old age! May this illness leave [name] of [name of home]. They are Oriel, Gabriel, and Raphael who pray for the cessation of all illness! May [full name] vomit it out!

The charm has been Christianized by the mention of the three archangels; it is from the Coptic Magic Papyrus in the Borgiano Museum.

 📖 Zoega, *Catalogus codicum copticorum manuscriptorum qui in museo Borgiano Velitris adservantur*, 627–30.

PLAGUE

In ancient times, the word plague *designated both the pestilence we are familiar with, and which was made famous by the great black plague of the fourteenth century, and various other afflictions. Saint Roch was invoked for his protection against it.*

 📖 Biraben and Le Goff, "La peste dans le haut Moyen Âge," Annales E.S.C. 24 (1969): 1484–1510; Naphy and Spicer, *The Black Death and the History of Plagues*; Coppin and Welpy, *La Peste: Histoire d'une épidémie*.

271 ◆ To Get Rid of the Plague

Say the following words:

> Disappear, bubo, as disappeared the man who braided and tied the rope that bound Jesus Christ when he was captured. You should do the same, bubo, disappear!

 📖 Middle High German, fourteenth century. Heidelberg, Universitätsbibliothek, Cpg 244, fol. 113r.

272 ◆ Blessing of Plague Patients

Recite a Pater Noster and the Credo while fasting, then say over the patient: † *Christus vincit* † *Christus regnat* † *Christus imperat*. Then write these words on a long parchment made from a stillborn calf, long enough to go around the neck, and tie it there with linen thread. It is

Saint Roch, patron saint of plague victims, visiting a hospital, 1484.

proven and true, the angel brought it from heaven to Rome and gave it to the pope at his instant request and insistent prayer.

> † *kay vinghan adonay satheos mire ineffabile omiginam ona animam misane dyas mode unde nemat gemasten orcamin sanguine berenisone irritas venas cansi dulis fervor fixiantis sanguinis siccatur. Fla fla gra gra frigela virgum et siden benedicite dominus.*

Then write on this same *bref*:

Our Lord be blessed as well as the day of his birth, may this person be likewise.

Write the name he is called on this *bref*. In the name of the Father, the Son, and the Holy Ghost. Amen.

The same spell can be found earlier in tenth- and eleventh-century England, against diarrhea, and in the Netherlands during the fifteenth century to stop bleeding. The corruptions[10] cannot be translated, but what survives of a coherent text indicates that it was a spell against bleeding.

📖 Middle Dutch, fifteenth century. London, British Library, Additional 39638, fol. 15r–v.

📖 Berthoin-Mathieu, *Prescriptions magiques anglaises du Xe au XIIe siècle.*

PLEURISY

273 ◆ To Cure Pleurisy
Write the following in a glass: *Dia Biz, On, Dabulh, Cnerih.*

📖 France, 1670, Honorius, *Le livre des conjurations*, 74.

POISON AND VENOM

274 ◆ Against Poison
If someone suspects the presence of poison in something, he should hold a dead starling over it. If there is truly poison, its wings will spread apart and start to move.

📖 Twelfth century. Hildegard von Bingen, *Physica*, VI, 50, "Starling"; Müller, "Krankheit und Heilmittel im Werk Hildegards von Bingen," in *Hildegard von Bingen, 1179–1979, Festschrift zum 800. Todestag der Heiligen*, 311–49.

275 ◆ To Stop the Effects of Poison

If someone has been poisoned let him write these words on three brefs of virgin parchment, and swallow one at noon, and one in the evening. Even is someone sought to kill him, the effect of the poison will be annihilated and the man will recover his health. Here are the words:

††† *Agla* ††† *effrecga* ††† *agla* ††† *refoa* †††

📖 Middle High German, fifteenth century. Kalrsruhe, Badische Landesbibliothek, MS Donaueschingen 792, fol, 138v.

276 ◆ Against Poison

Say the following verse:

> *Poison, in doing this I beseech you,*
> *In asking the aid of Saint Urh [Ulrich] and Saint Margarethe.*
> *Begging you before the living God*
> *To take back the poison from all venomous animals.*
> *If you no longer live, may your parents take it back for you.*

Make the sign of the cross, blow on the bread, and strike it three times with your knife. Recite the Our Father and the Angelic Salutation.

📖 Slovenia, nineteenth century. Monika Kropej, "Charm in the Context of Magic Practice: The Case of Slovenia," *Folklore* 24 (2003): 70.

277 ◆ To Drive Away Poison

There is a holy mountain, there is a holy seat. Saint Šempas is seated on a holy chair, holding a holy sword in his hands. The Virgin Mary comes looking for him, holding Jesus the Merciful in her arms, and says to him: "Why don't you drive away this poison and the beast from which it comes? Return it to the animal whence it came!" Say three Our Fathers in honor of Saint Šempas over a piece of bread and give it to the animal.

Saint Šempas is the popular alteration of the Latin name of

Saint Bassus (or Pass, in German), first changed to Saint Basso and then into Šempas buy fusing the two words. Šempas is also the name af a Slovenian village.

📖 Slovenia, nineteenth century. Slavec and Makarovič, eds., *Zagovori v slovenski ljudski Zupanič ter zarotitve in apokrifne molitve.*

278 ◈ Protection against Sudden Death

This orison was at the sepulaire [tomb] of Jesus Christ, and whoever carries it on their person shall not die a sudden death, not be attacked by a venomous beast, finally, wherever this orison is, no evil can occur.

> Jesus Christ, son of the living king, help me, savior of the world, save me.
> Holy Virgin pray to your dear beloved son for me poor sinner, Queen of Angels, mirror of the blessed, Virgin Mary at the time my soul departs my body. Forgive me all my sins. So be it.

This is a short narrative of the "legend-prayer of the Holy Sepulcher" that a priest is supposed to have discovered wrapped in a cloth. It is a variant of the "letters fallen from Heaven."

📖 *Revue du clergé français* 89, no. 529 (1917), 264ff.

PUSTULE

279 ◈ For Pustules Appearing Suddenly on the Tongue

Before speaking, touch the pustule with the edge of the tunic you are wearing and say three times: "May he who speaks ill of me perish!" and spit an equal number of times on the ground. You will be healed immediately.

Even in the twentieth century, it was believed that if someone was speaking ill about you, pustules would appear on your tongue; it was then necessary to bite the left edge of one's tunic or apron, or bite one's elbow, in this way the ill sayer would bite his own tongue. Or else spit three times into a handkerchief and knot it shut, and strike it with the hand. The pustules would boomerang back on the person speaking ill. (Cf. Wuttke, *Der deutsche Volksaberglaube*, 287.)

 📖 Latin, fourth century. Marcellus, *De medicamentis liber*, XI, 21.

280 ❖ Against Pustules

> *Jesus was following his path.*
> *He met a galloping pustule.*
> *"Where are you going"*
> *"I am going to the peasant's farm.*
> *To make holes there and break bones."*
> *"You shall not go there at all.*
> *With nine fingers of God*
> *And ten angels of God*
> *I send you beneath a rock stuck in the ground.*
> *There you shall live and you shall do no wrong to anyone.*
> *Shame on you, backsliding pustule,*
> *Cursed galloping pustule,*
> *You shall ride cats and claws,*
> *And all the dogs living in Hell!"*

 📖 Sweden (Medelpad), 1908. Klintberg, *Svenska trollformler*, 69, no 14, "stryga" (fulsang).

RABIES

281 ❖ To Cure Rabies

Write this on bread and give it to eat to the one with rabies and to all animals: *Bus gur raber sibis graon diton. Si gur ramina pax peun pax inpeon peopn pax ita amen.*

 📖 Latin, ninth–tenth century. *Archiv der Gesellschaft für ältere deutsche Geschichtskunde* 7 (1839), 1020–21.

282 ❖ Remedy for Treating the Bite of a Dog or Any Other Rabid Beast

Take a bread crust and on it write the following words: † *bestera* † *bestie* † *brigonay* † *dictera* † *sagragan* † *es* † *domina* † *fiat* † *fiat* † *fiat*.

 📖 France, ca. 1393, *Le Mesnagier de Paris*, 788.

283 ◆ Against the Bite of a Rabid Dog
Have [the victim] eat cantharides nine days in a row. One on the first day, two on the second, three on the third, and so forth. Then nine on the ninth, eight on the tenth, seven on the eleventh, and so on. They must be wrapped in paper on which has been written: "Saint Christopher, help me! *Pater, fili, spiritus*"; the person swallows the paper at the same time as the cantharides.

 📖 Saxons of Transylvania, nineteenth century Wlislocki, *Volksglaube*, 96.

284 ◆ For Rabies
Write this on the butter of three slices of bread that should be given the patient to eat in the morning, the evening, and the following morning:

> *Irijon + Sirijon + Karbon + Karfun + Stilida + Stalitara + Kakara + Idata + Stridata + Sijan + Beijan + Ad deus + Meus +*

 📖 Lithuania, nineteenth century. Vaitkevičienė, *Lietuvių užkalbėjimai*, no. 1395.

RASH OR OTHER OUTBREAK

285 ◆ To Get Rid of a Rash
The trunk of a tree should be split into two, without separating the two halves completely, and the patient should be passed between them. Next, one must say:

> May the three holy women examine my wounds, may they remain close to me until I am cured. May the wounds go hide in the wild woods so they may die there in the name of Lord God! Amen!

Then one draws a cross above the affected area.
This healing technique is called "transfer" (transplantatio morborum). *In it, an individual rids himself of an ailment by transferring it into a tree, a plant, the water, and so forth.*

 The Jesuit Martin Delrio provided another method of transfer in 161:

130   The Illnesses of Humans and Their Cure

Transplantatio morborum.

To heal the evil spell of hairs, needles, thorns, and similar things, which sorcerers stuff inside the body by means of the Devil, they should not be cut out of the body but once they have voluntarily emerged, seal them in the hollow of an oak or elder facing the east, and then plug the hole of same tree while saying certain words.

📖 Saxons of Transylvania, nineteenth century. Wlislocki, *Volksglaube*, 85.

📖 Bartholin, *De Transplantatione morborum dissertation epistolica*; Fischer, *Das Buch vom Aberglauben und falschen Wahn*, 168–70; Delrio, *Les Controverses et Recherches magique*, 989; Saintyves, "Le transfert des maladies aux arbres et aux buissons," *Bulletin de la Société préhistorique française* 15 (1918): 296–300; Grabner, "Die 'Transplantatio morborum' als Heilmethode in der Volksmedizin," *Österreichische Zeitschrift für Volkskunde* 21 (1967): 178–96.

RHEUM

Rheum is a sticky yellowish secretion that collects and hardens on the edge of the eyelids.

286 ◈ To Cure Rheum

Harvest the root of the *Rumex sylvestris* (a small sorrel or dock) during the waning of the moon and wear it; so long as you have it on your person, you will not suffer from rheum.

📖 Latin, fourth century. Marcellus, *De medicamentis liber*, VIII, 41.

287 ◈ To Cure Rheum

When rheum gets established, it can surely be cured in a marvelous fashion by writing on a virgin parchment: φυρφαραν, and that you attach this amulet to a cord, and that this be done in a state of purity.

📖 Latin, fourth century. Marcellus, *De medicamentis liber*, VIII, 56.

288 ◈ To Cure Rheum

With a copper needle, carve these words on a gold blade: Ορωνω συρωδη. Hang it by a ribbon around the neck of the patient; this will keep him well for a long time if the application is performed on a Monday and if you have been chaste.

📖 Latin, fourth century. Marcellus, *De medicamentis liber*, VIII, 59.

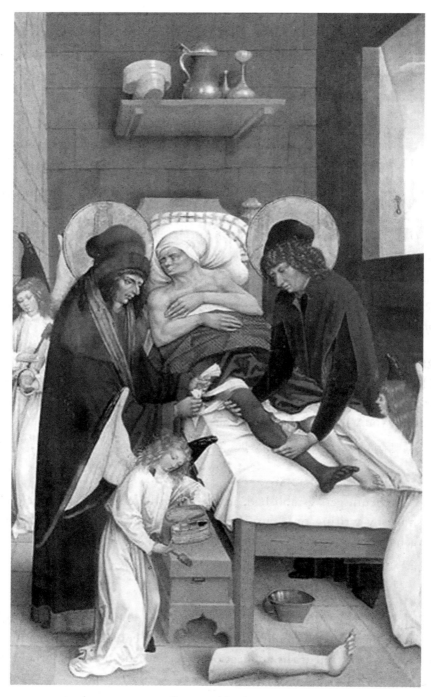

Cosmas and Damian.

RHEUMATISM

289 ❖ Against Rheumatism

Have the miller or the miller's wife strike with the mill hammer three times while saying: *in nomine patris,* and so on.

 📖 France, eighteenth century. Lebrun, *Superstitions anciennes et modernes,* 82; Coulon, *Curiosités de l'histoire,* 44.

290 ❖ To Heal Rheumatism

To heal rheumatism, which some call *enchappe,* by having the miller or miller's wife of three races strike the mill hammer three times near the patient while saying *In nomine patris,* and so on.

 📖 France, eighteenth century. Thiers, *Traité des superstitions* (1777), 4:337.

291 ❖ Orison for Rheumatism and Other Sufferings

Blessed Saint Anne who gave birth to the Virgin Mary, Virgin Mary who gave birth to Jesus Christ, God heal you and bless you, poor creature, of illnesses, wounds, fractures, and all kinds of disabilities in the honor of God and the Virgin Mary, like Saint Cosmas and Saint Damian healed the five wounds of Our Savior. Say three Paters and three Aves for nine days every morning while fasting, in honor of the agonies suffered by Our Savior Jesus Christ on Calvary.

In the nineteenth century, in the arrondissement of Verviers (Belgium), rheumatics would go to the cemetery in search of five coffin nails that they would wear around their neck in a small pouch. The local gravediggers made a business out of selling these "good nails."

 📖 France, M. Le Pesant, "Prières superstitieuses du pays d'Ouche," *Annales de Normandie* 3, nos. 3–4 (1953): 328.
 📖 Hock, *Croyances et Remèdes,* 3:161.

RICKETS

292 ❖ Against Carreau (*Tabes Mesenterica*)

Say these words:

 Holy Son, I am complaining to you because the carreau is

irritating me. The carreau in the liver and in the lungs. From wherever it came to me, may God and good Saint John heal me. In the name of God, amen.

Carreau or mesenteric atropia, is a form of rickets.

(Cf. Charles Blomme, *Dissertation sur l'atropie mésenterique vulgairement connue sous le nom de carreau.*)

 📖 Middle Dutch, fourteenth century. Leiden, MS Mij. Ned. Letterk. 960, fol. 2v.

293 ◈ To Heal a Child of Carreau

To heal a child of carreau, take up a church paving stone before sunrise and without letting anyone see you. Then apply it to the patient's stomach.

RINGWORM

In ancient times, ringworm, scabies, and impetigo were often commingled in prescriptions. In the first century, Pliny the Elder in Historia naturalis *(XXVII, 100) proposed the following remedy:*

> The stone customarily found near rivers bears a dry, gray moss. It should be crushed into powder to which is added saliva and another stone. With this latter, you rub the scaly part while saying: "Flee cantharides, the wolf is greedy for blood."

The spell in quotation marks is in Greek in the text. It is thought that moss mentioned here is peat moss (Sphagnum L.). *The spell can be understood this way: just as cantharides eats the wheat, scabies gnaws the flesh.*

294 ◈ To Cure Ringworm

Saint Peter upon the bridge of God was sitting; Our Lady of Caly went there and asked: "Peter, what are you doing here?" "Lady, it is for the pain of my head that I have come here." "Saint Peter, you will rise; to Saint Agert you will go; you shall take the holy ointment from the mortal wounds of Our Lord; you will rub them upon yourself and say Jesus Maria three times. You must make the sign of the cross over your head three times."

📖 France, seventeenth century. Honorius, *Le livre des conjurations*, 79; *Les Œuvres magiques de Henri-Corneille Agrippa*, 90.

295 ◈ PRAYER FOR RINGWORM

Paul was seated on a marble stone, Our Lord who was passing that way, asked him: "Paul, what are you doing there?" "I am here to heal the problem with my head." "Paul, get up and go find Saint Anne so that she can give you some oil, you will grease yourself lightly with it while fasting, once a day for one year and a day. He who does this will have no bad temper, scabies, ringworm, or rabies."

You must repeat this orison for one year and a day without missing a single day, every morning before breaking your fast, and at the end of this time you will be radically healed, and freed from all these evils for life.

📖 France (Troyes), ca. 1840, *Laissez dire et faites le bien: Le Médecin des pauvres*, 4.

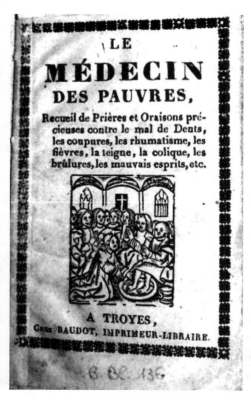
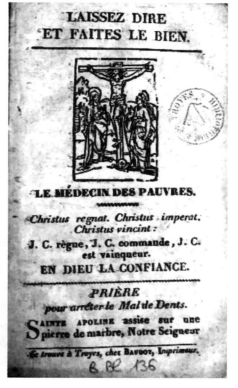

SAINT ANTHONY'S FIRE, HOLY FIRE

*An illness caused by rye ergot, a fungus. In 945, the annalist Flodard described what he then called the fire plague. Saint Anthony's Fire (*Thönigisfeuer *in Alemannic) is still called* ignis sacer *(holy fire), Saint Marcel's Fire, the burning disease, and ergotism. It is also used to designate erysipelas, shingles, and gangrenous ergotism.*

296 ❖ For the Holy Fire

Write on the part suffering from holy fire: "Flee, the pale Father Black shall follow you!" Also write this on the pain in the head: "YωωBBeVICI." Also write: "aOPOMalω."

📖 Latin, fifth century. Pseudo-Theodore, *Theodori Prisciani Euporiston*, 282: 19ff.

297 ❖ To Relieve the Pain of the Holy Fire

Moreover, do not forget to enchant holy fire with these words: "The fire increases, the door burns, the water is thirsty. Just as I command this error, may this fire not cause me to suffer, nor to redden, nor get worse."

The Pseudo-Theodore uses a figure of speech here called an adynaton, *which is based on something that is naturally impossible and whose absolutely affirmative nature is displayed by its negation. The oldest such European formula dates from the tenth century and is in Old High German:*

> *A bird who flew without feathers,*
> *Was perched on a leafless tree,*
> *A footless woman came along*
> *Who caught it without hands,*
> *Cooked it without fire,*
> *Ate it without a mouth.*

📖 Latin, fifth century. Pseudo-Theodore, *Theodori Prisciani Euporiston*, 282: 19ff.
📖 Gerhard Eis, *Altdeutsche Zaubersprüche*, 73; Archer Taylor, "Vogel federlos once more," *Hessische Blätter für Volkskunde* 49–50 (1958): 277–93; Max Lüthi, *Volksliteratur und Hochliteratur*, 181–224.

298 ◈ AGAINST THE HOLY FIRE
Repeat the following verse:

> *I was crossing through a red forest,*
> *In the red forest stood a red church,*
> *In the red church there was a red stone,*
> *On the stone lay a red knife,*
> *Omen. Amen.*

📖 Switzerland (Argovie), nineteenth century. Rochholz, "Aargauer Besegnungen," 104.

SCABIES

299 ◈ TO HEAL SCABIES
To heal yourself of scabies, wash yourself with dew that fell during the night of Saint John.

📖 France (Ardennes), nineteenth century. Meyrac, *Traditions,* 172, no. 38.

SCARLET FEVER

300 ◈ TO CURE SCARLET FEVER
Repeat the following verse:

> *Scarlet fever, what are you trying to do?*
> *Do you want to create a corpse?*
> *Scarlet fever, abandon your plan,*
> *Go far away into the greenery!*
> *There is a cold spring there*
> *Where you should flounder,*
> *Where you should bathe for eternity.*
> *In the name of G. t. F. a. t. S. a. t. H. G.*

📖 Germany, nineteenth century. Carly Seyfarth, *Aberglaube und Zauberei in der Volksmedizin Sachsens,* 81.

SCIATICA

301 ◈ TO CURE SCIATICA
Before sunrise, go the ocean's edge for three days in a row and swear not to eat garlic. You will recover.

📖 Latin, ninth century. Önnerfors, "Iatromagische Beschwörungen," no. 31; Floridus, *De viribus herbarum*, vv. 161–95; Camus, *Circa instans*, no. 15; Platearius, *Livre des simples médecines*, 2:67, chap. 18.

302 ◈ To Cure Hip Problems

Say the four following words aloud: *sista, pista, rista, xista*.

The spell seems incomplete. In fact, Jean-Baptiste Thiers presented it under this form: Huat hauat ista pista sista dannabo dannaustra, *and indicated it was for treating fractures and hip problems* (Traité des superstitions *[1777]*, 1:361).

📖 France, nineteenth century. Coulon, *Curiosités de l'histoire*, 46; Heim, "Incantamenta magica," 534.

303 ◈ To Get Rid of String (Sciatica, Lumbago)

To get rid of the string [sciatica, lumbago], one must repeat nine times several days in a row:

> String, I bid you good days; you have as many roots as the good Lord has friends, but the friends of God will profit and your roots will die. In the name of the Father, the Son, and the Holy Ghost.

📖 France, nineteenth century. Cabanès and Barraud, *Remèdes de bonne femme*, 288.

SCROFULA

Scrofula (Latin scrofulae) *is the common name for a tubercular deterioration affecting the lymph nodes in the neck. It is also know as the "king's evil." The kings of France and England were believed to have the power to cure this affliction by saying: "The king touches you, God heals you."*

Johann Weyer provided an ancient recipe in 1568:

> And the ancients believed that verbena (crushed with its root, sprinkled with wine, wrapped with a leaf, and heated in the ashes), when laid upon scrofulous tumors, would drive them away, if this was done by a fasting virgin for a fasting patient and if she touched him with her hand while saying: "Apollo forbids the spread of this plague, which a virgin extinguishes."

Healing of scrofula.

At this point she was supposed to spit three times (*De praestigiis daemonum*, 4.7)

📖 Du Laurens, *De mirabili strumas sanandi, solis Galliae regibus christianis divinitus concessa.*

304 ◆ To Cure Scrofula

Culled before sunrise and wrapped in wool that is the color known as native, and, moreover, coming from a ewe that has birthed a female lamb, the root of hibiscus* worn tied to the scrofula, even when suppurating; some believe that for this usage it should be plucked with a gold tool, and care taken to avoid it touching the ground.

📖 Latin, first century. Pliny, *Historia naturalis,* XX, 151.

305 ◆ To Cure Scrofula

Mallow root, or plantain, carried in cloth or tied to a string around the neck will cure scrofula, it is obvious.

📖 Latin fourth century. Marcellus, *De medicamentis liber,* XV, 48.

306 ◆ Orison for Requesting the Healing of Scrofula and Foul Humors

Repeat the following prayer:

> Jesus, who healed the lepers, deliver your servant from the vile evil that afflicts him.
>
> Great Saint Louis, you who touched the scrofulous and restored them to health and purity in their homes, pray so for God to protect this poor world, and for all its wounds to be closed.
>
> Blessed Saint Marcou, come to the aid of those who revere you, and pray so that the miracle of Reims will repeat in their favor.

📖 France, eighteenth century. *Le Médecin des pauvres,* 7; Trüb, *Heilige und Krankheit.*

307 ◆ To Heal Scrofula

To heal scrofula, a fasting virgin need only say:

> *Negat Apollo pestem posse crescere, quam nuda Virgo restringat.*

The phrase comes from Pliny the Elder (*Historia naturalis,* XXVI, 92) and concerns tumors:

---

*Pastinaca latifolia sylvestris.

The tumors are healed by nostrums with honey, by plantain with salt, by cinquefoil, by the root of the persolata used as for other forms of scrofula, by damasonium, and by verbascum mullein crushed with its root, sprinkled with wine, wrapped in its own leaves and heated in ashes, and applied hot. Individuals who have had the experience assure me that it matters a great deal that this application be made by naked young girl, who like the patient is fasting, and that this girl when she touches the afflicted area with the back of her hand, should say: "Apollo, prevent this fire of plague from spreading in the patient who has had it extinguished by a naked virgin." After turning over her hand, she will speak this phrase thrice, and she and the patient will spit three times.

This spell seems to have been spread by a translation appearing in 1584: Gaius Plinius Secundus, History of the World *(Lyon: Antoine Tardif), 2:344.*

In the following recipe negat was replaced by neque. Was this a typo or a reading error? There should be nothing surprising about the fact that the phrase "By Apollo, an evil driven away by a pure virgin cannot grow" turns to a healing god of classical antiquity for help, several centuries later.

📖 France, eighteenth century. Lebrun, *Superstitions anciennes et modernes,* 101.

308 ◆ To Heal Scrofula

Let a virgin girl heat a leaf of mullein in ashes, then apply it to the patient while saying:

> Necque Apollo pestem posse crescere quam nuda virgo.

📖 France, nineteenth century. Cabanès and Barraud, *Remèdes de bonne femme,* 211.

309 ◆ To Chase Away Scrofula

Worn around the neck, plantain roots chase away the evil scrofula and do not permit its afflictions to grow.

📖 Middle High German, Speyer, 1456. Berlin, Staatsbibliothek, Codex mgf 817, fol. 42r; Camus, *Circa instans,* no. 377; Platearius, *Livre des simples médecines,* 2:195, chap. 263.

SCURVY

310 ◈ Prayer for Scurvy

Say the following phrase:

> White canker, red canker, black canker, and all kinds of evil cankers, I enclose the scurvy inside, I curse you and conjure you to depart from me as quickly as the dew leaves before the sun on Saint John's Day, by blowing for three mornings in a row into the mouth of the person before the sun rises.

 📖 France, nineteenth century. *Le Médecin des pauvres* (1857), no. 7.

THE SHAKES

The shakes are characteristic of a feverish state that was once also known as "cold fever."

311 ◈ Protection from the Shakes

Whoever carries a sprig of mullein on his person will have no fear of the shakes and no illness will affect him.

 Mullein (Verbascum thapsus), *was also known as white broth, molene, or Saint Fiacre's herb; it was later used as an herbal tea.*

 📖 Latin, fourth century. Pseudo-Apuleius, *Herbarius*, 72.

312 ◈ To Get Rid of the Shakes and Fever

Say the following phrase:

> I adjure you, shakes and fevers, by all-powerful God and His son Jesus Christ, by the ascension and the descent of Our Savior into Hell, to withdraw from this servant of God and his poor body that Our Lord sought to illuminate. The lion of the tribe of Judah, David's lion, defeats you, he defeats you, he who cannot be defeated. The Christ is born, the Christ is dead, the Christ will come back, *Aius, Aius, Aius. Sanctus Sanctus, Sanctus.* This is why, entering the cities with a salutary stride, traveling through the capitals, the countryside, the hamlets, villages, and towns, He drives out all diseases and treats all bodies.

 📖 Old English and Latin, tenth century. *Læce boc* in Cockayne, *Leechdoms*, vol. 2, 136–38.

SHINGLES

313 ⟡ To Cure Shingles

Pass your hand over your chest several times, at the ailing area, in a clockwise direction, while saying: "Shingles, go away! This is not your place, neither here nor elsewhere. Between nine seas and nine mountains, there is your lodging."

📖 France, Brittany, nineteenth century. Cabanès and Barraud, *Remèdes de bonne femme*, 214–15.

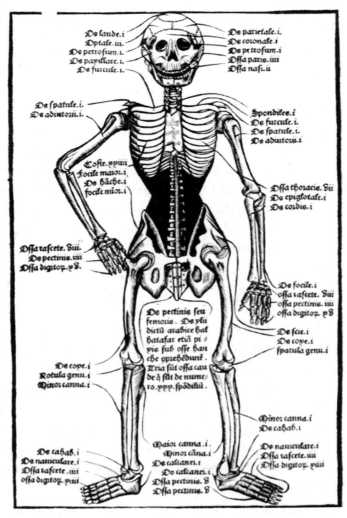

Anatomy, Johannes de Cuba, *Hortus sanitatis*, ca. 1501.

SHOT AND PROJECTILES

A distinction must be made between two different kinds of shot: those received in battle and the arrows shot by fantastic beings that carry disease.

314 ◆ To Extract a Bolt

Didymus pulled the nails from the wounds of Our Lord Jesus Christ. Here are his words:

> *Sunt veriterra amide ellus lancea aliusta carne velocimiliter istis ossibus* †. In the name of the Father † and the Son † and the Holy Ghost. Amen.

   📖 Latin, sixteenth century. Ghent, Universiteitsbibliotheek, MS 1021 A, fol. 142v.

315 ◆ To Remove an Arrowhead

When you reach the place where the wounded man lies and you wish to remove the arrowhead, you must fall down on your knee and say three Our Fathers and three Hail Marys and add: "Nicodemus took the nails from the hands and feet of Our Lord Jesus Christ. In the same way this arrow is pulled from the body of this wounded man. In the name of the Father, the Son, and the Holy Ghost. Amen." It will come out immediately by divine power.

   📖 Middle Dutch, fifteenth century. London, British Library, Harley 1684, fol. 31r.

316 ◆ To Make an Arrowhead Come Out

If an arrowhead has entered the body and cannot be extracted, place your right thumb over the wound, kneel, and say: *"Pater on. fyli. on spiritus. on Jesus Criste.* True God, hear us through the prayer of your servant Saint Blaise and hurry to heal your servant [name], amen." Repeat this prayer as long as the arrowhead has not been pulled out.

   The word on, "he who is" (the Greek ο ων), is regarded as the first name of God. It occurs frequently in charms against fevers, meteors, epilepsy, toothaches, and so forth.

   📖 Middle High German, Tyrol, fifteenth century. Zingerle, "Segen und Heilmittel," 316.

317 ◆ Charm against Shots

Odin's mother stood on a mountain and drew a line through the nine kinds of magical shots:

> Against the shot to the heart
> Against the shot to the lungs
> Against the shot to the liver
> Against the shot to the blood
> Against the shot to the flesh
> Against the shot to the intestines
> Against the shot to the stomach
> Against the shot to the kidneys
> Against all the nine kinds of shots
> Which travel between heaven and earth, beneath moon and sun,
> By the three names!

📖 Norway, Ringerike, 1885, Bang, *Norske hexeformularer og magiske-opskrifter*, no. 886, "For Fin Skød"; Reichborn-Kjennerud, "Krankheit und Heilung in der Frühgeschichte Norwegens," *Niederdeutsch Zeitschrift für Volkskunde* 14 (1936): 1–17.

318 ◆ For Healing of Shot from Arquebuses and Others, Both Old and New, without Ointment or Rags

You shall make a decoction from what I will write for you below: take round birthwort, the weight of two pennies, laurel seed, an equal weight of freshwater crayfish dried in the oven, and which have been caught under the full moon, powdered musk, the weight of a penny, the herb called self-heal [*Prunella vulgaris*], otherwise average comfrey, the weight of four pennies. This herb must be plucked with its flowers and dried in the shade between two cloths. You shall reduce all these drugs to a powder, and after blending them well, place them in a packet of new cloth, which will be tied or sewn shut with a thread. Then you should take a new glazed pot, in which you shall place your packet, with around twenty small branches of periwinkle and three bottles of the best white wine you can find, and after having sealed your pot with three or four sheets of paper, so the steam cannot escape, you shall light the charcoal, and make it boil until you believe that the decoction has been reduced by one-third. Then you shall remove it from the fire, and after letting it cool, you shall put the decoction into two layers of fine linen, and place it in a jar of strong glass, to be used as needed. Make especially sure that the jar is so well sealed that it cannot take wind.

> France, eighteenth century. *Petit Albert,* 157ff; Paré, *La Méthode de traicter les playes faictes par hacquebutes et aultres bastons à feu et de celles qui sont faictes par flèches, dardz, et semblables, aussi des combustions spécialement faictes par la pouldre à canon;* Honko, *Krankheitsprojektile: Untersuchungen über eine urtümliche Krankheitserklärung.*

SPASMODIC SOB

319 ◆ To Stop Crying

When a child is crying spasmodically and cannot sleep, his mother takes a wisp of straw from his mattress, puts it in his mouth and, while she fumigates the child with cow manure mixed with hairs from the mother and father, she whispers:

> With the hairs and the manure
> May the disease be burned!

> Gypsies of Transylvania, nineteenth century. Wlislocki, *Volksdichtungen,* 145.

SPLEEN

320 ◆ To Cure Pain in the Spleen

The fresh spleen of a sheep is placed, by a Magian prescription, over the painful spleen of a patient, the attendant saying that he is providing a remedy for the spleen. After this the Magi prescribe that it should be plastered into the wall of the patient's bedroom, sealed with a ring thrice nine times and the same words repeated. If a dog's spleen is cut out of the living animal and taken in food it cures splenic complaints; some bind it when fresh over the affected part. Others without the patient's knowledge give in squill vinegar the spleen of a two-day-old puppy, or that of a hedgehog.

> Latin, first century. Pliny, *Historia naturalis,* 30.51.

SPRAIN

321 ◆ To Heal a Sprained Foot
This healing must be started as soon as possible, not giving time for inflammation, and the sprain will be subtly healed. The person performing the operation should take off his left shoe, and and use his left foot to touch the patient three times while making the sign of the cross with this same left foot, and while saying the following words. The first time, say *Antè* †, the second time say *Antè te* †, on the third time, *super antè te* †. The ailing foot should be touched above the sprain, and this spell can be used to heal horses as well as men.

The spell Antè, *and so on, was still used in twentieth-century France to protect livestock. The oldest instance of its use can be found in England in a fifteenth-century charm against a sprain in a horse; in Holland,* † *Ante* † *Sus Ante* † *Per Ante* † *cures gout.*

📖 France, eighteenth century. *Petit Albert,* 161.

📖 Camus, *Paroles magiques, secrets de guérison: Les leveurs de maux aujourd'hui,* nos. 77, 79, 81, 87ff.; Camus, *La Sorcellerie en France aujourd'hui,* 101–4; J. van Haver, *Nederlanse Incantatieliteratuur: Een gecommentarieerd compendium van Nederlandse Besweringsformules* (Gand, 1964), nos. 231, 491.

322 ◆ To Relieve the Pain of a Sprain
Repeat the following:

> Sprain, sprain, sprain, if you are in the blood, jump into the marrow; if you are in the marrow, jump into the bone; if you are in the bone, jump into the flesh; if you are in the flesh, jump into the skin; if you are in the skin, jump outside.

📖 France, nineteenth century. Cabanès and Barraud, *Remèdes de bonne femme,* 216.

323 ◆ Prayer for Fixing Sprains, Hernias, and Fractures
Make the sign of the cross over the injury while saying these words three times.

> The four Evangelists, Saints Matthew, Mark, Luke, and John are present here to repair fractures and dislocations (sprains).

During the novena, say five Our Fathers and five Hail Marys while fasting.

 📖 France, nineteenth century. *Le Médecin des pauvres* (1868).

324 ◈ Against Sprains

> *Dåve crossed the bridge over the water*
> *And entered Tiveden Forest*
> *His horse tripped on a root*
> *And sprained its foot.*
> *Odin was passing by:*
> *I shall heal your wound;*
> *Flesh in flesh, bone in bone,*
> *I will place limb against limb,*
> *And never again shall your foot*
> *Suffer misfortune or pain!*
> ††† *Amen.*

This charm, featuring Odin, is reminiscent of the Second Merseberg Charm (late ninth or early tenth century), the oldest known example of the spell for healing a horse's sprain by Odin/Wodan.[11] The perennial nature of the thinking expressed by the Swedish charm is confirmed by the Apocalypse of Peter (third–fourth century), in which we read: "Bone, go to the other bones, in the joints, tendons, nerves, flesh, the skin with its hairs."

 📖 Sweden (Södermanland), ca. 1860–70. Klintberg, *Svenska trollformler*, 66, no. 6, "vrickning."

STERILITY

325 ◈ To Have a Child

Women who have a problem conceiving a child gather the threads of the *Metellina segmentata*, a spider, threads known as the Virgin's threads, and ingest them with their husbands while both say:

> *Keshalyi, spin, spin*
> *As long as water is flowing in the stream!*
> *We invite you to the baptism,*
> *When you will have spun, spun*
> *The red threads of happiness*

> *For the son that we have obtained*
> *By your grace, you Keshalyi*

The Keshalyia/Kešalya (singular Kešly) are fairies of the woods and mountains, the daughters of the King of the Mists who drove them out of his palace after the Sun King had burned his beloved wife. They live in the mountains and forests, sometimes in gold and diamond palaces, and let their hair hang down into the valleys. These are seen in the form of fogs that the Gypsies call "hairs of the Kešalya" (Kešalyakri). Their eyes shine with a green light. Sometimes they weave the invisible caul (amniotic membrane) and ensure the individual's good fortune for life. They are regularly invoked as a cure for sterility.

📖 Gypsies of Transylvania, nineteenth century. Wlislocki, *Volksdichtungen*, 142.

STING

326 ✦ ORISON FOR REQUESTING HEALING OF BEING PRICKED BY THORNS, AND FOR SCRAPES AND BOILS

Say the following orison:

> Sweet Jesus, the crown of thorns that was placed on your forehead left only holes of glory, however, the thorn is wicked, but it is powerless wherever faith reigns. I place my hope in you and pray to you with my hands clasped, my God, per *Christum natum, mortuum, resurrectum et vivum in aeternum, exi spina aut vermiculum.*

The phrase in Latin means: By the Christ who was born, died, resurrected, and lives eternally, leave thorn or little worm." What we find here is a spell that was widely used during the Middle Ages when illness or injuries were perceived as a worm.

📖 France, eighteenth century. *Le Médecin des pauvres*, 6ff.

STOMACHACHE
(SEE ALSO "COLIC" AND "STOMACH GROWLS")

327 ✦ GREAT RECIPE AGAINST THE PAINS OF THE STOMACH

On a silver blade write: "Aritmatho carry off the pains of this stomach that that one but into the world," then wrap the blade in the wool of a living sheep, hang it around the patient's neck, and while doing this, say: "May Arimatho take away the pain of this stomach."

Scholars have interpreted Aritmatho *as the Gallic* aruhmhath, *"the good demon."*

 Latin, fourth century. Marcellus, *De medicamentis liber*, XX, 66.

328 ◈ Against Stomachaches

Burn nine hairs of a black dog into ash, then add it to mother's milk and the excrement of a child. Make a paste from this that you will then place in the hold of a tree while saying:

> *Leave the belly,*
> *Here is a green house for you!*
> *Dwell there, live there*
> *I command you.*

 Gypsies of Transylvania, nineteenth century. Wlislocki, *Volksdichtungen*, 146.

329 ◈ Charm for Bellyaches

One rubs the belly with the hand, smeared with oil, with this incantation:

> Three sows fell from the sky, a shepherd found them, killed them without a knife, baked them without teeth: I have cooked them well, I have cooked them well, I have cooked them well."

*The part of the spell, "baked them without teeth," is based on the merger of two different adynata: "baked them without fire" (*coxit eas sine igni*) and "ate them without teeth" (*comedit eas sine dentibus*), a merger that creates a nonsensical term. In a charm against erysipelas, Marcellus of Bordeaux (chap. 28) writes: "Stolpus fell from the sky, shepherds found this disease, gathered it up without hands, and ate it without teeth." Stolpus personifies the disease, sometimes we also find Stupidus (Marcellus 10.35), and Stulta in a charm against bleeding (Heim, "Incantamenta magica," 498).*

 Latin, mid-fourth century. Pelagonius, *Artis veterinariae quae extant*, 58, no. 121.

 Addabo, "*Stupidus in monte ibat*: ub caso di interdizione verbale?" *Civiltá classica e cristiana* 12 (1991): 331–41.

330 ◆ Spell against Stomachache

Hor, son of Eset, scaled a mountain, wishing to sleep, he sang his songs, spread his nets, and captured a falcon, a bird of prey of the boulders. He cut it into pieces without a knife, he cooked it without a fire, and he ate it without salt. Then his stomach began to hurt around his navel, he started sobbing out loud and cried: "I wish to call home today my mother, Eset! I need a demon so that I may send it to the home of my mother, Eset!" The first demon that arrived, Agrippa, went in and asked him:

"Do you want me to go the home of your mother, Eset?"

He asked: "When will you get over there and when will you get back?"

The demon answered: "I will get over there in two hours and after two hours I will get back."

Hor answered: "Be off with you, that is not suitable."

Then the second demon Agrippa arrived and asked him: "Do you want me to go the home of your mother, Eset?"

He asked: "When will you get over there and when will you get back?"

The demon answered: "I will get over there in one hour and after one hour I will get back."

Hor answered: "Be off with you, that is not suitable."

Then the third demon Agrippa arrived and asked him: "Do you want me to go the home of your mother, Eset?"

He asked: "When will you get over there and when will you get back?"

The demon answered: "In one breath of your mouth I will get there, and in one breath of your mouth I will get back.

"Go, that suits me fine!"

He climbed up the mountain of On and found Hor's mother, Eset, there wearing her iron helmet and making a fire in a copper saucepan.

She asked him: "Demon Agrippa, why have you come?"

He answered her: "Your son Hor climbed a mountain wishing to lie down, sang his songs, spread his nets, and captured a falcon, a bird of prey of the boulders. He cut it into pieces without a knife, he cooked it without a fire, and he ate it without salt. Then his stomach began to hurt around his navel and it caused him great pain."

She told him: "If you do not find me and if you know not my true name that guides the Sun toward the west, that guides the Moon toward the east, and the six stars toward the propitiatory (i.e. star) on which Ra is seated, then conjure the three hundred veins surrounding the navel and say:

"May any illness, any suffering, and any evil that is in the body of [name], son of (the) [name], cease at once! I that am speaking is the Lord Jesus who heals!"

Hor is one of the names of the well-known god Horus, and Eset (Isis) is his mother. Readers cannot help but note the adynaton (combination of incompatible facts) here, such as "cut it up without a knife," and so forth, which can also be found in an old High German charm.

📖 Lexa, *La Magie dans l'Égypte antique,* 100ff.

STOMACH GROWLS

331 ❖ Charm for Rumbling of the Belly

Write the following on a strip of tin and attach it around the neck:
Ante cane corcu nec megito cantorem ut os ut os

Prepare a light wine you like and scatter some arête-boeuf (bull stopper) in the name of the God Jacob, in the name of the god Sabaoth.

Arrête-boeuf (Ononis spinosa)* *is a member of the family Fabaceae.*

📖 Latin, fourth century. Marcellus, *De medicamentis liber,* XXI, 3.

STYE

332 ❖ An Effective Remedy for Styes

Take nine barley seeds and prick the stye with their tips, and each time, say this charm once: φευγε φευγε χρεων σε διχει.

The use of the imperative "flee" (φευγε, fuge) *is extremely common in Greek and Latin charms.*

---

*[Spiny restharrow in English. —*Trans.*]

📖 Latin and Greek, fourth century. Marcellus, *De medicamentis liber*, VIII, 193.

333 ◆ A Cure for Styes

If a stye appears on your right eye, say: "The mule does not reproduce, the stone carries no wool. May this ailment not rear its head or grow, but let it perish."

📖 Latin, fourth century. Marcellus, *De medicamentis liber*, VIII, 191.

SWOLLEN GLANDS

334 ◆ A Cure for Swollen Glands

The person who undertakes the cure should begin by making the sign of the cross over the affected part and repeat three times: "Saint John had a veuble which flowed at nine pertins. From nine they shrunk to eight; from eight they went to seven; from seven they went to six; from six they went to five; from five they went to four; from four they went to three; from three they went to two; from two they went to one, from one they went to nothing; and in this way Saint John lost his veuble."

Veuble *is a word for "swollen gland" in the local dialect, and the method used here to heal it is known as counting down.*

📖 French (Isle of Guernsey), nineteenth century. Saintyves, *Les Grimoires*, 56.

SYPHILIS

335 ◆ A Cure for Syphilis

Tie the following letters over the vein of the man suffering from fever or the evil malady [syphilis]:

† *F E T R A*/† gra † ma † lum †

This form of treatment is still known today in Norway and is called årelating: *the patient is bled and a piece of paper with magic words is placed on top of the vein being treated.*

📖 Norway, 1790. Bang, *Norske hexeformularer*, no. 1036; Ohrt, *Danmarks trylleformler*, 2:128.

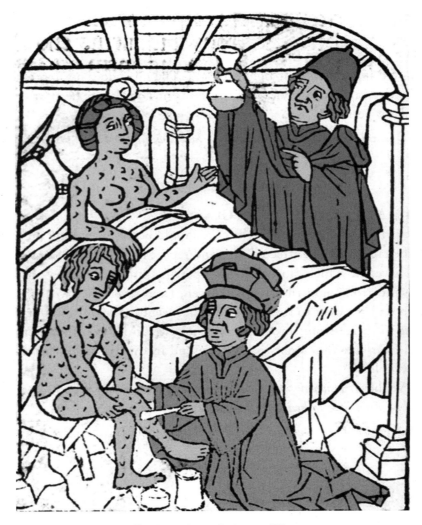

Treating patients who have syphilis.

THORN

336 ⟡ Orison for a Thorn

Points on points. My God, heal this point like Saint Cosmas and Saint Damian healed the five wounds of O.L.J.C. in the Garden of Olives (and say the name of the person).

Natus est Christus, mortuus et resurrexit Christus

After you have said this orison, take a man's linen and cut it as long and wide as the finger, then place it in a cross over the thorn, and next you will wrap it in that same linen. You will blow three times on the thorn, while saying the orison, and then you will wrap it as said; finally the blower will perform a novena while fasting, for the sufferings endured by Our Lord Jesus Christ on Calvary.

📖 France (Troyes), ca. 1840. *Laissez dire et faites le bien: Le médecin des pauvres*, 6; Laubach, *Krankheit und Heilung in biblischer Sicht*.

337 ◈ Cure for a Thorn

If a thorn has entered your finger, say the following over the wound three times:

> *Para fara gara*
> *Thorn, you shall leap forth*
> *A my wound will be healed*
> *By Saint John and Nicholas.*

📖 France (Vosges), nineteenth century. De la Salle, *Croyances et légendes du centre de la France*, 334.

THROAT PROBLEMS

338 ◈ Protection from Sore Throats

Whoever wears acanthus hung from their neck will not suffer from sore throats.

📖 Latin, fourth century. Pseudo-Apuleius, *Herbarius*, 69.

339 ◈ Charm against Sore Throat

This charm expels everything that could cause the throat to choke:

> *Heilen prosaggeri vome si polla nabuliet onodieni iden eliton.*

Recite this three times, spitting each time.

📖 Latin, fourth century. Marcellus, *De medicamentis liber*, XV, 105.

340 ◈ For the Mouth and Throat

For the mouth or anything that causes the throat to tighten, one must say this in his ear or write it on a parchment that will be tied around his neck in a cloth:

I feel myself turning white with fright at the thought that, from the depths of Hades, the noble Persephone could send us the head of Gorgo.

Nothing can resist this remedy.
This spell is, in fact, two verses from Homer's Odyssey *(11,634 ff.).*
This example of reuse is not isolated, and other extracts from ancient texts can be found in the charms of late antiquity. The Gorgon's head was a very widespread phylactery in antiquity.

📖 Latin and Greek, fourth century. Marcellus, *De medicamentis liber*, XV, 108.
📖 Roscher, *Ausfürliches Lexicon der griechischen und römischen Mythology*, vol. 1, col. 1695ff.

341 ◆ For Sore Throats
Say this with your hands turned up and wrapped in a hide:

VII anginas, VI anginas, V anginas, IV anginas, III anginas, II anginas, I angina, no angina.

📖 Latin, ninth century. St. Gallen, Stiftsbibliothek, Codex 751; Heim, "Incantamenta magica," 557.

342 ◆ To Dislodge a Bone from the Throat
If a fish bone or something else remains lodged in your throat, touch your head nine times with your left hand and a thorn with the other, and say nine times: "Lafana [?] sinner get out and do what Jupiter commands you," then spit.

📖 Latin, ninth century. St. Gallen, Stiftsbibliothek, Codex 751; Heim, "Incantamenta magica," 557.

343 ◆ For Ailments of the Throat and Neck
Carve the figure of Taurus in the third face, the sun being over the earth.

📖 France, 1658. Belin, *Traité des talismans*, 110.

344 ◆ For Sore Throats
To rid yourself of them, spit into an open grave and urinate on the wall of a synagogue while saying:

> *Absalon, my Absalon*
> *Take away my sore throat.*

📖 Saxons of Transylvania, nineteenth century. Wlislocki, *Volksglaube*, 95.

345 ◈ For the Ailments of the Mouth and Throat

Go in the morning before sunrise to the river's edge where the rushes grow. Take three of them without breaking them when pulling them up. Pass the root three times over the affliction and hang the rushes above the fireplace, tying them to the pothook with a coarse thread, then let them burn. Once the rushes have been consumed, the ailment will be healed, but it is necessary to say the following spell during this operation: "Mouth ailment, throat ailment, growing quinsy, you will heal as fast and as promptly as the dew melts beneath the rising sun on the hottest day of the month of August."

📖 France, nineteenth century. Cabanès and Barraud, *Remèdes de bonne femme*, 215.

346 ◈ Against Throat Ailments

Say the following phrase:

> Afflictions of the throat, grippe, group [?], scurvy, canker, I cut you, I overtrump you, I conjure you, I excommunicate you in the name of the good Lord and the holy Virgin, you will dry up, you will melt away in the mouth of [name] as quickly as the dew melts before the sun of the great Saint John.

📖 France, nineteenth century. Cabanès and Barraud, *Remèdes de bonne femme*, 281.

TONGUE BUMPS (TRANSIENT LINGUAL PAPILLITIS)

For Bernard de Gordon (circa 1270–1330) tongue bumps were a kind of tiny seed inside the tongue, and for Guy de Chauliac (1298–1368), they were pustules, apostemes.

347 ◈ Admirable Charm for Tongue Bumps

While saying this three times, spit on the ground and pull on these bumps with your thumb and ring finger while saying this charm.

White tongue bump, do no evil, cause no harm, create no chaumes [?] but dissolve like salt in water.

Do this before sunrise and after sunset so they diminish during both day and night.

📖 Latin, fourth century. Marcellus, *De medicamentis liber,* XV, 101.

TONSILLITIS
(SEE ALSO SORE THROAT, ANGINA)

348 ◈ CHARM FOR TONSILLITIS
With your hands turned over and your hair let down, say: "Queen of tonsillitis, daughter of Orcus, I abjure you by hell and heaven to quit this place!"

📖 Latin, ninth century. Önnerfors, "Iatromagische Beschwörungen," no. 15.

349 ◈ TO HEAL TOOTHACHE, PAIN OF THE UVULA, TONSILLITIS, AND SQUINANCY
When hung from the neck, the green woodpecker's beak heals toothache, pain of the uvula, tonsillitis, and squinancy [peritonsillar abscess].

📖 Latin, twelfth century. *Liber Kyranidorum,* 155, 11ff. Greek, fourteenth century. ΚΥΡΑΝΙΣ III, Δ; Mély, *Les lapidaires grecs,* 87–88.

TOOTHACHE

350 ◈ TO CURE A TOOTHACHE
The Magi tell us that toothache can be cured by the ash of the burnt heads of dogs that have died of rabies. This head must be burned without any flesh and the ash must be injected with cypress oil in the ear on the side where the pain is felt. The same affliction can also be cured by scraping the gum of the ailing tooth with the left eye-tooth of a dog, or with the spine of the dragon or water snake, the serpent being a white male. When the top teeth are so afflicted, two teeth from the upper jaw are hung around the neck, and when the pain is below, two teeth from the lower jaw are used. When they go in hunt of the crocodile they rub its fat on themselves. They also scrape the gums with bones taken from a lizard's forehead during a full moon, without allowing them to touch the ground.

The Illnesses of Humans and Their Cure 159

📖 Latin, first century. Pliny, *Historia naturalis,* 30.21.

351 ◆ Charm for Toothache

On a Tuesday or Thurday, during the waning moon, say these words seven times:

Argidam margidam sturgidam

You eliminate the pain when, wearing shoes, you stand under the heavens on the living earth and take the head of a frog, open its mouth, and spit inside. They you will ask him to carry away the pain of the teeth, and you will let him go with his life. Do this on the right day and at the right hour.

📖 Latin, fourth century. Marcellus, *De medicamentis liber,* XII, 24.

352 ◆ To Get Rid of Tooth Pain

Say this three times over the suffering teeth,

> In the name of Jesus Christ, may these words heal Your servant [name]. May the Lord direct his action upon the pain of the teeth.

Recite three Pater Nosters, then hang aroung the sufferer's neck these words written on a page and he will surely be healed.

> † *on* † *in* † *in* † *in* † *on* † *bon* † *bin* † *bin* † *bon*.

📖 Latin and Middle French, ca. 1300. Oxford, Bodleian Library, Digby 69, fol. 138v.

353 ◆ For Toothache

> † In the name of the Father † and the Son † and the Holy Ghost. Amen.
> † *loy* † *loye* † *nazir* † *oy* † *eloy* † by the holy names and the incarnation of Our † Lord † Jesus † Christ and by the passion of Christ.

Whoever carries these words on his person will no longer suffer from toothache. And if he has a worm, it will die immediately.

> † in the name of the Father † and the Son † and the Holy Ghost. Amen.

The belief that toothache is caused by a worm is one whose origin is lost in the depths of time. It can be found among the Babylonians,[12] *then in Homer's* Hymn to Demeter (*fifth century BCE*).

📖 Latin, sixteenth century. Ghent, Universiteitsbibliotheek, MS 1021 A, fol. 10r–v.

354 ◆ For Toothache

Write on a piece of lead that is the width of your hand:

> † Job Zarobabatos † Job Thanobratos † In nomine Patris et Filii

And recite five Our Fathers and Hail Marys in honor of God and Saint Apollonia.

The mention of Job indicates that the affliction is allegedly the work of a worm, and that of Apollonia refers to the martyrdom of the saint under the reign of Emperor Decius.

📖 Norway, ca. 1480, *Vinjeboka: Den eldste svartebok fra norsk middelalter*, no. 40; Pinon, "Une très vielle prière à sainte Apollinia," *Enquête du musée de la vie wallone* 169–72 (1960): 1–47.

355 ❖ To Cure a Toothache

Nail a nail into a wall to be cured of a toothache.

Scrape the gums with one of the teeth from a dead person who died a violent death, to heal a toothache.

> 📖 France, seventeenth century. Thiers, *Traité des superstitions* (1679), 322, 332.

356 ❖ Against a Toothache

> *Job was clinging to his rock*
> *And could only weep in desolation.*
> *Then Jesus happened by:*
> *"What have you got to weep about this way, Job?"*
> *"I cannot help but lament,*
> *I cannot help but weep*
> *From having larva in my teeth*
> *And larva in my lands."*
> *"Look at the sun," said Our Lord,*
> *"And spit upon the sacred land,*
> *You shall be healed at that very instant!"*
>
> † † †

This charm that is widespread throughout all Europe is known as "Job's Charm." It follows the meeting pattern. The larva are worms. In her study of folk medicine, Natalia Mazalova notes: "Teeth and bones can be attacked by zoomorphic illnesses. This is why cavities are due to little worms that get inside the teeth."

> 📖 Sweden (Småland), 1763. Klintberg, *Svenska trollformler*, 69, no. 15, "tandvärk."
>
> 📖 Mazalova, "La médecine populaire," 669.

357 ❖ For Toothache

Write the following spell:

> *Horiandus +*
> *Horiandu +*
> *Horiand +*
> *Horian +*
> *Horia +*

> *Hori +*
> *Hor +*
> *Ho +*
> *H +*

This is one of countless reducing spells used to cause misfortune to retreat.

> 📖 Norway, circa 1850. Bang, *Norske hexeformularer,* no. 1050, "For Tandpine." For more on this type of spell, cf. Lecouteux, *Dictionary of Ancient Magic Words and Spells,* 279–80.

358 ◆ Charm for Saint Apollonia

Write the following verse.

> *Saint Apollonia*
> *The divine,*
> *Sitting at the foot of a tree,*
> *On a marble stone,*
> *Jesus our Savior,*
> *By happy chance passed by,*
> *And asked her: "Apollonia,*
> *What is grieving you?"*
> *"I am here, divine teacher,*
> *For pain and not for grief;*
> *I am here for my head, for my blood,*
> *And for my toothache."*
> *"Apollonia, you have faith,*
> *By my grace, turn around,*
> *If it is a drop of blood, it will rise,*
> *If it is a worm, it will die."*

In thirteenth-century Belgium, this charm would be written on a page that the patient had to hold between his or her teeth. In the nineteenth century, in the Ouche region of Normandy, one added: "Five Pater and five Ave in the honor and to the intention of the five wounds of Our Savior Jesus Christ. The sign of the cross on the jaw next to where the pain is felt, and in a very short time, you will be cured." In Spain, the *Oracion de Santa Apolonia* replaces Jesus with the Virgin Mary.

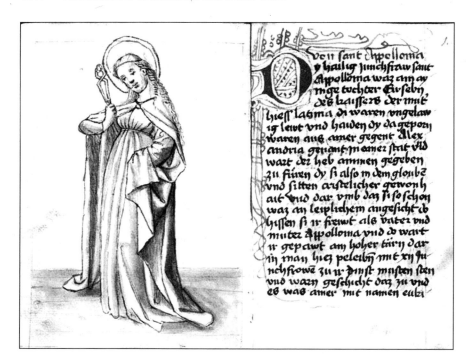

📖 Nisard, *Histoire des livres populaires,* 2nd ed., vol. 2, 76; *Le Pesant,* "Prières superstitieuses du pays d'Ouche," 328.

359 ◆ For Violent Toothaches

Take a new needle and scratch the teeth with it until it is spattered with blood, then, before sunrise, stick the needle in a place in a corner of the cellar where neither the sun nor the moon shine. At the first blow, name the name of the patient you wish to help, at the second, say: "Toothache, disappear!" and at the third: "Toothache, off with you!" †††

📖 Denmark, nineteenth century. Peuckert, "Die Egyptischen Geheimnisse," 88.

360 ◆ Against Toothaches

The toothache sufferer should wrap a stone with a blade of barley straw and toss is into running water while saying:

> *Pain, o pain in my tooth,*
> *Do not attack me so!*
> *Remove yourself, leave me,*

My dog is not home!
Do not visit me,
Since I curse you constantly!
Follow this straw in the torrent,
Follow it peacefully."

📖 Gypsies of Transylvania, nineteenth century. Wlislocki, *Volksdichtungen,* 137.

361 ◆ To Avoid Toothaches

To never again suffer from toothaches, one must never cut one's nails on a day of the week starting with an R.

📖 France (Ardennes), nineteenth century. Meyrac, Traditions, 172, no. 40.

362 ◆ To Cure Toothaches

To cure yourself of a toothache, you must take a brand new nail and stick it into the cavity until the tip of the nail is red with blood. Then race to bury the nail with a single hammer blow in the trunk of a very young tree and you will be cured.

This is another example of healing based on a transference of the affliction. In the Lower Poitou region, it is recommended to bury the nail in a wall (Cabanès and Barraud, Remèdes de bonne femme, *151). Elsewhere, a small piece of willow bark is pulled off, then a small piece of sapwood is removed, which is stuck inside the ailing gum. Next the now bloodstained piece of sapwood is put back where it came from and covered by the piece of bark.*

📖 France (Ardennes), nineteenth century. Meyrac, *Traditions,* 174, no. 54.

363 ◆ To Heal a Toothache

Take a nail from a horseshoe, commonly known as a spike, and bury it in the trunk of a tree with three blows from a hammer. At the first blow say: *enbornus!* At the second: *et dognus.* And at the third: *et diminuet!* And the toothache will vanish.

This means of transference, the imprisonment of the affliction in a tree is common throughout Europe. Ronald Grambo has shown that people caused the tooth to bleed with a splinter of wood that was subsequently put back into the tree, as close as possible to the roots, where it was covered by bark and then the trunk was wrapped in bandages to ensure that "the illness crossed into the tree." This was believed in Germany, Sweden, and Norway. The Norwegian bishop, Anton Christian Bang, collected this recipe that dates from 1897:

> One carves three needles from a young spruce tree in the forest and pricks the gums with them until it bleeds. Then, stick these needles into the spruce, and one should never have to return there. (Bang, *Norske hexeformularer,* no. 990)

A tree like this was taboo and chosen as standing apart from others.

📖 France, twentieth century. Le Pesant, "Prières superstitieuses du pays d'Ouche," 322.

📖 Wuttke, *Der deutsche Volksaberglaube der Gegenwart,* 328–30; Grambo, *Norske tannbønner, Småskrifter fra Norsk etnologisk gransking* 9, 11.

TUBERCULOSIS

364 ❖ To Heal Consumptives
Wear the stones from the sea bream's head around the neck to heal consumptives.

📖 Greek, fourteenth century. *ΚΥΡΑΝΣ* IV, C; Mély, *Les lapidaires grecs,* 123.

TUBERCULOSIS OF THE BONE

365 ❖ Against Bone Tuberculosis
Say the following verse:

> *Go into a maple tree*
> *Take a leaf from the maple*
> *Carry it to the mountain,*
> *There where no bell sounds,*
> *No pew is to be found,*
> *No barrel stands,*
> *No fire cooks,*
> *No mouth is eating.*
> *You are there; this is not your place!*
> *I beg you [to disappear]*
> *In the name of the Father, the Son, and the Holy Ghost.*

📖 Slovenes of Carinthia, nineteenth century. Kropej, "Charm in the Context of Magic Practice," 69.

TUMOR

366 ◈ To Heal a Heart Tumor

If a man is suffering from tumors in his heart region, a virgin should go the spring that is flowing dead east, and draw a cup from it in the direction of the current and sing over it the Credo and Our Father. She should then pour it into another container while she again sings the Credo and Our Father. Do this in a way to have three of them and proceed this way for three days. He will soon get better.

📖 Old English, tenth century. *Lacnunga* in Cockayne, *Leechdoms*, vol. 3, 74.

ULCER

367 ◈ To Heal Ulcers and Swollen Ear Glands

When hung around the neck, verbena root is very beneficial for ulcers and swollen ear glands (parotids).

📖 Latin, fourth century. Pseudo-Apuleius, *Herbarius*, 3§1.

368 ◈ Charm for Ulcer, Boil, or Wound

Take a piece of lead, and have it pounded until it is as thin as a leaf and you are able to bend it here and there, then, with a knife, draw five crosses as follows:

> When making the five crosses, recite five Our Fathers in honor of the five wounds of Our Lord Jesus Christ. When you make the three holes, two on the right and one on the left, say three Our Fathers in honor of the holy Trinity and the three nails with which Our Lord Jesus Christ was crucified. Then, recite the Our Father in honor of the passion and speak this charm: "In the name of the five wounds that Our Lord Jesus Christ suffered, in the name of the holy Trinity and the three nails with which Our Lord Jesus Christ was crucified, in the name of the holy passion, I conjure you to heal [name] of ulcers, boils, or wounds, without injuring him and without any risk of injury."

Next, place the lead on the afflicted area with the cross-side in, and make sure that the lead is washed each day and put back in place, and that once it has been charmed, it never touches the ground. And, each time you speak this charm, bless the lead.

📖 Middle French, fourteenth century. London, British Library, Harley, 273, fol. 85v.

369 ◆ To Dissolve Tumors

Rub the wens (tumors) with the robe of an executioner shortly after he has performed an execution, in order to dissolve them.

📖 France, seventeenth century. Thiers, *Traité des superstitions* (1679), 325; *Traité des superstitions* (1777), 4:331.

UVEITIS

370 ◆ To Cure Uveitis

Cull the root of navelwort before sunrise with the thumb and ring finger of your left hand in the name of the person suffering from uveitis, and hang it around his neck in a cloth.

📖 Latin, fourth century. Marcellus, *De medicamentis liber*, XIV, 65.

VARICOSE VEINS

371 ◆ To Heal Varicose Veins without a Blade, and the Lesions That Form Ulcers in the Leg and Body

For the varicose veins of man and the pregnant woman, mash ox manure with vinegar and stick a cloth inside this warm bath; do this during the waning moon while saying these words: "Just as the horns of the ox are dry and tight, may it proceed the same, *illi Gaio Seio*, that the varicose veins dry and close up." Duck fat blended with wax placed on varicose veins will heal you.

illi Gaio Seio *replaces the name of the person afflicted by the ailment. In the Middle Ages, and later, we simply find* N. (name) *or* N. N. (full name).

📖 Latin, fourth century. Pseudo-Theodore, Theodori *Prisciani Euporiston*, 292, 19ff.

372 ◈ To Heal Varicose Veins in the Feet

The thighbone of the white-tailed eagle tied to the hip is healthful for varicose veins of the feet.

📖 Latin, twelfth century. *Liber Kyranidorum*, III, Φ.

VEIN SPASM

In the countryside a sprain or twisted limb that can be healed with prayer is called a jumping vein.

373 ◈ To Heal a Jumping Vein

Repeat the following:

> Jumping vein, twisted vein, dislocated vein, may God restore you to the place you have left, in the name of the Father †, the Son †, and the Holy Ghost †. So may it be.

At each cross, you must make a cross on the patient with your thumb dipped in holy water.

📖 France, nineteenth century. Cabanès and Barraud, *Remèdes de bonne femme*, 279.

VERTIGO

374 ◈ To Dissipate Dizziness

You can dissipate the pains of the head that cause dizziness by tying a branch from elm around your head and if you sleep thus crowned for three days. This is verified.

📖 Latin, fourth century. Marcellus, *De medicamentis liber*, III, 2.

375 ◈ To Cure Headaches and Vertigo

Tied around the neck with red thread, the bones of the vulture's head will cure headaches and vertigo.

📖 Latin, twelfth century. *Liber Kyranidorum*, 152, 16–17.

WARTS[13]

376 ❖ To Get Rid of Warts

To get rid of warts, some lie in a footpath on their back when the moon is at least twenty days old, looking at this astral body while extending their arms above their head and rubbing themselves with anything within their reach.

📖 Latin, first century. Pliny, *Historia naturalis*, XXX, 86.

377 ❖ To Make Warts Fall Off

Rub the warts with broom (*Cytisus scoparius*) and tie it on as low as you can in order to make them fall off.

📖 France, seventeenth century. Thiers, *Traité des superstitions* (1679), 321; *Traité des superstitions* (1777), 4:326.

378 ❖ To Make Warts Disappear

Take the lard of a freshly slaughtered pig that has not yet been smoked or salted, and rub the warts when the moon is waning; then bury the lard in the ground. As it rots, the warts will disappear.

📖 Germany, 1750, Staricius, *Grimoire ou la Magie naturelle*, 345.

379 ❖ To Make Warts Go Away

To make warts go away, you must run water over your hands during the full moon and say: "Meuntien, Meuntien."

📖 Netherlands, nineteenth century. Van Haver, *Nederlanse Incantatieliteratuur*, no. 541.

380 ❖ To Drive Warts Away

At the hour the new moon first appears, touch each wart with a certain pea, next tie the peas into a rag and toss them behind you, in this way they will vanish. Or else you can smear them under the waning moon with the fresh lard of a pig that has just been slaughtered, then bury it in the ground. The warts will vanish as the meat putrefies.

📖 Sweden, nineteenth century. Peuckert, "Die Egyptischen Geheimnisse," 90.

> *& ceremonieux.* 173
>
> 7. *Contre toute fieure.*
>
> Portez vne ataigne viue dans vne noix, pendue au col.
>
> 8. *Contre la fieure quarte.*
>
> Qv'vn frere mendiant la vous demande pour l'amour de Dieu : vous la perdrez, & il la prendra.
>
> 9. *Pour faire perdre ses verrues.*
>
> Touchez en la robe d'vn que vous sçachiez bien estre coqu: en quelque endroit de son habillement que vous le touchiez, sans qu'il s'en aduise, vos verruës se perdront. On dit aussi, que si voulant trancher vn leuraut, connil, perdrix, volaille, &c. vous estes empesché à trouuer les iointures, pensez à vn coqu, & vous les trouuerez.
>   Item pour perdre les verruës, faites les conter à vne personne qui soit plus ieune que vous: elle les prendra & les pourra aussi donner à vne autre plus ieune, par semblable moyen.
>   Item, faites les toucher auec autant de poix, à qui que ce soit, & il les vous prendra.
>   Item, prenez vne poignee de sel, & allez tout courant le ietter dans vn four, & les verruës s'esuanouyront.
>
> 10. *Pour guerir de l'hydropisie.*
>
> Il faut pisser durant neuf matins sur le marrube, auāt que le Soleil l'ait touché: & à mesure que la plante mourra, le ventre se desenflera.

Laurent Joubert, *La Première et seconde partie des Erreurs populaires touchant la medicine at le régime de santé,* 1601.

381 ◆ To Remove Warts

Say this verse at the time of a full moon:

Salud, loar gan	Hail, full moon
Kas sar re-man	Take these [the warts] away
Gan-ez ai han	Far, far way!

📖 France, nineteenth century. Sauvé, *Lavarou Koz / Proverbes et dictons de la Basse-Bretagne,* 140.

382 ◈ To Heal Yourself from Warts

To heal yourself of wens or warts, you must rub them with a rind of pork lard, and next, take pains to put this rind beneath a large stone so it can rot. It is also sufficient to hide the peas under a stone or bury them: when the peas have rotted, the wens and warts have disappeared.

Another recipe commands the casting of the peas or lard into a well, or even tying a slug to a thorn bush: as the slug disappears, so do the warts.

📖 France (Ardennes), nineteenth century. Meyrac, *Traditions*, 179, no. 90.

383 ◈ To Make Warts Disappear Overnight

When you see the new moon, if you have warts and wish to heal them do this: kneel down, rub the wart thrice then say "Angels of God" three times. It has happened that people using this magic have observed the next morning that their warts had disappeared.

📖 Lithuania, twentieth century. Vaitkevičienė, *Lietuvių užkalbėjimai*, no. 1483.

WHITLOW (FINGER OR TOENAIL ABSCESS)

384 ◈ To Cure Whitlow

You must take a promissory note and write on it with chalk: " † *vir* † *clarus* † *demens* † *probune* † *augens* † *ego* † *letus* † *alpha* † *et o* †." Then plunge the promissory note into water and give it to the patient to drink. He will be healed.

📖 Middle Dutch and Latin, fifteenth century. Ghent, Universiteitsbibliotheek, MS 697, fol. 20r.

WORMS

All the illnesses eating away a part of the body were attributed to worms, which people tried to banish far away or kill with magical recipes.

385 ◈ Against Tooth Worms

Repeat the following:

† *bon* † *pen* † *na* † *ason*

On the top of Mount Celion stayed seven sleeping brothers † Marcius † Marcellinus † Serapion † Alexander † Vitalis † Phillipus † Dyonisius † by these seven brothers I conjure you, worm, to withdraw and not harm this man.

According to legend, the Seven Sleepers of Ephesus took refuge in a cave on Mount Celion to escape persecution. They are also invoked against insomnia, demons, and quartan fever.

📖 Latin, twelfth century. Codex Engelbergensis 45, fol. 157; Heim, "Incantamenta magica," 555.

📖 *Acta Sanctorum Julii,* 6.375–97; Bonser, "The Seven Sleepers of Ephesus in Anglo-Saxon and Later Recipes," *Folklore* 56 (1945): 254–56; Lecouteux, *The Book of Grimoires,* no. 30; Storms, *Anglo-Saxon Magic,* no. 37ff.

386 ◈ TO GET RID OF STOMACH WORMS

Take milfoil and cumin, vinegar and verjuice. Cook this blend and apply it to a cloth while still quite hot and which you will bind over the navel; this will heal the affliction.

📖 France, thirteenth century, Cambrésis. Coulon, *Curiosités de l'histoire,* 58, no. 26.

387 ◈ A CHARM AGAINST WORMS

Here is the charm that the angel Gabriel brought to Saint Susanne on behalf of Our Lord to deliver Christians of worms, fistulas, gout, tumors, cankers, and all kinds of gout.

First, have a mass of the Holy Ghost sung in the morning in the patient's presence, then you will have him sing: "*In nomine Patris et Filii et Spiritus Sancti.* Amen. As true as God exists, as true as when He did things, He did them well, as true as He took flesh from the holy maiden, as true as He was crucified, as true as He suffered from five wounds to save all sinners, as true as He was hung on the cross, and as true as it was between two thieves, as true as He was wounded on the right side by a spear, as true as His head was crowned with thorns, as true that the nails were hammered into His hand and His feet, as true that His body rested in the holy tomb, as true as He resurrected three days after his death, as true as he descended into Hell, as true as He broke the gates of Hell, as true as He bound the devil there, as true as He brought the saints there, as true as he sits at the right of His father, as true that the day of Judgment will come, as true as each man aged thirty years will rise again in flesh and blood, as true as Our Lord will judge as he deems fit, as true as this is true, as true as God, Father, Son, and Holy Ghost, that I will see the simple, gentle, debonair, humble, pitiful, merciful kings for all the anguish You suffered on the holy cross—heal [name] of this illness." Urge the patient to abstain from eating any meat and recite this charm secretly at mass.

📖 Latin and French, ca. 1300. London, British Library, Additional 15236, fol. 29r.

388 ❖ A Charm for Worms
Repeat the following prayer:

> Lord, by Your death I beg You to make die these worms by reason of Your martyrdom. When, Lord, you hung on the holy cross; these wounds caused Your death. By Your distress, I beg you to cause the death of these worms in these bones, amen.

Recite five Our Fathers and five Hail Marys in honor and glory of the five wounds of Our Lord and five for the worthy poor.

alivia † *zorobamur* † *tronus* † *tron* † *sonus* † *abrota* † *an* †.

📖 Alemannic (Alsace), fifteenth century. Birlinger, "Aus einem elsässichen Arzbeibuch," 219–32.

The word zorobamur *in this unintelligible spell, sometimes garbled into* zorobantur *or* zorobantiz, *can be found in several Dutch charms against worms.*

389 ❖ To Dry Up Worms
Repeat the following prayer:

> Worm, I conjure you to dry up like the grass dried under the feet of Judas when he betrayed Our Lord Jesus Christ! In the name of the Father, the Son, and the Holy Ghost. Amen.

📖 Dutch, 1597. Gelinden, Parochiaal Archief, no. a, fol. 85r.

390 ❖ Against Worms
Repeat the following prayer:

I adjure you worm, to not eat the flesh of this man, [name], nor drink his blood.

I adjure you, by the living God to not have the power to eat and drink!

I adjure you, by Jesus Christ † who was born in Bethlehem and was baptized in the Jordan, to no longer drink his blood and no longer eat his flesh!

📖 Latin, circa 1400. Erfurt, Wissenschaftliche Allgemeinbibliothek, MS Ampl. D 17, fol. 40r.

391 ❖ Against Worms

On the first day, draw a cross on your forehead and say: "Easter Day, Christ was taken †, on Friday, he was hung on the holy cross †, on Saturday, he was resurrected." All the worms will fall to the ground when you draw this cross on your stomach.

📖 Germany, sixteenth century. Vienna, Nationalbibliothek, Codex 2999, fol. 204r.

392 ❖ To Rid an Animal of Worms

Before sunrise, collect in a bowl the sap of the plant called "wolf's milk" (a kind of euphorbia), then add salt, garlic, and water to it, and boil it. Rub the animal with one part of the liquid and throw the rest along with the bowl into running water, while saying:

> Worm, go into the wolf's milk,
> From the wolf's milk into the garlic,
> From the garlic into the water,
> With the water, go home to your father,
> Go to Nivaši's home
> He will tie you with a bond
> Of ninety-nine rods!

The water spirit is sent back by tracing out the path he should follow. All the ingredients used have a history; garlic, for example, has always been used to repel spirits because of its strong odor . . .

📖 Gypsies of Transylvania, nineteenth century. Wlislocki, *Volksdichtungen*, 153.
📖 Gubernatis, *La Mythologie des plantes*.

393 ◆ To Rid a Pig of Worms
Before dawn, stand in front of a nettle that you water with the urine of a sick animal, while saying:

> *Good day, good day!*
> *I have many cares:*
> *My pig has worms,*
> *I am complaining of it to you!*
> *They are white, black, or red*
> *May they die from this tomorrow!*

📖 Gypsies of Transylvania, nineteenth century. Wlislocki, *Volksdichtungen*, 153. For more on the nettle, see Gubernatis, *La Mythologie des plantes*, 2:271–74; Grabner, "Der 'Wurm' als Krankheitsvorstellung," *Zeitschrift für deutsche Philologie* 81 (1962): 224–40; Höfler, *Deutsches Krankheitsnamenbuch*, 822–35.

WOUNDS

394 ◆ For a Wound
Repeat the following verse:

> *Christ was wounded on earth,*
> *Heaven learned of it.*
> *He did not bleed,*
> *Nor suffer at all;*
> *It was a blessed wound.*
> *Wound, be healed!*

In the name of Christ, may this be your cure! Say three Our Fathers and add three times, "I conjure you by the five wounds. Heal, wound! May it be so! May it be so! In the name of the Father, and the Son, and the Holy Ghost. Amen."

📖 Old High German, late twelfth century. Ebermann, *Blut- und Wundsegen*, 43.

395 ◆ A Good Benediction for Wounds
Three good brothers were walking quite swiftly along their path. Our Lord Jesus Christ came forth to meet them and said: "Where are the three of you going?" "Lord and Father Jesus Christ, we are hunting for an herb

The Illnesses of Humans and Their Cure 177

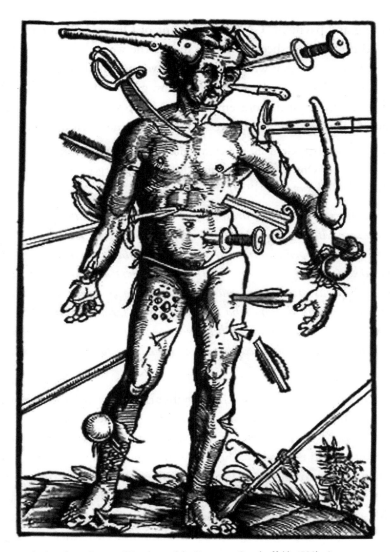

A plate from *Surgery (Wundarznei)* by Hans von Gersdorff (d. 1529) gives us a brief overview of the wounds caused by sharp and blunt instruments.

that is good for wounds, whether they are caused by a thrusting or cutting blow, by stones, by arrows, or by speech; what means were used to inflict it, this herb should provide a remedy." Christ responded: "Kneel down and swear to me, by the blood of Our Lord and the milk of Our Lady, that you will chant this charm before this person and no other, without accepting any payment. Go to the Mount of Olives, take the oil of the tree and the wool of sheep, and pass it over the wounds and they will be entirely healed. Say that what befalls these wounds shall be like unto what befell the one that Longinus, the blind Jew, gave to the right side of Our Lord Jesus Christ: it did not enflame, fester, or go septic. The same will happen to these wounds as I have said. In the name of God. Amen."

 📖 Middle High German, fifteenth century. *Zeitschrift für deutsches Altertum* 38 (1875), 80; Ohrt, "Über Alter und Unsprung der Begegnungssegen," *Hessische Blätter für Volkskunde* 35 (1936): 49–58.

The charm of the three brothers has been shown to have first appeared in Germany during the twelfth century and can be found in a number of other European countries, such as Denmark, for example (Ohrt, *Danmarks trylleformler, no. 1125). The bothers are sometimes named Ylinius, Cosmas, and Damianus, these last two (Cosmas and Damian) being brothers and doctors who healed for free. Jacob Grimm* (Deutsche Mythologie, *3:501) provides a later version of this extremely widespread charm in which it is specified that it must be worn for twenty-fours under the right arm:*

A charm to be worn beneath the right arm for twenty-four hours: Three blessed brothers who were walking met Jesus Christ. Our sweet Lord Jesus Christ asked: "Where are you going? "We are going behind the hedge," they answered, "we are seeking the herb that is good for all wounds, whether they be caused by thrust or cut." Our Lord Jesus Christ answered: "Go to the Mount of the Messiah, take the wool of sheep, the moss of stones, and the oil of [olive] trees, press them on and in the wound, whether they are from stabbing, cutting, or breaking, or due to something else; it will not become inflamed or fester." Just as Luke has spoken on Mount Severin when the Jews surrounded and struck Our Lord Jesus God. May God the Father reign, and so on.

 📖 Olsan, "The Three Good Brothers Charms: Some Historical Points," *Incantatio* 1 (2011): 48–78; Artelt, *Kosmas und Damian, die Schutzpatrone des Ärzte und Apotheker: Eine Bildfolge.* On wounds in general, cf. Whipple, *The Story of Wound Healing and Wound Repair.*

CHAPTER 3
EVIL SPELLS

¶ Incipiunt remedia contra maleficia.

Vir quidam qui maleficiis impediti cū suis vxo-
ribus coire nō possunt de quorū
suffragio librū nostrū volumꝰ de
nudare ꝙ medicamētū nisi fallo:
est sanctissimum. ergo si tibi ꝺue
nit speres de deo z ille dabit benignitate. sz qm̄ male
ficia sunt multiplicia. Primo de eis disputemꝰ. Cū si
leficio:. itaꝗ q̄dā de aiatz fiunt vt testiculi galli sup-
positi lecto cū san. efficiūt ne ꝺcubet i lecto iacet. q̄dā
de caracterib' scripti cū sang. vespertilionis. q̄daz xo de
terre nascētib'. vn si nux vel glans sepes qm̄ medietas
et via pre vir ponat z alia ex alia pte ex qua spōsus z
spōsa dz ventre. sunt alia q̄ de granis fabarū coficiunt
q̄ nec aq ca. mollificanf nec igne coquāf qd maleficiū
est pessimū si. iiij. illarū vel. iij. sub lecto vel in via vt supra hostiū vt circa ponāt. sunt et alia q̄ fiunt metallica
q̄ fiūt ex ferro vel plūbo z ferro sed q̄ fiūt ex acu q̄ mor
tui vel mortue suuntur in sudariis z qz hec dyabolica z
maxime in mulieribus fiunt alij diuinis alij humanis
curant auxiliis. ergo si spōsus vel spōsa hmōi cōtrahū-
tur maleficiis / sanctius quidem est de his speculari ꝙ
si non succurratur his separanf z deciuntur z per hoc
maleficium nō solum exercetur in pa-oximis sed etiā

Malleus maleficarum, 1496.

Evil Spells

> *None are safe from witches. .... The other diseases that come are curses that should be considered to be supernatural as they are inflicted by the power of demons with the permission of God.*
>
> MALLEUS MALEFICARUM, 2, 1.

Evil spells were particularly feared, and it is surely no accident that one of their personifications was called Envy! The following countermeasures focus on curses, the evil eye, enchantments levied by means of the figurine known as the voult, which is mistreated, thereby inflicting a thousand misfortunes on its target from a distance. Martin Delrio (1611) notes: "There are sorcerers who help themselves with certain wax images that they roast or stick with pins, causing their enemies to languish, for as long as they continue to keep their images intact (Les Controverses et Recherches magiques, *396).*

Seligman, *Der böse Blick und Verwandtes;* Arnaud, "La baskania ou le mauvais œil chez les Grecs modernes"; Pócs, "Evil Eye in Hungary"; Camus, *La Sorcellerie en France aujourd'hui; HDA,* vol. 7, 1537, "Malefizwachs"; Hole, "Some Instances of Image-Magic in Great Britain."

Quod imagines de ere plumbo vel cera alba vel rubea vel alia materia baptisatę exorcizatę immo potius exsecratę per artes magicas & quod sub diebus certis habeant virtutes mirabiles quę in libris talium artium recitatur error est cótra fidé.

Quod imagines de ere vel plumbo vel auro vel cera alba vel rubea vel alia materia baptizatę vel exorcitatę confecratę :

Martinus de Arles, *Tractatus de superstionibus* (1559).
The opening of his discussion on voults.

396 ◆ To Get Rid of Evil Spells

If a man falls under the power of the devil or an evil spell, take the heart of the cypress, bore a hole into it, draw water from a spring with a clay container, pour it into the hole and retrieve it with the same container while saying: "Water, I pour you through this hole. Flow with the strength given you by nature and with divine virtue, enter into this man and destroy in him all that attacks him. Restore him to the right path to which God in His true intelligence and His true science has assigned him." Give this water to the possessed or cursed man for nine days in a row, while fasting. He will get better.

 📖 Twelfth century. Hildegard von Bingen, *Physica*, 3.20, "On the Cypress."

397 ◆ To Rid an Evil Spell of Impotence from a Man

If an evil spell falls on a man and his wife so that he is unable to know her carnally, take a long plate or platter, in the center of which you will draw a cross and at whose four corners you will write these four names: *Avis, Gravis, Seps, Sipa*. In the center write the entire Gospel of Saint John. Next, take holy water, or wine, or another liquid if you have no holy water, and pour it into the platter. Dilute the letters with your finger, and have the husband and wife devoutly drink it in God's name. This is proven.

In the same way, if you know how to write, write this name in the four corners: *tethragramaton*, as I said earlier. Say what this name means.* It will be even more effective if written in Hebrew letters. Next, do as above. If the Gospel is written down by a virgin child, it is even better.

 📖 Latin, thirteenth century. Arnaldus de Villa Nova, *Opera*, fol. 215v; Franz, *Die kirchlichen Benediktionen*, 2:481.

This is a case of unknotting the cord [the laces of the breeches], in other words, restoring to a man his sexual potency.

It was also believed that witches had the power of removing your sexual equipment, as illustrated by a fifteenth-century woodcut (next page).

The Petit Albert *also provides recipes for lifting the curse that makes one impotent:*

---

*The word means "God in four letters."

Our elders swore that the bird called the green woodpecker is a sovereign remedy against the evil spell of the knotted [breeches] laces; if one eats it roasted after fasting with blessed salt ... if one inhales the smoke from the burning tooth of a recently dead man, one will likewise be freed of the charm.... The same effect occurs if one puts quicksilver in a drinking straw made from a blade of oats or wheat, and then places this drinking straw made from a blade of oats or wheat under the side of the bed in which the person stricken by this evil spell sleeps.... If the man and the woman are afflicted by this charm, it is necessary, to be healed, that the man pisses through the wedding ring that the woman will hold while he is pissing.

📖 *HDA*, vol. 6, 1014–16, "Nestelknüpfen"; Le Roy Ladurie, "L'aiguilette"; *Petit Albert*, 20–21.

398 ❖ To Lift an Evil Spell from a Husband or Wife

If a man or woman is cursed and unable to love his or her spouse, he should deposit his excrement (*merda*), or whatever he expels into his right shoe and then put it on. As soon as he smells the stench, the evil spell will be lifted. This is proven.

📖 Latin, thirteenth century. Arnaldus de Villa Nova, *Opera*, fol. 215v.

399 ❖ Against Evil Spells from the Devil

Lord Jesus Christ, son of the living God, and the blessed Virgin Mary, miraculously fertilized by the operation of the Holy Ghost, Logos, God, and flesh, we implore your mercy so that we may be delivered from any snare and evil spell of the devil, and give us the ability to engender, conceive, and nurture children for eternal life. In the name of the father †, the Son †, and the Holy Ghost †. Amen.

📖 French, nineteenth century. Nisard, *Histoire des livres populaires*, 78.

400 ❖ To Cure the Bewitched

He who is bewitched should sleep completely wrapped in a blessed sackcloth; on waking, he will be cured. She who is bewitched need only drink, on Sunday, the holy water in which the priests have dipped the aspersorium.

📖 France, thirteenth century. Cambrésis, Coulon, *Curiosités de l'histoire*, 66, nos. 61–62.

401 ❖ To Lift Curses

If one has coral in the house, all curses shall be lifted. Similarly, the blood of a black dog on the walls of the dwelling in which it is found carries away all evil spells. Mercury sealed in a reed or a walnut and placed on the bewitched one's head, or beneath the threshold of the door by which he enter, removes the curse. Placed in a hollow platter placed above or beneath the threshold, mugwort prevents any evil spell from harming this house [or its inhabitants].

📖 Latin, thirteenth century. Arnaldus de Villa Nova, *Opera,* folio 215v; Macer Floridus, *De viribus herbarum,* vv. 1–30.

402 ❖ To Break an Enchantment

When someone is enchanted, write this on a new cup and have him drink water from it: Χιστι

📖 Italian in Greek letters, sixteenth century. Schneegans, "Sizilianische Gebete, Beschwörungen und Rezepte in griechischer Umschrift," *Zeitschrift für romanische Philologie* 32 (1908): 574; Pradel, *Griechische und süditalienische Gebete, Beschwörungen und Rezepte des Mittelalters.*

403 ❖ Against the Evil Spell

Sweep the house three times while thinking: "I am not sweeping the house clean of straws, rubbish, but I am sweeping away evil spells, curses, yawns, shouts, all the ugly things, and all the illnesses." And once you have piled the trash at the door, place three burning coals in the rubbish, and place them in a sack whose bottom is worn out, and carry them to the river, and say: "Who gives it to me with one hand, I give it to him with two." And say this until nine hands, and when you say: "Who gives it to me with nine hands, I give it to him with both of mine and who gives it to me coldly, I give it to him quite ardently, and gives it to me with the mouth, I give it to him by his back, so that it* travels from one house to the next house, from one village to the next village, from one wave into another wave until it falls upon the head of the one who cast it upon me."

📖 Romania, eighteenth–nineteenth century. Bucharest, Biblioteca Academiei Române, MS Romanian BAR 4917, fol. 2r, "De fapt"; Timotin, *Descântecele manuscrise românești,* 343. For more on beliefs connected with sweepings, see *HDA,* vol. 4, 1211ff., "Kehrricht."

404 ❖ Against the Curse Cast on Children

Fill a pot with water drawn from a river following the direction of the current, in it drop seven coals, seven handfuls of flour, and seven heads of garlic, and place it all over the fire. When the water boils, stir

---

*The curse.

it with a piece of wood that resembles a fork with three tines saying:

> *May perish here*
> *The evil eyes that watch you!*
> *May seven crows*
> *Have quickly eaten you!*
> *May perish here*
> *The evil eyes that watch you!*
> *May a great deal of dust*
> *Blind them quickly!*
> *May perish here*
> *The evil eyes that watch you!*
> *May they burn, burn forever*
> *And may lightning carbonize them!*

 📖 Gypsies of Transylvania, nineteenth century. Wlislocki, *Volksdichtungen*, 142.

405 ❖ A Charm against Demons and Envy

Our Lord Jesus and Saint Peter stepped on to the large bridge where they met the demons and Envy, the infamous one. "Where are you going?" asked Our Lord Jesus Christ. "I am going to see the farmer's wife and take the best of her breasts and the best of her smooth churns, and from there go to the farm of a peasant where I want eggs, and there, I wish to be shorn." "No!" said Our Lord Jesus who struck him with His sacred hand. "I command you to go back to the envious man that sent you out of wickedness and with anger!" And listen to my words as if they counted for the Name of Our Lord Jesus. In the name [of the] Father, [the] Son, and [the] Holy Ghost. So may it be!

 📖 Norway (Hallingdal), 1843. *Svartebok in Ål*, 15, Norwegian Folklore Archives (NFS), University of Oslo (Blindern), "For Auguns Taaver."

Envy (Ovundshugen, Avindsh*) *is the personification of the person who sends the evil eye (Danish* avund*), one of the anthropomorphic figures of evil that attack Christians. For* auguns taaver *is the title of countless charms against the evil eye.*

In The Hammer of Witches *(1496), the inquisitors Jacob Sprenger*

---

*There are countless terms for designating Envy: *avindsmand, Avunsman, ovund*.

and Heinrich Kramer note that witches "can sometimes bewitch men and animals with a simple glance, without touching them, and thereby cause their death" (2, 2, fol. 48v).

406 ◆ AGAINST THE EVIL EYES

Repeat the following:

> Two evil eyes look at you, three kings oppose it: God the Father, God the Son, and God the Holy Ghost. May they protect the eyes and flesh of this child, in the name of the Father, and so on.

📖 Transylvanian Saxons, nineteenth century. Schuster, *Siebenbürgisch-sächsische Volkslieder*, 293.

407 ◆ AGAINST THE EVIL EYE

Mary was standing before the door of the church when her dear son approached. "O my very precious son, why are you so sad?"

"O mother, my very dear mother, how could I not be sad? Two gray eyes have stared at me."

"O, my very dear son, the two gray eyes have stared at you and broken your heart,"

In nomine, and so on.

📖 Transylvanian Saxons, nineteenth century. Schuster, *Siebenbürgisch-sächsische Volkslieder*, 293.

408 ◆ TO KNOW IF A CHILD HAS BEEN CURSED BY THE EVIL EYE

Go to the immediate proximity of some running water and say this charm. If the noise of the water swells while you are saying it, it is because the child has been bewitched.

> *Brooklet, little brooklet, flow!*
> *Child, look up high, look down low!*
> *So much water is flowing,*
> *May as much flow into the eyes*
> *Of the one who gazed at you!*
> *May he die this very day!*

 📖 Gypsies of Transylvania, nineteenth century. Wlislocki, *Volksdichtungen*, 142ff.

409 ❖ Against Curses

Cut a branch from three different trees; put them in a pot of stream water that has been collected beneath a bridge and in the direction of the current. Add three handfuls of flour and cook a puree; next, in one of the branches stick an upside-down sewing needle wrapped in the hair from a horse's mane in another trough into which the pot is turned. The child presumed to be bewitched is then held above it, and the following charm is said nine times before throwing into the river the water of the trough, the pot, and its contents.

> *Stay here never again!*
> *May the one who bewitched this child*
> *Resemble this leaf*
> *In this pot, in this pot*
> *That we are offering to Nivashi!*

The Nivashi (Nivaši) *are water spirits. The males have puffed-up bodies, horse hooves, red hair and beards, and are sometimes hairy. When a man crosses over a bridge, they drag him into the water and drown him, then imprison his soul in a pot and regale in its wailing; they will not allow it to leave until the corpse has decomposed.*

The Nivaši *women are very beautiful, their eyes shine like stars, and they have thick hair that serves them for clothing. They can also be found wearing clothes that are as white as snow and red shoes. The live in splendid palaces to which they bring the mortals with whom they fall in love.*

 📖 Gypsies of Transylvania, nineteenth century. Wlislocki, *Volksdichtungen*, 143.

410 ❖ To Cure a Bewitched Child

The mother of the bewitched child takes salted water and drips it on the child's limbs while saying:

> *False eyes that have gazed upon you*
> *Should disappear like water!*
> *Evil illness should move on,*
> *Leave from your head,*
> *From your chest,*

From your stomach,
From your leg,
From your arm!
May it flee far away
And enter the false eyes!

📖 Gypsies of Transylvania, nineteenth century. Wlislocki, *Volksdichtungen*, 144.

411 ❖ INCANTATION AGAINST CAST CURSES

Repeat the following spell

Bless me, lord, Christ of Truth! In the name of the Father, the Son, and the Holy Ghost, amen! In the same way as the spell-caster, the sorcerer, the spell-caster, the witch, cannot swallow the white foam of the sea or measure its depth, may they be unable to harm or enchant me: neither in my bold head, nor in my fierce heart, nor in my lungs, nor in my liver, nor in my white chest, nor in my kidneys. I seal myself against the spell-caster, the sorcerer, the spell-caster, the witch, and every kind of enchanter with a solid lock, an iron key, and I have let fall, I [name], servant of God, this key into the ocean sea. Even when the spell-caster, the sorcerer, the spell-caster, the witch will have swallowed the foam, measured the depths of the sea, and the heights of the heavens they will still not be able to enchant me [name], servant of God, in the centuries upon centuries.

By assigning impossible tasks to spell casters, one protects oneself against their evil spells. The reader will note the list of what the most important parts of the body were in the eyes of the people who used this incantation.

📖 Russia, nineteenth century. Gruel-Apert, *La Tradition orale russe*, 106.

412 ❖ LIFTING A CURSE

If a stranger [to the village] must lift a curse, she should take three coals and toss them one after another into a glass of water, make a sign of the cross over it, and say each time: You, curse, you who are causing the suffering, leave the brain, from the head into the face. If you come from the ground, may the grass dry! If you come from the sun, may its rays die!

📖 Romania, nineteenth century. Schullerus, Rumänische *Volksmärchen,* 41ff.

413 ◈ A Charm for Lifting a Curse
Repeat the following words:

> I conjure and curse all the spirits issuing from wicked men and their houses. By the prayers of the saints, and they are legion, we drive off and push far away all wickedness and maleficence, and envy, and jealousy, knotted curse, evil spells, bewitchment, evil eye, backbiting, slander, diabolical words, and the oaths and conjurations that are harmful to the body and damaging to the soul, and the illnesses, and the mortal wounds, and all the misfortunes of life tending to impoverish and reduce life through all sorcery by enchanters. May the evil depart from the slave of God, [name]!

📖 Russia, nineteenth century. Rybakov, *Le paganisme des anciens Slaves,* 154.

414 ◈ Against Curses So That God May Aid You
Make the sign of the cross and say: "I cast a spell for curses so that you may receive the help of God. The first *norokas* and the second *prorokas.*" Then recite the Ave Maria. You should say this three times.

📖 Lithuania, nineteenth century. Vaitkevičienė, *Lietuvių užkalbėjimai,* no. 1422.

Norokos *is most likely derived from the Polish or Byelorussian* uroki, *"evil eye";* prorok *in Polish, Russian, and Byelorussian means "the prophet," sometimes designated as a saint by the charms.*

Medals against the evil eye.

415 ◆ For No Magic to Harm You

Write the following spell on paper and carry it on your person:

> *X osa x osa asa x so x ea x aa x*
> *sax, nn, Patres x exx Filyxax*
> *Spiritus x sanctinomen*

We can recognize in this spell fragments of Eax Filiax Artifex; "x exx" *seems to refer to* Christus rex.

📖 Poland, nineteenth century. Vaitkevičienė, *Lietuvių užkalbėjimai*, no. 1534.

CHAPTER 4

DEVILS AND DEMONS

We should not be led astray: when the texts talk about the devil and demons, these names often overlie fantasy beings from folk belief, as I have shown in various studies. These creatures are gathered together and commingled in the same anathema by the Church. "Devil" and "demon" are generic terms that designate everything that is unorthodox, at the same time they mean the Christian devil.

416 ◆ A Charm against Demons
Repeat the following charm:

> Saint Anatole, you lord Severus, deliver so-and-so from the power of noon, the power of the sorcerers, the power of the devil, of all wicked enemies!
> Angel Michael †, angel Gabriel, angel Ariel, angel Rachoel, angel Parachoel, angel Oriel, angel Raphael, deign to save so-and-so, in the name of the Father, the Son, and the Holy Ghost! Saint Yriex, Saint Donat, Saint Severus, by the virtues of the present list we invite you to not allow the servant of God here present [name] to be attacked or obsessed by anything, by any demon of the hour of noon or of the night. Take pains to not act otherwise. Saint Donat. Amen.

📖 Latin, thirteenth century. Paris, Bibliothèque nationale, MS Lat. 13246, fol. 253v.

This is one of the rare Latin charms that mentions the demon of noon, the famous daemonium meridanum. *The angels Oriel, Parachoel, and Rachoel are not in the Bible; they are most likely the seven angels of Revelation (8:6). The saints invoked are those from the third to sixth centuries.*

📖 Lecouteux and Lecouteux, *Contes, Diableries et Autres Merveilles au Moyen Âge*, 45–47.

417 ◈ To Destroy Evil Spells

Mugwort puts demons and noxious substances to flight.

In 1843, "Aaron" (Simon Blocquel) wrote that, to destroy evil spells, it was necessary to take stems of mugwort and steep them for three days in the urine of a virgin girl, then seal these stems in a belt that one had to wear.

📖 Latin, fourth century. Pseudo-Apuleius, *Herbarius*, 10§1.
📖 *La Magie rouge*, 113.

418 ◈ To Send Evil Away

Repeat the following charm:

> † Enemy, by the passion of Our Lord, I conjure you to spare, not strike! † Enemy, by the blood of Our Lord Jesus Christ, I conjure you to spare, not strike! † Enemy, by the resurrection of the Lord, I conjure you to spare, not strike! The tormentor is tormented, Christ heals, Christ saves.

Enemy is the customary name for the devil. The reader will note the triple command that should lead to sending the evil back upon its author.

📖 Latin, thirteenth century. Paris, Bibliothèque nationale, MS Latin 13246, fol. 253v.

419 ◈ Remedy for Demoniacs

To put demons to flight, say this natural remedy:

> *Ocopo oxφ.e. Γ.e.i*

📖 Latin, ninth century. Önnerfors, "Iatromagische Beschwörungen," no. 36.

420 ◈ Potion for the Possessed, to Be Drunk in a Church

Take corn-cockle, bugloss, milfoil, lupine, betony, barnyard grass, sedge, iris, fennel, lichen taken from a church, lichen taken from a cross, and lovage.

Prepare the potion with light beer, sing seven masses over the plants, add garlic and holy water and pour this into the beverages that he will later drink. Also sing the psalms *Beati immaculi* and *Exsurgat*, and *Salvum me fac Deus*. The possessed person should then drink the potion in a church steeple, after a priest has sung *Domine sancte pater omnipotens* over him.

The use of the Psalms for magical purposes was widespread. The recipe here calls for Psalms 119, 68, and 69. The Domine sancte pater omnipotens *is a prayer found in France in the* Rituel romain pour l'usage du diocese de Toulon, *by the Bishop Louis-Albert Joly of Choin (Lyon: Chez led Frères Perisse, 1778, 279).*

📖 Old English and Latin, tenth century. *Læce boc* in Cockayne, *Leechdoms*, vol. 2, 136–38.

📖 On betony, cf. Macer Floridus, *De viribus herbarum*, vv. 429–91.

421 ◈ Protection against Night Terrors

When set in gold, chrysolite is said to be an amulet. It is a solid protection against night terrors. If pierced and threaded on the bristles of a young donkey, it will terrorize demons and, it is believed, torment them. When it has been set like this, it is best to wear it on the left wrist.

📖 Latin, eleventh century. Marbode, *De lapidus,* 11.

422 ◈ To Make Demons Flee

Whoever makes a ring from the iron bit of a donkey and wears it, will send demons fleeing and deflect fevers.

In itself, iron has always had the reputation for forming an obstacle to spirits, but this is the sole prescription that recommends the provenance and form. Pliny the Elder noted: Iron offers other remedies besides that of making incisions. For if a circle is traced with iron, or a pointed weapon is carried three times round them, it will preserve both child and adult from all evil spells: also, nails that have been removed from a grave, if driven into the threshold of a door, will prevent nightmares. (*Historia naturalis,* XXXIV, 44)

📖 Latin, twelfth century. *Liber Kyranidorum,* 123, 1ff.

📖 *HDA,* vol. 2, 717ff., "Eisen"; Mozzani, *Le Livre des superstitions,* 717–20.

423 ❖ To Drive Away Demons

The beak of the needlefish, also called belonis, drives away demons if one wears it or uses it in suffumigations.

📖 Latin, twelfth century. *Liber Kyranidorum,* 198: 7–8.

424 ❖ Another Charm to Drive Away Demons

The needlefish from the sea is also called belonis. . . . Its beak, worn or suffumigated, drives away demons.

📖 Greek, fourteenth century. KURANIS III, R; Mély, *Les lapidaires grecs,* 117.

425 ❖ To Eclipse the Devil's Malice

Betony can sometimes eclipse the devil's malice like other plants, because it appears with the dew and thus possesses the virtues of simples.

📖 Latin, twelfth century. Hildegard von Bingen, *Physica,* 1.56, "On Betony."

Betony (Betonica officinalis) is a veritable panacea. The Pseudo-Augustus Antonius Musa (first century BCE) listed forty-seven therapeutic properties in his De Herba vettonica. *It protects the body and soul from all charms and dangers. In the Germanic regions, this plant lent its name to a witch,* Patonnyerinn, *"she who digs up the betony."*

📖 Latin, first century. Pliny, *Historia naturalis,* XXV, 101; Heim, "Incantamenta magica," 503; Musa, *De herba vettonica;* Müller, *Die pflanzlichen Heilmittel bei Hildegard von Bingen;* Feyringer, *Das Speyrer Kraüterbuch mit den Heilpflanzen Hildegards von Bingen.*

426 ❖ To Drive Away Evil Spirits

The fern possesses certain virtues reminiscent of the sun, and the devil flees from it. It drives away phantasmagorias, which is why evil spirits do not like it. Wherever it grows, it is rare for the devil to work his tricks; it execrates the place and dwelling where lurks the demon. The one who carries the fern on his person is safe from diabolical snares and attacks on his body and life.

In early antiquity, the fern was a sacred plant, a remedy against wounds, sciatica, and hypochondria. It was said to resist magic charms. In Russia, it was harvested in accordance with a strict ritual: before midnight on Saint John's night, with a white napkin, a cross, the Gospel, and a glass of water, one went into the forest where it grew. One drew a circle with the cross that was then placed upon the napkin with the Gospel and the glass of water. Toward midnight, the fern was expected to flower. . . .

 📖 Latin, twelfth century. Hildegard von Bingen, *Physica*, I, 47, "On the Fern."
 📖 Floridus, *De viribus herbarum*, vv. 678–710.

427 ❖ To Get Rid of Demons and Wild Beasts

Carried on your person, a vulture heart will send fleeing all demons and wild beasts.

 📖 Latin, thirteenth century. Arnold of Villanova, *Opera*, fol. 215v.

428 ❖ To Drive Away Demons and Ghosts

Worn around the neck, the teeth of the joulie drive demons away and ghosts; its eyes repel curses.

 📖 Greek, fourteenth century. ΚΥΡΑΝΙΣ III, I; Mély, *Les lapidaires grecs*, 111.

429 ❖ To Expel a Demon from the Body

Write on the right or left hand [of the possessed individual] *tetragramaton*, on the nape of his neck: *Emanuel;* on his chest: *Sabaoth*, and on his forehead: Agla.

 📖 Middle French, fourteenth century. London, British Library, Harley 273, fol. 162v.

430 ❖ To Drive Away a Demon

To ensure that a demon or any air spirit depart the body of a person, he should carry *panicaut* (eryngium) root in his clothing and *confitabitur tibi* (Psalm 48:19), the evil spirit will immediately leave.

 📖 Middle French, late fourteenth century. Paris, Bibliothèque de l'Arsenal, MS 2872, fol. 41v, a.

431 ❖ Protection against the Devil

You should always wear salad burnet around your neck, in this way the attacks and temptations of the devil will not harm you, nor will the magic potions you may drink or the bewitched food you may eat.

 📖 Germany (Speyer), 1456, Berlin, Staatsbibliothek Preussische Besitz, Codex mgf 817, fol. 14v.

Gian Battista della Porta recommended salad burnet against snakebite and kidney stones.

 📖 Gubernatis, *La Mythologie des plantes,* 2:287–89.

432 ❖ For Demon Possession

Take the nemecite stone and on it carve the image of a maiden standing on a fixed wheel, and who is holding a rule in her left hand and a rod in her right, and one of her feet is resting on an ox. Beneath the stone place some mullein and pilot fish, and set it all in a gold or silver ring when the sun is in the sign of Scorpio. Know that this ring has marvelous virtues: whoever gives it to one possessed by the demon, that individual will confess his incontinence and the demon shall flee, and the man will remain sensible and virtuous. It is good against the dreams and fantasies to which the demon-possessed are prey, and against the fears of small children, and against all evil things that occur at night. . . . It is necessary for this individual to abstain from sin.

Many virtues have been lent to mullein, and it was used to treat skin disorders, rheumatism, and snakebite.

 📖 Middle French, late fourteenth century. Paris, Bibliothèque de l'Arsenal, MS 2872, folio 41v, a.

433 ❖ To Drive Away Demons and Thwart the Evil Eye

Mugwort is an herb; of all it is mine; its virtue is dear, it drives away all demons. If you fear curses, put three bouquets of it in your chamber, in this way demons will be unable to harm you, nor children, nor livestock nor anything at all; no kind of illness will affect the infant of a woman when she brings it into the world.

Mugwort (Artemisia vulgaris), *nicknamed "mother of all herbs," is one of the herbs of Saint John. According to Macer Floridus's* De viribus herbarum *(ninth century), it helps with childbirth, gall and kidney stones, and destroys the effect of poisons. Apuleius claims that it drives demons away and thwarts the evil eye.*

 📖 Middle High German, Tyrol, fifteenth century. Zingerle, "Segen und Heilmittel," 323.

434 ◈ Against the Devil

When a priest speaks these words in the ear of someone possessed by the evil Enemy, he will manifest at his request:

> *Amara Tonta Tyra post hos firibis ficaliri Elypolis starras poly polyque lique linarras buccabor uel barton uel Tiram celi massis Metumbor o priczoni Jordan Ciriacus Valentinus.*

 📖 Middle High German, Tyrol, fifteenth century. Zingerle, "Segen und Heilmittel," 319.

435 ◈ To Chase Away Nightmares, the Devil, and Ghosts

The smoke of birthwort chases away nightmares, the devil, and ghosts. This is why it should be used to suffumigate newborns to provide them assistance.

 📖 Middle High German, Speyer, 1456. Berlin, Staatsbibliothek, Codex, mgf 817, fol. 7v.

436 ◈ Against the *Năjit*

Lord, Lord, victor, vanquish! A *năjit* was coming out of the Red Sea and met Jesus Christ, [the Christ asked him]: "Where are you going, *năjit*?" It answered: "I am going to so-and so's house to suck out his brain, spill his blood, and break his ribs." And he said: "I conjure you, to not go to so-and-so's home but to go to deserted areas, to find stags there and enter their heads, and drink the brains you find there, to break their ribs, and to curdle their blood. Go and never return, until the day that has been prepared for judgment. Fear God who is seated on the throne of the cherubim, which frightens all those who see it and all those who do not. And you, be even more frightened of the Lord, whose glory lives forever, amen."

📖 Slavonic, Romania, tenth–eleventh century. Timotin, *Irodia, doamna zânelor,* 179–94.

Năjit designates both neuralgia and a demon that sends illnesses and fevers. The text was carved on a lead amulet that was worn around the neck. We find the same charm among the Serbians. It is based on a very common motif throughout Europe: the encounter of a major figure of Christianity with a demon.

📖 Timotin, "Les Charmes roumains manuscrits," 72–108; Timotin, *Descântele manucrise Româneşti (secolele al XVII-lea – al XIX-lea).* Bucarest: Editura Academiei Române, 2010, pp.251-259; Timotin,"The *Năjit* between Prayers and Charms," in *The Power of Words: Studies on Charms and Charming in Europe,* 216–30.

437 ◈ INCANTATION TO CHRIST FOR DRIVING THE DEVIL AWAY

Repeat the following incantation:

> I conjure you, O devil, by the terrifying name of Our Lord Jesus Christ. I conjure you, O devil, with Saint Mary, the holy mother of God, and with all the saints. I conjure you, O devil, with Saint John the Baptist.
>
> I conjure you, O devil, with the head of the archangels Michael and with Saint Gabriel and Uriel and Raphael and will all the holy celestial powers that serve around the throne of the lord. I conjure you, O devil, with all the saints of On High, with Zachariah and Simon.
>
> I conjure you, O devil, with the martyred saints Demetrius and George, and with the hierarchical saints John Chrysostom, Basil, and Gregory, with our brother [Saint] Nicholas and with the saints Sisinnius and Sinodor. I conjure you, O devil, with the life-giving holy cross that drives demons and all unclean spirits away. So that you may have no power from this day of today forward over the servant of God George Bratul. In the name of the Father, the Son, and the Holy Ghost, and now, and so forth.
>
> I conjure you, O devil, with the all-powerful, vigilant God. Unclean spirit, have fear of His holy name.

I conjure you, O devil, by He who breathed life into all beings and who is revered in trembling by all creatures.

I conjure you, O devil, with He who predicted fire would come from the heavens. I conjure you, O devil, with He who preached at the temple of Moses, with He who revealed himself in the bush on the mountain.

I conjure you, O devil, with He who slew the Egyptian official and caused drinkable water to gush from the stones. I conjure you, O devil, with He who said, "Heaven is my throne and the earth is my footstool."

I conjure you, O devil, by the great name of Christ, of Sabaoth.

I conjure you, O devil, with He who restored life to Lazarus after he had been dead for four days.

I conjure you, O devil, with He who commanded the sea, "May your springs dry up and earth come to judgment before the living God."

I conjure you, O devil, with He will come from heaven to earth and by the voice of the trumpet and fire of Whom will be shaken the pillars of heaven and the stars will fall.

I conjure you, O devil, with He who sits on the throne in glory and before Whom stand the countless crowds of angels, archangels, cherubim, and seraphim bursting into hosannas and singing and saying "holy holy holy."

This phylactery carved on lead sheets was discovered in Oltenia, Romania. It was obviously designed to be worn. It is a veritable incantation based on anaphors and taking the form of an exorcism.

📖 Slavonic Serbian, first half of the seventeenth century. Stahl, "L'organisation magique du territoire villageois roumain," 52ff.

438 ◈ A Spell against the Demon
Repeat the following:

> Flee from here, wicked scourge! Flee from here, wicked plague! Go far away from the naked skin. I will supply you with a dashing steed to carry you away and save you, a courser whose

hooves never slip on the ice, never trip over a rock. So flee then, as I command you, on hell's courser, on the wild stallion of the mountains! Flee by way of the deserts of Hell! Jump into the eternal abyss and never return! So flee then, as I command you, into the deep forest of the Lapps, into the dark Pohjola!

The Turju mountains designate neighboring Lapland, and Pohjola is the name of the polar regions, a mythical region that holds the roots of the world. What we have here is a spell for banishing evil into uncultivated wilderness.

📖 Finland, nineteenth century. Bartels, "Über Krankheits-Beschwörungen," 26ff.

439 ◈ Spell against Gylou

Saints Sisinnios and Synidôros, help God's servant [name] and his wife [name], and their children having this phylactery. And bind, and seal with lead any apparition and any aerial [spirit] and the unclean Gylou, who will have neither the power or the strength to approach the house of God's servant [name], nor his wife [name], nor their children, neither at night, nor day, nor midnight, nor noon. Saint Marina bind and gag and vanquish any aerial [spirit] and demoniac and the unclean Gylou, far from the house of God's servant [name] and his wife and his children. Saint George, Saint Theodore of Tyr and General, aid God's servant [name] and his wife and his children. And vanquish and drive off and bind and seal with lead any demonic [spirit] and any apparition and any aerial [spirit] and any evil spirit far from the house of God's servant [name] and his wife and his children.

Gylou (Gylloy, Gyllou) is a demoness with twelve names: she is responsible for infant mortality and often appears in the Byzantine exorcisms known as "Gylou's papers."

📖 Greece, nineteenth century. *Cahiers Mondes anciens* 1 (2010), §23.
📖 Greenfield, "Saint Sisinnios, the Archangel Michael, and the Female Demon Gylou," *Byzantina* 15 (1989): 83–142; Oeconomidès, "Yello dans les traditions des peuples helleniques et roumains," *Laografia* 30 (1975): 266–78.

LEO ALLATIVS

VIII. Alii fe ad Amuleta & Periapta convertunt, quorum ftultitiam ut rideas, nonnulla, mutila illa ac detruncata, ut potui habere, exſcribo: * * * * μήπως σφ́ή ἐν τῷ πύργῳ, καὶ καταφάγῃ μκ τὸ βρέφος, καθὰ ἓ πεποίηκεν. οἱ ἢ ἅγιοι ξ θεῦ Σισώιος, καὶ Συνίδωρος, ὡς εἶδον τὴν ἀδελφὴν αὐτῶν κοπτομένην, ἔκλαυσαν καὶ αὐτοὶ ἐ μετρίως, καὶ ἐυθὺς κλίναντες τὰ γόνατα αὐτῶν ἐν τῇ γῇ, ἐδέοντο ξ θεῦ, ξ δοῦναι αὐτοῖς ἐξεσίαν, καὶ ἰσχὺν κξ τ μιαρᾶς Γυλᾶς, ὅπως αὐτὴν χειρώζωσ). Καὶ δὴ λαβόντες ἐξεσίαν ἐκ θεῦ παντοκράτορος, ἐχαλίνωσαν τοὺς ἵππες αὐτῶν εὐθὺς. Καὶ ἤρξαντο καταδιώκεν τὴν μιαρὰν Γυλοῦν, καὶ ἐλθόντες ἐν τῇ ὁδῷ ηὕρωκεν, καὶ ἠρώτων εἴ τι δὲ ἂν ἔθελον. ὑπελύτησαν ἢ τὴν ἰτέαν, καὶ ἠρώτησαν αὐτὴν, λέγοντες. ἴδες ἐδῶ τ μιαρὰν Γυλᾶν πεπομένην; ἡ ἢ ἠρνήσατο, ὅτι οὐκ οἶδα. Καὶ ἐκατηράσατο αὐτὴν οἱ ἅγιοι, λέγοντες, μηκέτι ἐκ σῦ καρπὸς γλύκητε εἰς τ αἰῶνα. Καὶ ἄνθρωπος ε φάγεται ἀπ' αὐτῦ. Καὶ πάλιν οἱ ἅγιοι δρομαῖοι ἔτρεχον ἔμπροσθεν. Καὶ ὑπελύτησαν τὴν βάτον. Καὶ ἠρώτησαν αὐτὴν, λέγοντες. ἴδες ἐδῶ τ μιαρὰν Γυλᾶν πεπομένην, καὶ ἠρνήσατο κ αὐτὴ ὁμοίως, ὅτι οὐκ οἶδα. Καὶ ἐκατηράσαντο ἓ αὐτὴν οἱ ἅγιοι λέγοντες. Ἡ ῥίζα σε ποιήσοι κορυφᾶς, καὶ ἡ κορυφή σε ῥίζας, καὶ ὁ καρπός σε ἀνόφελός ἐστι, καὶ ἄνθρωπος ε ζήσεται ἐξ αὐτῦ. Καὶ πάλιν οἱ ἅγιοι δρομαῖοι ἔτρεχον ἔμπροσθεν, κ ὑπελύτησαν τὴν εὐλογημένην ἐλαίαν. Καὶ ἠρώτησαν αὐτὴν οἱ ἅγιοι λέγοντες. Ἴδες ἐδῶ τὴν μιαρὰν Γυλοῦν πεπομένην. Ἡ ἢ λέγει πρὸς τοὺς ἁγίες. Δράμετε ἅγιοι ξ θεῦ ἐν τάχι, ἔτι ὑπάγει πρὸς τ αἰγιαλόν. Οἱ ἢ ἅγιοι ξ θεῦ Σισώιος κ Συνίδωρος ηὐλόγησαν αὐτὴν, καὶ εἶπον, ὁ καρπός σε πολὺς ἧς, καὶ οἱ ἅγιοι ὑπ' αὐτῦ φωτισθήσωνται, καὶ βασιλεῖς, καὶ πτωχοὶ ἐξ αὐτῦ εὐφρανθήσονται. Φθάσαντες οὖν οἱ ἅγιοι εἰς τ αἰγιαλὸν ἴδον τὴν μιαρὰν Γυλῦν πεπομένην, καὶ ὡς ἴδεν τοὺς ἁγίες ἡ μιαρὰ Γυλᾶ ἐγίνετο εὐθὺς, ὡς ἰχθύς. Καὶ οἱ ἅγιοι ξ θεῦ ἁλιεῖς, καὶ ἡλίθον αὐτὴν. Καὶ πάλιν ἡ μιαρὰ Γυλᾶ ἐγίνετο ὡς χελιδών. Καὶ οἱ ἅγιοι ξ θεῦ ὡς εἶχον τὴν χάριν

Leo Allatius (1586–1669),
De templis Graecorum recentiorbus (Cologne, 1645),
on the "papers of Gylou."

CHAPTER 5

FANTASTIC BEINGS AND SPIRITS

The fantastic beings that appear in the charms and recipes for healing and protection bear different names depending on the eras and the cultures. It is important to know though that these names have a long history and they blur the specificity of those that carry them. For example, in modern times, the troll is no longer a dwarf or giant but a simple devil. Elves, meanwhile, were demonized in the tenth and eleventh centuries. In the European cultures after the Middle Ages, as the influence of the Christian Church shrank, these creatures enjoyed a resurgence. This is particularly evident in Romanian and Gypsy charms.

📖 Lecouteux, *The Secret History of Poltergeists and Haunted Houses*; Lecouteux, *Eine Welt im Abseits: Studien zur niederen Mythologie und Glaubenswelt des Mittelalters*; Lecouteux, *Demons and Spirits of the Land*; Lecouteux, *Les Nains et les Elfes au Moyen Âge*.

440 ◆ Protection from the Night Gods and Fauns
The Magi assure us that those who are tormented by the night gods and fauns will be freed of their visions if they rub themselves in the morning and in the evening with the tongue, eyes, bile, and intestines of a dragon that have been boiled in wine and oil, and left to chill overnight in the open air.

📖 Latin, first century. Pliny, *Historia naturalis*, XXX, 84.

441 ◆ Protection against Elves, Night Spirits, and Those Who Copulate with the Devil

To make an ointment against the race of elves, the spirits that walk the night, and those who copulate with the demon.

Take hops, wormwood, marsh mallow, lupine, verbena, henbane, cudweed, viper's bugloss, plants of blueberry, leek, garlic, seeds of cleaver, corn cockle, and fennel. Put the plants into a pot, place them beneath the altar, and say nine masses over them. Boil them in butter and mutton fat, add a good quantity of blessed salt, and filter it through linen. Toss the plants into running water.

If he displays some evil temptation, or an elf, or a nocturnal spirit, smear his face with this ointment, place it over his eyes and wherever the affliction appears, make suffimigations of incense to it and bless him often with the sign of the cross—his condition will improve.

Elves and dwarves had the reputation of sending illnesses by means of invisible shot called aelfscot, dvergscot. *In the Old English texts, there is often mention of the magic of the elves* (aelfsidene) *who suck the blood and cause an illness called* aelfsogopa; *another affliction is the water elf disease* (wæterælfdle). *The Scandinavian world has preserved a large number of charms against dwarves.*

 📖 Old English, tenth century. *Læce boc* in Cockayne, *Leechdoms*, vol. 2, 346.

 📖 Lecoutuex, *Les Nains et les Elfes au Moyen Âge*, 152–56; Berthoin-Matthieu, *Prescriptions anglaises;* Bang, *Norske hexeformularer*, no. 42ff., "Dværge-besværgelse" and "Vise dvergin" no. 111, "For dverge-slag." For more on wormwood (absinthe), see: Macer Floridus, *De viribus herbarum*, vv. 52–114; Camus, *Circa instans*, no. 1; Platearius, *Livre des simples médecines*, 2:70, cap. 22.

442 ◆ Holy Beverage against the Activities of Elves and against All Temptations of the Devil

Write several times on a paten: "In the beginning was the Word," until "comprehended it naught" (John 1:5); "And Jesus went all about Galilee, teaching" until "followed him great multitudes" (Matthew 4:23–25); "God by your name" until the end (Psalm 54); "God be merciful unto us" until the end (Psalm 67); and "Make haste to help me, O Lord" until the end (Psalm 70).

Take pulicaria [small fleabane], disme [musk], zedoary [white turmeric], canche [tussock grass], and fennel. Take a pitcher of consecrated wine, ask a person who is a virgin to go fetch in silence a half pitcher of running water taking it against the current. Then take the plants, put them all in the water, carefully take off the inscription on the paten by washing it in this water, then pour the consecrated wine over this beverage. Bring the entire thing to the church and have three masses sung over it, the one being *Omnibus sanctis,* the other being *Contra tribulation,* and the third, *Sanctam Marian.*

Sing these invocatory psalms: *Miserere mei Deus* (Psalm 57), *Deus in nomine tuo* (Psalm 54), *Deus misereatur nobis* (Psalm 67), *Domine Deus* (Psalm 70), *Inclina Domine* (Psalm 85), then the Credo, the Gloria, the Litanies, and Our Father.

Bless the beverage ardently in the name of the all-powerful Lord and say: "In the name of the Father, the Son, and the Holy Ghost, may it so be blessed!" Then use it.

 📖 Old English and Latin, tenth–eleventh century. *Lacnunga,* in Cockayne, Leechdoms, vol. 3, 10–12. For more on zedoary *(Curcurma zedoaria)* see Floridus, *De viribus herbarum,* vv. 2131–40.

443 ❖ Protection against Airy Spirits

When airy spirits start habitually appearing, it is necessary to burn a little whale's liver over hot coals. The spirits will leave without being able to return because of the odor.

 📖 Twelfth century. Hildegard von Bingen, *Physica,* V, 1, "Whale."

444 ❖ Protection against the Attacks of Demons and Spirits

Wearing a jasper adorned with an image of a hare that does not correspond to the celestial sign provides protection against the attacks of demons and spirits.

 📖 Latin, Italy, 1502. Leonardi, *Speculum lapidum,* 3:19, 5.

445 ❖ Conjuration of the Spirits

I've been told that you, male elf, female elf, are able to abduct the king from the queen and steal the bird from the nest. You shall know no rest or respite before being in the bushes so that you are unable to harm anyone.

📖 Germany, eighteenth century. Grimm, *Deutsche Mythologie*, vol. 3, 502.

446 ❖ AGAINST ALL EVIL SPIRITS

To protect yourself against all evil spirits, you must make a silver ring in the second house of the moon and set in it a crystalline stone on which ŋ has been carved; then write "Gabriach" with the blood of a white dove on virgin parchment perfumed with aloe.

📖 France, eighteenth century. London, British Library, Landsdowne 1202 4to, fol. 175.

447 ❖ TO WARD OFF EVIL SPIRITS

Our Lord Jesus Christ went down to his green field. There he met the Tuss and the troll, the vile one. "What are you going to do?" asked Jesus. "I am going to the home of the man named _____ to break his bones and suck his blood." "I am going to send you back," said Jesus, "under a huge rock where you will rot and where you are going to break yourself."

📖 Norway, nineteenth century. Nergaard, *Skikk og bruk: Folkeminne fraa Østerdalen*, 111; Amilien, *Le Troll et autres creatures surnaturelles*.

448 ❖ PRAYER AGAINST THE DEMONS (MEANING TROLLS)

To expel nine kinds of demons out of men and, after, as many others that walk and fly between heaven and earth—of these remote evils that oppose us and which, in complete serenity, take pleasure in sating themselves:

> I went out into the open meadow; there I met Envy. Virgin Mary, lend me your keys, I wish to paralyze all the animals with talons in the forest, their mouths, and their tongues and their livers and tongues, so that none among them can touch or harm anyone, may your rock sit in the ground of the forest or at the rounded top of the mountain.

The demons are clearly identified here with the emissaries of evil, they are personified and animalized. Their activity is incorporated into that of devouring.

📖 Norway, Archives of the Cultural Studies Institute of Oslo (Blindern): "å fordriva torv (tövr) kjå [leu] ist"; Nelson, *Charmes et bénédictions. Reflets de l'univers mental du monde médiéval, étude d'un corpus germanique.* 8.

449 ◆ AGAINST THE IELE

Repeat the following:

> I, [full name], I am very happy that you have come and here I have been fasting since three Fridays, and here I am preparing you a large meal, specifically for your arrival. And I am sending prayers so that you may forgive me for any transgressions I have committed, because henceforth I keep a close eye on myself to avoid offending you ever again. And if I do sin again, have pity on me for I am the servant of God, and then your servant, me, [full name].

The Iele *are wicked fairies. Iele is the third-person feminine pronoun of the first-person she. They paralyze people, crippling them and making them blind, mute, or mad, or they kill those they encounter. The meal mentioned in the spell has been around in the West since the Middle Ages; it is a propitiatory rite.*

📖 Romania, late eighteenth century. Bucharest, Biblioteca Academiei Române, MS Romanian BAR 1517, fol. 44r.

📖 Lecouteux, "Romanisch-germanische Kulturberührungen am Beispiel des Mahls der Feen"; Timotin, *Paroles protectrices, paroles guérisseuses. La tradition manuscrite des charmes roumains (XVIIe-XIXe siècle)*, 227.342–72; Timotin: *"Irodia, doamna zânelor:* Notes sur les fées roumaines et leur cohort fantastique," in *Les Entre-Mondes: Les Vivant, les morts,* 279–94; "Un aspect méconuu des fées roumaines: Observation sur un texte magique manuscript," *Revue des Études sud-est européennes* 45 (2007): 433–43.

450 ◆ AGAINST THE SPIRIT LOVER

One day when the saint and holy martyr George was taking his sheep to pasture, one of those that are called spirit lovers fled before him and went quite quickly to corrupt all his things and all the dishes of his master. And this cursed being became child, woman, and girl, and could assume a male appearance or several appearances. And the saint, when he grabbed him, tied him with a large restraint.

So, when you meet [full name], do not offend him for he is the servant of God, and do not offend anyone in his family or anything they own. Me, I was seized and freed this way, and anyone who was exposed as I was, should write these letters, burn them, suffumigate himself with them:

ⰏⰓⰜⰈⰔⰁⰟⰔⰓⰔⰈⰏ
ⰔⰀⰔⰓⰜⰄⰟⰏⰀⰟⰓ

The spirit lover (zburător) comes from erotic desire, and this is the reason why it assumes the semblance of the beloved individual in both form and appearance; it is close to the nightmare. To protect oneself, it is necessary to barricade all the exits of the home and arrange four knives in the shape of a cross at the entrance to the chimney.

📖 Romania, late eighteenth century. Bucharest, Biblioteca Academiei Române, MS Romanian BAR 1517, fol. 44r, "Pentru cei cu zburători"; Timotin, *Descântecele manuscrise românești*, 325.

📖 Vinagradova, "Les croyances slaves concernant l'esprit-amant," *Cahiers slaves* 1 (1997): 237–53; Lecouteux, "Un démon des croyances populaires: l'esprit-amant," *Mythes, Symboles, Littératures* 2 (Nagoya, 2002): 21–32.

451 ◈ Against the Bite of the Mountain Trolls

Spit and spread [the saliva] over the wound and then say this prayer:

> The troll blows, while sitting in the mountain with a ring around the neck and slobber around its mouth. Hold on, I am going to give you something else to do now! I command you to return with staff and crutch into the mountain and sit down, ashamed and upset, so that you are unable to do anything more, and I command you to stay there until the day of the Last Judgment.

📖 Norway, Bøyun 5, 26, Archives of the Cultural Studies Institute of Oslo (Blindern), "Åtgjed mot tusse-bit"; Nelson, *Charmes et bénédictions. Reflets de l'univers mental du monde médiéval, étude d'un corpus germanique*, 281.

452 ◆ AGAINST THE NASTY BITE

>Nåsse and Tåsse were going their way
>When they met Jesus Christ in person.
>"Where are you going?"
>Asked Jesus Christ.
>Then they told him:
>"I am going to [name]'s home,
>I intend to afflict his flesh,
>Suck his blood,
>And break his bones."
>"No!" answered Jesus Christ in person,
>"I forbid you this thing.
>You shall not afflict his flesh,
>Nor suck his blood,
>Nor break his bones;
>You shall no longer do anymore harm
>Than a mouse does to a rock stuck in the ground."
>In his name:
>††† Amen.

Nåsse and Tåsse are personifications of evil. Here again we find the theme of the encounter.

 📖 Sweden (Västergötland), 1722, Klintberg, *Svenska trollformler*, 68, no. 13, "mot onda bettet."
 📖 Tillhagen, Folklig läkekonst, 277–79.

453 ◆ AGAINST THE BITE OF THE TUS OR TROLL

Christ and Saint Peter were crossing through a cemetery. They met Tus-Tas taking a stroll. The father strolling, the mother strolling. "Brother Tus," asked the Lord, "where are you going?" "I am going to the peasant's farm, to strike, strike blood, and break a leg." Christ struck him with his divine hand. "I command you to turn away from that you great traitor, by your Lord Jesus, and with one leap, to disappear again! By the three Names, by the Father, Son, and Holy Ghost!" Say the Our Father three times.

 The Tuss are mountain trolls; in Norwegian, Berg-Troll.

📖 Norway (Hallingdal), 1834, Svartebok in Ål, 11, Norwegian Folklore Archives (NFS), University of Oslo (Blindern), "For Tud sebide og Troldet."

454 ❖ To Protect a Woman in Labor

In order to keep the evil spirits away until the newborn is baptized, a fire should be kept burning continuously in front of the tent of the gypsy woman giving birth: the women will fan the fire by singing:

> *Fire, fire, burn quick,*
> *Burn rapidly,*
> *And keep far from my little infant,*
> *My little child*
> *Phuvush; Nivashi too*
> *Should flee away from your smoke!*
> *Attract the good Urmen*
> *So that this child may be blessed;*
> *On this earth, on this earth*
> *That he may be happy, happy!*
> *Branches of the broom, branches of the broom,*
> *And once more, branches of the broom,*
> *Branches of the broom, branches of the broom,*
> *And once more, branches of the broom,*
> *I place into the blazing fire;*
> *Fire burn fast,*
> *Listen, the little child is crying.*

Heinrich von Wlislocki collected the following variant from the Hungarian gypsies (Volksdichtungen, *141*):

Eitrá Pçuvuša, efta Nivašya	Seven pçuvuš, seven nivašya
André mal avená	Arriving by way of the field
Pçabuven, pçabuven, oh yákhá!	Fire, seize them!
Dáyákri punro dindálen	They want to bite the mother's leg
Te gule čaves mudáren	Wish to kill her little infant
Pçabuven, pçabuven, oh yákhá!	Fire, fire, burn quick
Ferinen o čaves te daya!	Save the mother, save the child!

📖 Gypsies of Transylvania, nineteenth century. Wlislocki, *Volksdichtungen*, 140.

455 ◈ For Nursing

When a child does not wish to take the breast, it is believed by the gypsies that the wife of a Phuvush has nursed it in secret. The mother places some onion greens between her breasts while saying:

> *Wife of the Phuvush, wife of the Phuvush,*
> *May illness devour your body!*
> *May your milk turn to fire!*
> *So burn then in the ground!*
> *Flow, flow my milk,*
> *Flow, flow white milk,*
> *Flow as long as I wish,*
> *To soothe the hunger of my child!*

📖 Gypsies of Transylvania, nineteenth century. Wlislocki, *Volksdichtungen*, 144.

456 ◈ A Prayer against the Exposed Child

Say the following prayer:

> *I arrived small;*
> *I am as big as a horse*
> *It is with men and women*
> *That I wish to be worse!*
> *I want to be a sucker of the head—No says Jesus!*
> *I want to be a sucker of the neck—No says Jesus!*
> *I want to be a sucker of shoulders, arms, and fingers—*
>   *No says Jesus!*
> *I want to be a sucker of entrails, stomach, and back—*
>   *No says Jesus!*
> *I want to be the new worms, sucker of kidneys and feet—*
>   *No says Jesus!*
> *I conjure you and make you disappear out of the skin and*
>   *into the wall;*
> *Out of the flesh and into the humus; out of the blood and*
>   *into the river;*
> *Out of the marrow and into the mountain,*
> *And in the blue mountains, I command you to stay*
> *Until judgment has passed!*

The child left to die of exposure in the forest transforms into a demon. He can busy himself with people, sometimes in the middle of the day, sometimes in the morning, and sometimes in the evening, and he can suck out their organs completely, sometimes the head and/or back, and, if not, all their limbs. He was a particularly dreaded figure. In Scandinavian charms, it was common to banish a wicked spirit to the Blue Mountain (Heimman blaa, Bjergethla), a mythical place incorporated to Hell.

    📖 Norway, "Ei segla mot útbore," Archives of the Cultural Studies Institute of Oslo (Blindern); Nelson, *Charmes et bénédictions. Reflets de l'univers mental du monde médiéval, étude d'un corpus germanique*, 346.

457 ◆ To Dispel Evil Spirits

Each morning upon rising, you will say: "O all-powerful Father! O mother, the gentlest of mothers! O admirable example of the feelings and tenderness of all mothers! O son, the flower of all sons! Farm of all farms, soul, spirit, harmony! O number of all things, preserve us, protect us, lead us, and be favorable to us in all times and all places!"

    Then you will say three times: "My God, I place my hope in you, the Son, the Holy Ghost, and in myself."

    📖 France (Troyes), ca. 1840, *Laissez dire et faites le bien: Le Médecin des pauvres*, 8.

CHAPTER 6

HEALING OF ANIMALS

BLOOD FLOW

458 ◈ FOR BLOOD FLOW FROM THE NOSTRILS OF A BEAST OF BURDEN

Write this on a virgin parchment and hang it around the animal's neck with a string: "The fire is cold, the water is thirsty, the mule gives birth; *tasca mascas venas omnes.*"

The spell is an adynaton (see entry 297) listing impossibilities. "The mule gives birth" can be found earlier, but reversed, in Marcellus de Bordeaux's De medicamentis liber (8.191) in the series: "Neither gives birth, not the stone bears wool. . . ."

📖 Latin, sixth century. P. Vegetius, Digestorum artis, 4:26, in P. Vegeti Renati *Digestorum artis mulomedicinae libri*, 306.

BOUQUET (SHEEP SCAB)

The bouquet is a pustular disease specific to sheep and goats.

459 ◈ AGAINST THE CANKEROUS BOUQUET, FEVERS

Take the first sheep you see that has been attacked by this evil. Turned toward the rising sun, open the animal's mouth and speak inside it the words that follow:

Brac, Cabrac, Carabra, Cadebrac, Cabracam, I cure you.

Blow into the sheep's mouth each time, and then cast it among the others, they will all be cured. You must make as many signs of the cross as there are marks. These same words, written on a paper, worn around the neck for nine days, will heal fever.

This spell is a variant of Abracadabra.

📖 France, 1670, Honorius, *Le livre des conjurations,* 119.

CANKER

Canker is a cancerous disease that appears in the hooves of ruminants.

460 ◆ To Cure an Ox from the Canker

If your ox has the canker, lead him into the meadow and cut a round of sod that he would have stepped on, then hang this sod above the hearth; as the sod dries up, the sickness of your ox will diminish.

Hanging a plant in the chimney so it will dry out is a very common technique when people are seeking to counter illnesses or curses.

📖 France (Ardennes), nineteenth century. Meyrac, *Traditions,* 178, no. 86.

CHARBON (ANTHRAX)

Bacterial charbon first affects sheep, then cows and horses, in whom it is displayed by fever, and by pustules and edemas in humans.

461 ◆ A Charm against the Charbon Disease

> In the name of the Father, the Son, and the Holy Ghost, amen. "I conjure you, evil charbon, in the name of God, creator of heaven, earth, hell, the sun, the moon, and the seven stars, and all creatures, and all angels, and all the confessors, bishops, and all the one hundred abbots ready to sing on winter solstice night, that you neither enter nor stay any longer [in this animal], in the name of the Father, the Son, and the Holy Ghost." Say this for the horse.

The mix of pagan elements (the celestial bodies) and Christian elements show how easy it was to make a charm orthodox: all it required was the addition of God, Jesus, the saints.

📖 Middle English, fifteenth century. London, British Library, Sloane 963, fol. 137v.

FARCY

Farcy is a cutaneous form of glanders, an infectious disease affecting Equidae.

462 ❖ A Charm for Farcy

In the name of the Father, the Son, and the Holy Ghost, amen. In the honor of Our Lord Jesus Christ and Our Lady Saint Mary and Saint Job and the soul of his father and that of his mother and the soul of all his ancestors, say three Our Fathers and three Hail Marys. Then: "Saint Job had nine worms, had eight worms, had seven worms, had six worms, had five worms, had four worms, had three worms, had two worms, had one worm, he had no more ulcers." Speak these words for the horse and he will be healed by God's grace.

📖 Middle English, thirteenth century. London, British Library, Sloane 692, fol. 133v.

FERTILITY

463 ❖ To Increase Fertility

To increase a mare's fertility, you should give it its first oats in an apron or gourd while saying:

> *Three asses, three dogs*
> *Racing up the mountain.*
> *May your body swell, eat and drink!*
> *Three asses, three dogs*
> *Racing down the mountain,*
> *Sealing all the cavities!*

> *They are placing a moon there.*
> *You will soon be impregnated.*

📖 Gypsies of Transylvania, nineteenth century. Wlislocki, *Volksdichtungen,* 139.

GANGLIA

464 ◈ To Cure Ganglia on a Horse

If a horse has ganglion cysts behind the jaw, you must recite, with three Our Fathers, these words three times:

> † *abgla* † *abgli* † *alphara* † *asy* † Our Father, and so on.

📖 France (Paris), circa 1393, *Le Mesnagier de Paris,* 470.

LAMINITIS

465 ◈ To Ward Off Demons in Your Horse

Begin by reciting an Our Father into the horse's right ear. Then say the verse below.

> *Leave, demon!*
> *Harm nothing.*
> *There was a protection.*
> *There was a demon.*
> *From where did you come?*
> *Depart into the mountains, into the seas.*

Then say an Our Father three times for the healing.

📖 Latin and Middle High German, twelfth century. Zurich, Zentralbibliothek, MS C. 58, fol. 47r; *HDA,* vol. 6, 1676ff., "Pferdesegen."

466 ◈ Charm against Laminitis

Say the following words:

> *Hinnitus quisitys vena vacca bane barra.*

And say a *Pater* and an *Ave* three times, for this is most effective, as many blacksmiths can attest.

📖 Latin and Middle English, fifteenth century. London, British Library, Sloane 692, fol. 136v.

NAIL WOUND

This is a wound caused by the blacksmith who when putting a shoe on a horse's hoof, drives one of the nails into the soft tissue, which causes an abscess. But this is also an evil spell against human beings. A person will take the nails from an old coffin and plant them in the footprint left by the person they want to make suffer.

467 ◆ Against Nail Wounds

In the same way for the nail wound of a horse, say this charm: "God, as patiently as you were bound [on the cross] at the roadside, when Longinus pierced your heart with a spear, save this horse!" And say three Our Fathers and three Ave in the name of the Holy Ghost.

📖 Middle English, fifteenth century. London, British Library, Sloane 692, fol. 134v.

468 ◆ To Treat a Horse Injured by a Nail

To treat a horse hurt by a smith's nail, take a piece of white bread and the herb that is called misery [spiderwort]; blend them together and give the mixture to the horse two or three times and it will recover. Ah, sweet Lord Jesus Christ, as true as your father and son and holy ghost, three persons and one God, and as you give chaplains the virtue of making flesh and blood from wheat bread,* and as true as you suffered from grave wounds in your flesh and your blood on the cross by iron nails to save the sinners, and as true as you have given powers to stones, herbs, and words, give this power to this bread and to this herb so that may heal without delay the nail-caused hurt of this animal, in the honor of the Father, the Son, and the Holy Ghost.

📖 French, beginning of the fourteenth century. Oxford, Bodleian Library, MS 57, fol. 217v.

PARALYSIS OF HORSES

469 ◆ To Heal Paralysis in a Horse

First of all, say an Our Father. Then repeat the following verse:

---

*A reference to transubstantiation.

> *A fish swam in the water, it dislocated its fins,*
> *Then Our Lord healed it.*
> *May the same Lord who healed the fish,*
> *Heal this horse of paralysis.*

📖 Old Saxon, ninth century. Vienna, Österreichische Nationalbibliothek, Codex 751, fol. 188v.

SPRAIN

470 ◈ Against Sprains

If a horse has twisted its leg, speak these words:

> Nabor, return whence you came!
> By three times
> I had faith, when I said
> By three times.
> *Alpha et O initium et finis.*
> The crosss is life for me and death for you, enemy!
>
> [Recite] an Our Father.

📖 Latin, tenth–eleventh century. London, British Library, Harley 585, fol. 181v–182r.

471 ◈ For Healing Sprains and Twisted Limbs

You must repeat the following phrase three times while striking the horse's hoof. If it is on the side of the mounting block, strike the left hoof. This works for men as well.

> "*Atay de satay suratay avalde,* walk!"

📖 France, 1670, Honorius, *Le livre des conjurations,* 120.

TRENCHES OF HORSES

Trenches are violent attacks of colic.

472 ◈ To Heal Horse Colic

To heal horse colic, say five Pater, five Ave, and, making the sign of the cross with your left foot on the horse's stomach, add: "Red trenches, white trenches, sharp and other trenches, I conjure you, in the name of the great living God, to depart from the body of this animal as quickly as Our Lord left the Garden of Olives, as true as Joseph of Arimathea was the first to enter holy paradise after Our Lord Jesus Christ."

📖 France, Ardennes, nineteenth century. Meyrac, *Traditions,* 188, no. 207.

473 ◈ To Cure a Horse of Trenches
Repeat the following:

> Saint George, patron of riders, and you blessed Saint Eligius, who shod the horses of the great King Dagobert, we confide to your cares the horse or mare of so and so, of such robe (say the name of the person and the color of the hair).

Lay one hand on the horse's croup and use the other to support its stomach while saying: "If you have the vives, no matter their color, whether they are red trenches, or the illness has some entirely different cause, may Saint George and Saint Eligius come to your aid and may God heal you, in the name of the Father, the Son, and the Holy Ghost. May it be so."

In Normandy, people add: "Say five Pater and five Ave while on your knees. For this, concerning the horse, open the horse's mouth and blow

Saint Eligius, patron saint of horses.

inside it three times [while] speaking these words: in tes dulame bonis vint diver nos Sathan."

📖 Nisard, *Histoire des livres populaires,* 77; *Le Pesant,* "Prières superstitieuses du pays d'Ouche," 331.

474 ❖ CHARM TO CURE HORSE TRENCHES

Black or gray horses, because it is important to distinguish the animal's hair color, belonging to [name], if you have the vives of whatever color they may be, or red trenches, or one of the thirty-six other illnesses, whatever the case may be, God heal you and blessed Saint Eligius. In the name of the Father, the Son, and the Holy Ghost.

And you will say five Pater and five Ave to thank God for his grace.

📖 France (Troyes), ca. 1840, *Laissez dire et faites le bien: Le Médecin des pauvres,* 10.

UNSPECIFIED DISEASES

475 ❖ FOR LIVESTOCK DISEASES
Say the following words.

✳ *chavit rauto † ad qui bany † de p̄ corte ut maxime rector* ✡

📖 Latin, ninth century. St. Gallen, Stiftsbibliothek, Codex 751; Heim, "Incantamenta magica," 564.

476 ❖ TO HEAL A HORSE
Rub the back of the purchased horse with powdered goat dung while saying:

> *May all the sickness*
> *Leave your body!*
> *The dung of goats quickly chases*
> *All the illnesses from your stomach,*
> *From your hooves, from your back,*
> *From your eyes, from your ears!*
> *Be henceforth like a newborn,*

> *Follow no other person but me,*
> *Stay, stay, stay here!*

📖 Gypsies of Transylvania, nineteenth century. Wlislocki, *Volksdichtungen*, 148.

477 ◈ Against the Sickness of Animals

Take two birds, quail if possible; kill the first then sprinkle the other with its blood before letting it fly away. The remaining blood is used to feed the ailing animal while saying:

> *May the sickness in you depart!*
> *Here is a good dwelling*
> *For the malicious spirit!*
> *When the blood dries up*
> *The illness leaves.*
> *Evil Spirit, get out,*
> *This dwelling is not good!*
> *Hold on, here is blood!*

📖 Gypsies of Transylvania, nineteenth century. Wlislocki, *Volksdichtungen*, 148.

478 ◈ To Cleanse a Cow's Milk

When a cow gives bloody milk, pour this milk into a field where there are quails while saying:

> *Here is some blood for you;*
> *It is not good!*
> *That of Our Lord Jesus Christ*
> *Is the sole that is useful;*
> *May he be with us always!*

📖 Gypsies of Transylvania, nineteenth century. Wlislocki, *Volksdichtungen*, 151.

479 ◈ To Cure a Cow of Disease

When a cow urinates while it is being milked, this urine should be boiled with onion peels and the egg of a black hen, then her feed should be watered with this blend while saying:

> *May what is within come out!*
> *Three good Urma are calling it,*

Three good Urma are expelling it
Into an eggshell.
May it live there, reside there,
Warm itself by the fire
And cool down in the water!

📖 Gypsies of Transylvania, nineteenth century. Wlislocki, *Volksdichtungen,* 148.

The Urma are spirits that appear as women of unnatural beauty; they are the fairies of fate. Their life is held in three golden hairs on their occiput. They live in glittering palaces built on mountains created by the Sun King and called "the happy mountains" (baçtalo bar) where they sing and dance at night under the moon. There are three of them. The eldest is named Lace Urme, "the good fairy," and she is the guardian spirit; the middle one, Šilale Urme, "the cold fairy," bears this name because her desires and prophecies are halfway between those of her two sisters. The last one, Miseçe Urme, "the evil fairy," brings only evil and suffering to people; she resembles a horrible old crone and lives in a castle surrounded by a sterile wasteland.

CHAPTER 7

PROTECTIONS

Magical protection essentially assumes two forms in our accounts: prayer or amulet. Every time there is a recommendation to carry or wear something on your person, the mental process conforms with the etymology of the word amulet, *which comes from the verb* amoliri, *"to ward off," "to protect." The object—plant, mineral, artifact—is a phylactery to which is attributed a preventive virtue against illnesses, afflictions, accidents, and evil spells. People seek protection when starting a journey, by land or sea, and, when staying at home, against anything that could possibly befall them.*

📖 *HDA,* vol. 7, 1611–16, "Reisesegen"; Charles A. E. Wickersheimer, "Figures médico-astrologiques des IXe, Xe et XIe siècles," *Janus* 19 (1914): 157–77; Evans, *Magical Jewels of the Middle Ages and Renaissance, Particularly in England;* Lecouteux, *The High Magic of Talismans and Amulets.*

PROTECTIONS OF THE INDIVIDUAL

480 ❖ For Protection while Traveling

If you carry verbena on your person while traveling, you should have no fear of thieves, as it sends them fleeing.

📖 Latin, fourth century. Pseudo-Apuleius, *Herbarius,* 73.

481 ❖ For the Dangers of the Road
Repeat the following:

> I enter today upon the path taken by Our Lord Jesus Christ. May he be as gentle and good to me. May His pink and holy blood come aid me, and His five sacred wounds, so that I may never be captured or bound. May he guard me from all my enemies, may he protect me from drowning, swords, shot, and all manner of perils, bad company, and misadventure. May all bonds be removed from me, at once, as Our Lord Jesus Christ was liberated when he rose to heaven.

📖 Middle High German, fifteenth century. Grimm, *Deutsche Mythologie*, 3:499.

482 ❖ For Protection on a Journey
Repeat the following:

> I shall go and travel among you[1] with God's love, Christ's humility, the holiness of Our Blessed Lady, Abraham's faith, Isaac's justice, David's virtue, Peter's power, Paul's steadfastness, God's word, Gregory's authority, Clement's prayer, and the waves of the Jordan.
>
> *ff p c g e g a q q est p t 1 k a b 2 a x t b a m g 2 4 2 1 qp x c g k q a 9 9 p o q q r.*
>
> O one Father ✠ O one Lord ✠ And Jesus passed among them ✠ pursuing his path ✠ In the name of the Father ✠ the Son ✠ and the Holy Ghost ✠

The letters are the initials of words that form a charm or orison, but we have not been able to pierce the secret.

📖 England, 1584, Reginald Scot, *The Discovery of Witchcraft*, 12.9.233.

483 ◈ A Pentacle for Journeys by Land and Sea

📖 *The True Minor Keys of King Solomon by Armandel,* London: British Library, Lansdowne 1202 4to, 134.

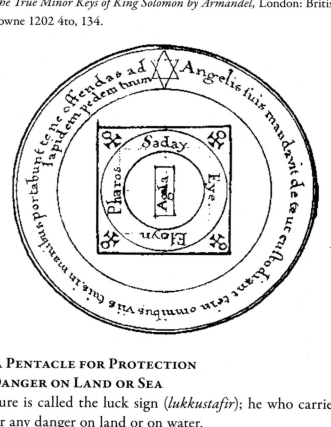

484 ◈ A Pentacle for Protection from Danger on Land or Sea

This figure is called the luck sign (*lukkustafir*); he who carries it will not incur any danger on land or on water.

📖 Iceland, seventeenth century. Davidsson, "Isländische Zauberzeichen," 277.

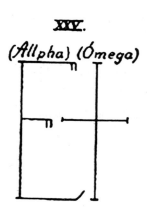

485 ◆ Protection for the Journey

Repeat the following verse:

> *I have crossed my threshold,*
> *May Jesus be my companion!*
> *Let my enemies sleep,*
> *Assist me in all my actions,*
> *On the water and on solid ground,*
> *Be my solid help!*
> *In the forest, against spirits and brigands,*
> *In the plains against the laggards,*
> *At day, against the invisibles,*
> *At night, against the devils,*
> *Without stop, for eternity,*
> *Protect my blood and flesh. Amen.*

📖 Saxons of Transylvania, nineteenth century. Wlislocki, *Volksglaube*, 112.

486 ◆ Protection *Bref*

Joseph of Arimathea found this *bref* on the wounds inflicted on the side of Jesus Christ, written by God's finger when His body was taken down from the cross. Whoever carries it on his person will not die an evil death if he believes in Christ, and he will be immediately delivered from any awkward situation, fear, and danger.

> *Fons ✠ alpha & omega ✠ figa ✠ figalis ✠ Sabbaoth ✠ Emmanuel ✠ Adonai ✠ O ✠ Neray ✠ Elay ✠ Ihe ✠ Rentone ✠ Neger ✠ Sahe ✠ Pangeton ✠ Commen ✠ a ✠ g ✠ l ✠ a ✠ Mattheus ✠ Marcus ✠ Lucas ✠ Iohannes ✠ ✠ ✠ titulus triumphalis ✠ Iesus Nazarenus rex Iudeorum ✠ ecce dominicae cruces signum X fugite parte adversae, vicit leo de tribu Iuda, radix, David, alelujah, Kyrie eleeson, Christe eleeson,* Pater Noster, *ave maria, & ne nos, & veniat super nos salutare tuum: Oremus,* and so forth.

In addition to the names of God, such as *Agla*, and some unidentified words, what we have here is an extract of the Mass of the Invention and exaltation of the Holy Cross, otherwise used as an exorcism, notably in the Roman Breviary and the Feasts of the Spanish Saints. *Folk tradition mentions the Orison of the Holy Cross used against the temptations of the devil.*

The prayers indicated here are the Our Father, the Angelic Salutation, the sixth request of the Pater Noster, and the Litany of the Saints, with a gap. It should read: Et veniat super nos misericordia tua Domine. Et salutarre tuum secundum eloquium tuum.

📖 England, 1584, Scot, *The Discovery of Witchcraft*, 12.9.233ff.

487 ◆ The Sixth Pentacle of Jupiter for Protection

Sixth pentacle of Jupiter; it is used for protection against all kinds of dangers on land [and] if one looks at it with devotion every day while repeating the verse that encircles it (Psalm 21:17), you will never perish.

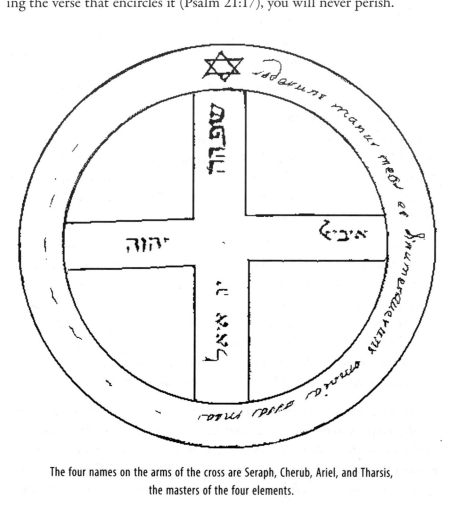

The four names on the arms of the cross are Seraph, Cherub, Ariel, and Tharsis, the masters of the four elements.

📖 *The True Minor Keys of King Solomon* by Armandel, London, British Library, Lansdowne 1202 4to, 134.

488 ◆ THE SECOND PENTACLE OF THE MOON FOR PROTECTION

The second pentacle of the moon; it helps against all the perils and dangers found on the water.

📖 French, eighteenth century. London, British Library, Sloane 3091, fol. 69r.

The second pentacle of the Moon.

489 ◆ Protection against the Dangers of Water

You must wear this sign under your right arm; it protects against the dangers of the water.

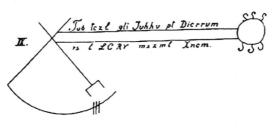

Written on it is: "May God grant happiness and blessing in the name of Jesus. Amen."

 📖 Iceland, seventeenth century. Davidsson, "Isländische Zauberzeichen," 276.

490 ◆ Protection from Lightning and Thunder

The *ceraunia* protects from lightning and thunder the one who carries it, and protects him from his enemies. Write these names on this stone: Raphael, Gabriel, Michael; you will defeat all enemies.

 Ceraunia, *or "thunderbolts," are stones with magical properties that were thought to have fallen from the sky when lightning hit the ground.*

 📖 Middle French, late fourteenth century. Paris, Bibliothèque de l'Arsenal, MS 2872, fol. 37r, a.

491 ◆ Protection against the Wolf

Say the following verse:

> *Listen, golden foot!*
> *Do not take my foot of wool!*
> *I would like you to be a good distance*
> *Away and not close to me.*
> *Shame on Holland!*
> *Shame on Hell!*

 In eighteenth-century France, for protection *"from the inconvenience one might receive from wolves,"* the following was recommended:

 If you carry on your person the eyes and the heart of a mastiff that has died violently, have no fear of the wolf that approaches you, as to the contrary, you shall see him flee like a timid rabbit. . . . If you hang the tail of a wolf you have savagely killed in the manger or stable of fat or thin livestock, no wolf will come close. . . . The same effect will occur for an entire village, if you bury pieces of wolf on the avenues.

 📖 Sweden (Bohuslän), ca. 1920–30, Klintberg, *Svenska trollformler,* 99, no. 94, "vargen."
 📖 *Petit Albert,* 41ff.

492 ❖ For Protection If You Meet a Bear
Say the following verse:
> *You are bear, I am man*
> *You were not baptized at the same fonts as me*
> *You should flee into the forest*
> *And bite the trees,*
> *But don't bite me at all!*

 📖 Sweden (Värmland), ca. 1880–90, Klintberg, *Svenska trollformler,* 99, no. 90, "vid björnmöte."

493 ❖ For Protection against Wolves
For a guaranteed protection against wolves, when crossing though the woods at night, and one fears encountering one, say:

> *Saint John, lock his teeth together,*
> *Saint Gregory, lock his jaw shut,*
> *Saint Remo, lock his intestines,*
> *Saint Gesippe, lock up his guts.*

The choice of saints is based on their consonance with the part of the body* mentioned. Gesippe is Saint Hegesippus, and Saint Remo is Saint Remy.

 📖 France (Ardennes), nineteenth century. Meyrac, *Traditions,* 180, no. 100.

494 ❖ Phylactery for Children against the Evil Eye or False Witness
Hang mandrake around the child's neck in a piece of clean linen cloth so that, when the time comes, no one speaks his or her name.

---

*[In French, respectively, *dents, mâchoire, boyaux,* and *tripes.* —*Trans.*]

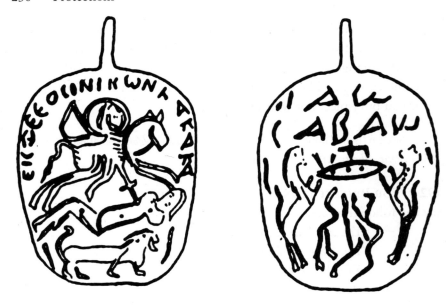

Byzantine amulet against the evil eye.

 📖 Latin, fourth century. Pseudo-Apuleius, *Herbarius*, 131. On mandrake, Gubernatis, *La Mythologie des plantes*, 2:219ff.; Elworthy, *The Evil Eye: An Account of This Ancient and Wide Spread Superstition*.

495 ◆ PROTECTION FROM THE EVIL EYE OR GOSSIP

Whoever carries on his person a man's eye and a wolf's eye, cannot be obstructed by an evil eye or wicked gossip.

 📖 Latin, Spain, thirteenth century. Ritter and Plessner, *Picatrix*, 3.11.

496 ◆ PROTECTION FOR CHILDREN FROM CURSES AND ILLNESSES

Put a live [fish] in oil and keep it there. Carried by children it will ward them from curses and illnesses.

 We should note here that in nineteenth-century France people used a charm for healing weever stings: "Little fish blessed by God † by the five wounds of Our Lord † do not cause harm to this person † [first and last name]."

 📖 Latin, twelfth century. *Liber Kyranidorum*, 35, 13. Greek, fourteenth century. ΚΥΡΑΝΙΣ III, Δ; Mély, *Les lapidaires grecs*, 15.

497 ◈ Protection against Demons and Enemies

In the name of the living Father Our Lord Jesus Christ, take very pure gold and melt it when the sun enters Aries, which is to say on the fifteenth day of the calends of April. Make a round seal of it and, while doing this, say: "Arise light of the world, Jesus, true lamb, you who remove our sins and cast light into our darkness." Then recite the Psalm *Domine, dominus noster* [Psalm 8], and so on. This done, set it aside.

Next, when the moon is in Cancer or Leo, carve on one side the figure of Aries and on the circumference: Arahel Tribus Juda V and VII. On the other side, carve these very holy words: *Verbo carum factum est es habitavit in nobis* with the A and the Ω in the middle and sanctus Petrus. This precious seal is proof against all demons and the principal enemies, against evil spells . . . against lightning, storm, inundations, the impetuosity of the winds and pestilential airs. . . . Nothing will be able to harm the inhabitants of the house where it is kept. It works against the demoniac, the frenzied, the maniac, those who suffer from tonsillitis and for the ailments of the head and eyes, the catarrhs, and, as it is said everywhere, wards off all evil and brings good fortune. May he who wears it avoid all uncleanliness as best he can, as well as lust and mortal sin. One wears it on the head with reverence and honor.

 📖 Latin, thirteenth century. Arnold of Villanova, *Opera,* fol. 301v.

498 ◈ For Protection from Evil Spells

The dried end of a lion's tail provides protection from evil spells, and a person should always keep it with him. It is especially important that it be placed near the food when he eats and drinks. If it contains poison, the food moves about the plate and the poisoned food will start to swell. This is how the presence of poison can be detected. If, despite all this, it has been ingested, he should stick the end of the tail in warm wine and drink it, the poison will be eliminated immediately when he goes to the toilet.

 📖 Latin, twelfth century. Hildegard von Bingen, *Physica,* VII, 3, "On the Lion."

499 ◈ Protection against Voults

If someone makes a voult of a man to kill, harm, or bewitch him, nothing will happen to him if he carries fern on his person.

The voult is a wax figure that resembles the individual targeted, into which pins are stuck. It is also called a dagyde. The Hammer of Witches (2.1.11, fol. 68v) *says this about them:*

> When a sorcerer crafts a wax image (*imaginem ceream*) in order to bewitch someone ... everything done to harm this image—a sting or cut [*punctura vel alia lesura*]—by a witch or another

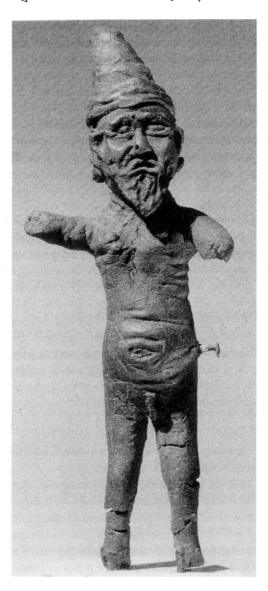

person, in order to strike the bewitched man, the demon of the aforementioned wound strikes the cursed individual invisibly.

The inquisitors cite the case of an inhabitant of Innsbruck who had been bewitched and fallen ill. They found beneath the threshold of her house "a wax image a palm's length, pierced through everywhere, with two needles going from side to side. . . ." (ibid., 2.1.12, fol. 68r).

📖 Germany (Speyer), 1456, Berlin, Staatsbibliothek Preussische Besitz, Codex mgf 817, fol. 27r.

📖 Roland Villeneuve, *L'Envoûtement; Descormiers, Étude sur l'envoûtement, les chaînes invisibles.* On fern, see Camus, *Circa instans,* no. 189; Platearius, *Livre des simples médecines,* 2:156, chap. 172a.

500 ❖ Apotropaic Spell

Repeat the following spell:

> *Nine they were, the sons of Nockunden,*
> *That Noren led,*
> *Who carried their dead mother.*
> *Why were they carrying her dead this way?*
> *Because she knew how to hide and conceal all things.*
> *As she did, so shall I:*
> *I will bind the fire to where it has burned,*
> *I will bind the cauldron to the place it ahs reached,*
> *I will bind the man to where he has ridden,*
> *I will bind the boat to where it has sailed,*
> *I will bind the iron houses**
> *To make them weep tears of blood.*

This is a sorcerer speaking. Since the time of antiquity we have found a mythic individual in charms who has seven or nine demonic children. This charm is definitely not in its original state because others have corrupted it. The names Nockunden *and* Noren *appear to be incomprehensible. The second is likely a garbled version of* Moren, *"the mother."* Nockunden *may designate a woman with a hooked nose. In Norse literature and especially in the sagas of ancient times* (fornaldsögur), *there are giantesses with hooked noses.* Nock *means "hook" (Norwegian* nokke).

---

*The word *järngårder* most likely designates the houses of trolls and giants.

📖 Sweden (Blekinge), 1679, Klintberg, *Svenska trollformler*, 92, no. 71, "Skyddsformel."

501 ◆ Protection against All Magic

This rune protects from all magic. Write it on a seal's shoulder blade with mouse blood and carry it on your person.

📖 Iceland, Strandgaldur, Museum of Icelandic Sorcery and Witchcraft, Hólmavik.

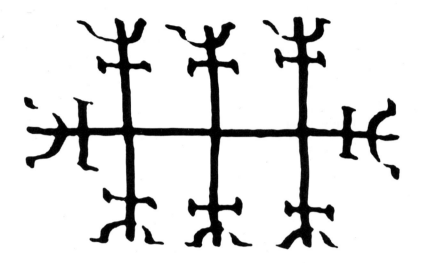

502 ◆ Protection from Charms and Curses

Attach nail heads to the doors of houses in order that the people and animals living there will be protected from charms and curses.

📖 France, seventeenth century. Thiers, *Traité des superstitions* (1679), 322.

503 ◆ Protection against Witches

Repeat the following verse:

> *Jesus went on to the flaming mountain*
> *And saw the evil women:*
> *I urge you, evil woman,*
> *Give back to me what is mine:*
> *Plain as an egg.*
> *Sweet as mother's milk,*
> *Red as a flower,*

In three settings of the sun,
Drawn or marked with the sign of the cross
As well as blown
Three times over salt.
†††

📖 Sweden (Ångermanland), 1674, Klintberg, *Svenska trollformler*, 92, no. 72, "trollkvinnor."

504 ◈ PROTECTION SO THAT NONE MAY BEWITCH YOU

Write these words on paper on a Thursday before sunrise in large letters, then carry it secretly beneath your right armpit:

Merida, Meron, Mionda, Ragon

📖 Norway, ca. 1770, Bang, *Norske hexeformularer*, no. 1094.

505 ◈ FOR PROTECTION AGAINST ALL DAMAGE

Write the characters listed below on paper and always carry it with you:

+B: +N: +G: +N: +R: +4
O: +B: +C: +B: +4:+
C: +C: +M: +N: +S: +B+e

📖 Poland, nineteenth century. Vaitkevičienė, *Lietuvių užkalbėjimai*, no. 1621.

506 ◈ CHARM AGAINST REVENANTS

Cross over the sky, cross over earth, cross over this place where I sleep. There is a cross, there is also a citadel with precious stones and Saint Nicetas sat there, a sword and a stout whip in his hand, and he kept watch from midnight to cockcrow and from cockcrow until dawn, like a block of stone in front of the door.

The beginning of the text is a fragment of prayer that is rarely used in the charms of the oral tradition. Saint Nicetas the Goth, martyred in 372 and whose feast day is September 15, is depicted as clad in armor and battling against the devil.

📖 Romania, text written by a scribe of Oltenia around 1777, Bucharest, Biblioteca Academiei Române din București, MS Romanian BAR 2183, fol. 161v, "Pentru strigoi descântec."

507 ◆ Protection against Ghosts
Suffumigations with peony root drive away demons and evil ghosts.
 📖 Latin, twelfth century. *Liber Kyranidorum*, 33, 66.

508 ◆ Protection against Diabolical Glamors
A certain kind of jasper drives ghosts away and protects its bearer from all manner of diabolical glamors.

According to the medieval lapidaries, this would be green jasper. Other stones possess this same power: gorgonian, coral, polophos.

 📖 Latin, thirteenth century. William of Auvergne, *De universo*, 2, 3, 1061 A.

509 ◆ Protection to Ward Off All Ghosts
Suffumigations or beverages of peony root drive demons away and, if worn, it will ward off all ghosts.
 📖 Greek, fourteenth century. ΚΥΡΑΝΙΣ I, Γ; Mély, *Les lapidaires grecs*, 13.

510 ◆ Protection against Phantoms
He who carries the heart fat of a dragon in buckskin or chamois, and ties it to his arm or beneath the elbow, will fear no phantom at night, even if he had been fearful before.
 📖 Germany, 1546, Herr, *Das neue Tier-und Arzneibuch*, chap. 47.

511 ◆ Protection against Ghosts and Evil Spirits
To drive off ghosts and evil spirits, you must carve these signs on oak and paint them with blood from your hand. Hang them above your door to ward off ghosts and evil spirits.

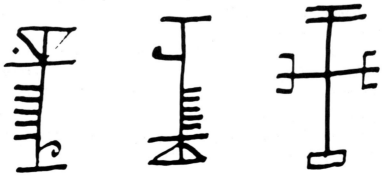

Iceland, Strandgaldur, Museum of Icelandic Sorcery and Witchcraft, Hólmavík.

512 ◆ PROTECTION AGAINST EVIL SPIRITS
The Seal of David (*Davíds innsigli*) protects its bearer against evil spirits.

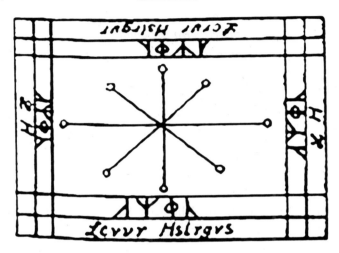

The runes signify Amen. I and H designate Christ.

 Iceland, seventeenth century. Davidsson, "Isländische Zauberzeichen," 277.

513 ◆ PROTECTION AGAINST ENEMIES
May he who has enemies listen to a mass in honor of God the Father, the Son, and the Holy Ghost, amen. Three Pater Noster with three genuflexions, one Ave Maria, three Pater Noster with three genuflexions, then say at the moment he stands up: "May my enemies be as dead men before the name of Jesus Christ! May they have no more power to harm me than those who have been buried thirty years! They have the vengeance of the dead in their mouths, they have the pain of the dead in their hearts. It is also true that Milady Saint Mary conceived and begat a son for all [incomprehensible passage]. Eya, the name of Jesus Christ is always a truth! Eya, the name of Jesus Christ is always a truth! Eya, and so on. May the Father be with me, may the Son be with all my enemies,

and may the Holy Ghost be between us. May he separate us into bodies and virtues." To be spoken three times.

 📖 Mixture of Latin and late Middle High German, fifteenth century. London, British Library, Additional 17527 in folio, fol. 14v.

514 ◈ Protection against Hate and Jealousy

> *I arose one morning*
> *Against all my cares,*
> *I girded myself with the bond of anger*
> *Against man and woman,*
> *Against the sword, against the world,*
> *Against all my misfortunes.*
> *This is how hatred and jealousy will melt*
> *Over me today*
> *As salt dissolves*
> *In cool water.*
> ✝✝✝ *Amen.*

 📖 Sweden (Uppland), 1646, Klintberg, *Svenska trollformler*, 93, no. 73, "ovänner."

515 ◈ Against an Enemy

Say the following prayer:

> In the same way the impetuous winds extinguish the stars, may the heart and lips of my enemy go pale; and like death is voiceless, may my enemy be voiceless unable to speak a word against me; and like death cannot see the light, may my enemy be unable to see me and speak evil about me [name], God's servant. Amen.

 📖 Russia, nineteenth century. Gruel-Apert, *La Tradition orale russe*, 108.

516 ◈ Protection Charm

> *Today I put on my right foot*
> *The hood of victory,*
> *A foot of steel*

And the power of the eagle
And the sacred force.
Victory I will have
And victory I will speak,
Victory shall enter my clothing
And victory shall travel on my roads!

I place chains around the feet of my enemies
And shackles around the legs of my enemies
And bars around the root of my enemies' tongue.

May my enemies mutter,
May my enemies fall silent,
But I, I am speaking.

My words will be feared
And my pages will be spread
First and foremost before God in the heavens
And next before all the good men of God!

And if I had burned towns
And raped virgins,
If I had committed adultery and murder
And if I had sent father and sister into the ground,
None of all that will shine over me
Except the sun in its purity.
   ✝✝✝ *Amen.*

This charm is borrowing the ancient form of the lorica, "armor"— magical armor, of course. For binding, cf. Mircea Eliade, Images and Symbols *(London: Harvill Press, 1961), 92–124, "The God Who Binds and the Symbolism of Knots."* We find this notion of a breastplate in a nineteenth-century French charm intended to provide protection against any evil act:

> I enter into the shirt of Our Lady; may I be wrapped in the wounds of my God, the four crowns of heaven, of Saint John the Evangelist, Saint Luke, Saint Matthew, and Saint Mark; may they be able to guard me; may neither man, nor woman,

nor lead, nor iron, nor steel, be able to wound me, cut me, or break my bones; to God, peace.

📖 Sweden (Blekinge), 1679, Klintberg, *Svenska trollformler*, 91, no. 70, "Skyddsformel."

517 ◆ SPELL FOR DULLING YOUR ENEMY'S SWORD

OFfüsa † O Amplustra † O Geministra. In nomine Patris † Filii † et Spiritus Sancti. Amen.

The first term garbles the Latin fuse *("abundantly"), and* geministra *is the merger of* gemma *("gem," or "stone") and* minister *("servant"). What we have here are the fragments of a Latin spell that was passed on orally without being understood.*

📖 Norway, circa 1480, *Vinjeboka*, no. 7.

518 ◆ PROTECTION AGAINST WEAPONS
Repeat the following:

Today is Friday, tomorrow is another day, when God the Son was crucified on the holy cross. His large and small wounds were flowing, and he was sorely struck and hit. In [His] name I will arise, and I will carry it upon me; it will guard me from all arms and blades so they cannot strike me, either by thrust or cut. May no evil tongue break this charm!

It is next necessary to recite five Our Fathers, five Ave Marias, and five Credos, every Friday.

📖 Switzerland, 1552, Wackernagel, "Ein schweizerischer Waffensegen aus dem 16. Jahrhundert," *Schweizerisches Archiv für Volkskunde* 40 (1942–44): 122.

519 ◆ PROTECTION AGAINST ALL KINDS OF ARMS
You take three roots of cardoon or fuller's teasel that no longer has its tip, like a brush used to clean tin pots, and take them on the eve of Saint John the Baptist, after the sun has set everywhere, at that very moment you will harvest them while saying: "I am taking you for all the virtue that you may hold," or else, "I take you that you may have the

strength, by the virtue given you by God, to defend me against swords and bullets, and against all kinds of firearms, In the name of the Father, the Son, and the Holy Ghost." Wrap them in a piece of black cloth that is brand new and never dyed, and once you have your root above you, you shall never be wounded by any arm, whether you find yourself in battle or elsewhere, for with the help of God and the virtue of this root, you will be safe from all danger.

To protect against all kinds of weapons, individuals would also make a wheat cake with flour and holy water, that would then be brought near a hanged man or someone who had died violently. Once returned home, the individual would make little balls out of the cake that would be wrapped in white paper on which was written: 1. u. n. ; 1. a : Fau., 1. Moot, and Dorbort, Amen. *These balls would be swallowed while reciting Our Father and the Ave five times.*

 📖 Switzerland (Vaud canton), ca. 1808, Georges Hervé, "Superstitions populaires suisses concernant les armes, le tir, la guerre, les blessures," *Revue anthropologique* 26 (1916): 361ff.

520 ◆ Protection from Peril and Sickness
Take the aetite stone,* carve an eagle on it, and, beneath his foot, stick a seed of bryony and a little piece of eagle wing. Place all of this in a ring and wear it. It will protect you from all peril and all sickness.

 📖 Middle French, late fourteenth century. Paris, Bibliothèque de l'Arsenal, MS 2872, fol. 39r, b.

521 ◆ Protection to Repel Fever
Torn out before sunrise, the eyes of a frog that you will throw back alive into the water, will repel fever once you have tied them to your person.

 📖 France, 1548, Fernel, *De abditis rerum causis libri duo*, 244.

522 ◆ Protection against the Miasms of Earth and Air
This *"Helmet of the children of Heaven"* (Himinsbarnahjálmur) *offers protection against the miasms of earth and air.*

---

*[Found in the neck or stomach of an eagle. —*Trans.*]

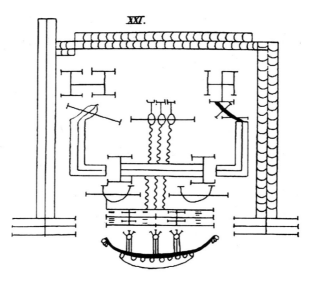

 Iceland, seventeenth century. Davidsson, "Isländische Zauberzeichen," 277.

523 ◆ THE CHARM OF LONGINUS
Repeat the following verse:

> *Lord God, protect me, [name], today,*
> *By the strike of the very holy spear*
> *That Longinus stuck into your side,*
> *When your sacred heart broke.*
> *May it protect me the blood*
> *That flowed from your wound,*
> *So that all dangers are driven far from me,*
> *That all weapons become blunted,*
> *That all steel and iron*
> *Cannot bite me at all,*
> *Like the Virgin retained her virginity*
> *When God incarnated within her.*

The apocryphal story of Longinus is, in fact, used quite frequently in charms against bleeding that form a family that experts have called "Charm of Longinus."

 Middle High German, fourteenth century. Vienna, Österreichische Nationalbibliothek, Codex 2817 [med. 9], fol. 25v.

524 ◆ Protection of the Eyes

The eyes and eyesight of the person who always wears a dried fox tongue tied to his right arm will never know pain or impairment, even if there is a predisposition to it.

 📖 Germany, sixteenth century. Herr, *Das neue Tier-und Arzneibuch*, chap. 5.

PROTECTION OF PROPERTY

525 ◆ Protection of the Garden

On certain days of the year, touch the herbs and vegetables of the garden with a broom to prevent ants, grasshoppers, snails, caterpillars, worms, and other insects from bothering them.

 📖 France, seventeenth century. Thiers, *Traité des superstitions* (1679), 326.

526 ◆ Prayer of the Martyr Saint Tryphon for Gardens, Vineyards, and Fields

Say the following prayer:

> God, you answer the prayers of those who trust in You. Send an angel from his home so he may overcome all the kinds of animals that devastate the vineyard, field, and garden of God's servant [full name]. And I know exactly the names of these animals and am thinking of caterpillars, worms, earthworms, grasshoppers, crickets, locusts, ticks, calobates [flies], ants, lice, sedge, fleas, bugs, blight, snails, earwigs, and everything that attacks and annihilates the grapes and other kinds of plants.
>
> I conjure you by the holy cherubim with four eyes and by the seraphim with six wings that circle the Throne shouting: "Holy, holy, holy, Lord Sabaoth" for the glory of God the Father.
>
> I conjure you by all the holy angels and all the powers and the ten thousand times ten thousand and the thousand times thousand that are plunged into profound terror at the sight of the Lord's glory.
>
> Do not destroy the vineyard, nor the garden with its trees and plants, of God's servant [full name], but go to the deserted woods of wild mountains that divine grace has given you for your daily food.

I conjure you by the venerable blood and body of Christ, the true God and our Savior, who offers us deliverance and redemption and in whose name we shall die. Do not harm this field, this vineyard, nor this garden, nor any tree, whether it bears fruit or not, nor a leaf of a vegetable around and within the domain of God's servant [full name].

If you do not obey this and go beyond the ban of my conjuration, you will not be acting against me, weak and insignificant Tryphon, but against the God of Abraham, Isaac, and Jacob who will come to judge the living and the dead. This is why I am telling you, retreat to the uncultivated forests of the wild mountains. If you do not obey this, I will appeal to the friendly God to send me His angel assigned to vermin and he will strike you and kill you because you will have annihilated the conjuration and prayer of the weak Tryphon, and even the birds sent by my prayer will devour you.

I conjure you again by the majestic name carved on the rock that you are not able to withstand at all—you will melt before him in the way the rock melts like wax in the presence of fire—leave this land, as I have commanded! Depart for the inaccessible deserts and sterile places. Depart from the home and surrounding of God's servant who has asked me for help, assistance, and salvation, so that in all this the most holy name of the Father and the Son and the Holy Ghost be glorified and the request of the weak Tryphon be granted, because, for all eternity, to God goes the power and the glory. Amen.

📖 Greece, eighteenth century. Malzew, *Blitt-, Dank- und Weihe-Gottesdienste der orthodox-katholischen Kirche des Morgenlandes* (Berlin, 1897), 744.

527 ◈ Conjuratory Benediction to Kill Garden Pests
Repeat the following:

I conjure you, abominable mice [or grasshoppers, crickets, worms, and other animals] by the all-powerful God, by Jesus † Christ, his son incarnate, by the Holy † Ghost who comes from both of them, to immediately depart our fields and meadows

Quod per diuina verba licitum est arcere lupos: serpentes: & locustas: & alia huiusmodi & quó hoc licite fiat & quomodo illicite.

EX quibus dicit sanctus doctor.ii.ii. vbi supra & etiam in quod libeto. xii.arti.xiiii.quod prędictus seruatis conditionibus per diuina verba licitum est arcere serpentes & eadem ratione quecūq; animalia si solus respectus habeatur ad sacra verba & ad diuinam virtutem. Quibus conditionibus obseruatis dico similiter quod licite potest fieri cóiuratio contra lupos vt arceantur à raptu, vel pręda pecorū & aliorū animaliū. Similiter contra locustas & contra mures vastantes fructus terrę: si nihil superstitiosum dicūt docent vel faciūt: vt dicit Guilhermus lugdunen. vnde si quęra

Martinus de Arles, *Tractatus de superstionibus* (1559).
"Is it permissible to use divine names to get rid of pests?"

and not stay a moment more, but to depart for where you cannot harm anyone. I curse you in the stead of all-powerful God and all his celestial court and the Holy Church, may you be cursed or may you be on your way! Get weaker mutually every day and die, until none of you remain, save that which is useful and salutary to men! May God grant [us] this, He who will come to judge the living and the dead, and the world by fire.

In 1583, in his Three Books of Charms, Sorcery, and Enchantments, *Leonard Vair teaches us an odd technique for getting rid of grasshoppers:*

> When the villagers wished to drive away grasshoppers and other noxious vermin, they chose a certain conjurer as judge before whom two lawyers were selected, one to represent the people while the other pleaded the side of the vermin. The people's lawyer demanded justice against the grasshoppers and caterpillars, to drive them out of the fields. The other responded that they should not be expelled. Finally when the ceremonies were fulfilled, a sentence of excommunication was handed down against the vermin if they did not leave the fields within a certain period of time.

In 1611, Martin Delrio noted (Les Controverses, *6.11, 1098ff.):* *"There are others who attribute to themselves a certain art of particular power, as granted by God, to drive away and kill caterpillars, locusts, and other insects and vermin of the fields, who chew and spoil all the seed, fruits, and roots, and disappoint the hopes of the poor laborers," and follows with a summary of what Leonard Vair said.*

The Petit Albert *mentions a very interesting practice because its includes a circumambulation:*

> Prayer for protecting from bugs, snails, worms, or caterpillars, fields and parks of vegetables or grains.
>
> After making the sign of the cross, say: "Our Lady of the Hyssop, on my path I found worms eating the leaves; make it Mary so that they leave the heart. I pray to the God of Abraham, Isaac, and Jacob, to ensure that the insects and worms of this earth do not touch at all the heart of the plants or grains sowed in this field, as they left alone the heart of Our Lady of the Hyssop."

This prayer is said three times. The first while walking around the edge of the field or park; the second, while crossing it from the first corner to the third; the third time from the second corner to the fourth, as depicted on the following diagram.

📖 Latin, Italy, twentieth century. *Rituale Romanum Pauli V Pontificus Maximi* ... (Rome, 1955).

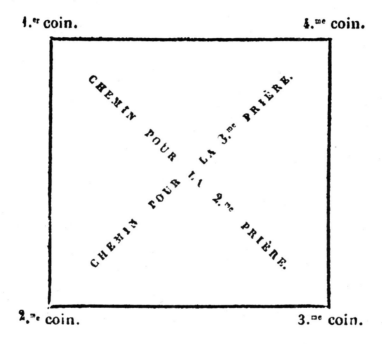

528 ◆ For Protecting Fruits

It is said that hanging a frog in the barn will protect the fruits stored there.

And from the same source: if one imprisons a frog in a new pot that is then buried in the field, no bad weather will harm the sowings.

📖 Germany, sixteenth century. Herr, *Das neue Tier- und Arzneibuch*, chap. 34.

529 ◆ For Protection of Fruits and Harvests

If you find on any kind of precious stone the image of an armed man with, above his right hand, a cross encircled by stars, know that it will be helpful for fruits and harvests; and storms cannot strike the place where it is located.

📖 Latin, Italy, 1502. Leonardi, *Speculum lapidum*, 3:15.16.

530 ◆ PROTECTION FOR CROPS
Repeat the following:

In nomine domini nostril Iesu Christi ad saluandum fructus terre † Christi † Christi: sed fortiter descendisti ad terram, etc.

📖 Spain, 1559, Martinus de Arles, *Tractatus de superstionibus;* Lebrun, *Superstitions anciennes et modernes.*

PROTECTION OF CROPS AGAINST METEORS

For protection from meteors, which were reputed to be sent by weather witches or sorcerers, people had recourse to a variety of methods: for example, appeal to the saints—Colomban, Donat, Ely, George, John the Evangelist, and so on.
Leonard Vair notes:

> There is no cause for surprise if the Demons procure this easily. In similar fashion, lightning, hail, rain and other disturbances of the air are excited by several spoken words that denote the pact one has made with the demons. . . .

📖 Wilhelm Fiedler, Antiker *Wetterzauber;* Lecouteux, "Les maîtres du temps: tempestaires, obligateurs, defenseurs," in *Le Temps qu'il fait au Moyen Âge;* Ohrt, *Fluchtafel und Wettersegen;* Vair, *Trois Livres des charmes, sorcelages, ov enchantemens,* 306.

531 ◆ PROTECTION AGAINST HAIL
Say: *Uno,* apostle *un abe,* one apostle *coro me.* May God keep us from the hail, the storm from the sky, weather, two apostles, two sobe [?], two crowned apostles. May God keep us from the hail, the storm, and the bad weather. May God keep us from the storm from heaven, the storm of heaven. Continue until twelve apostles.

📖 France, nineteenth century. *Le Médecin des Pauvres* (1875).

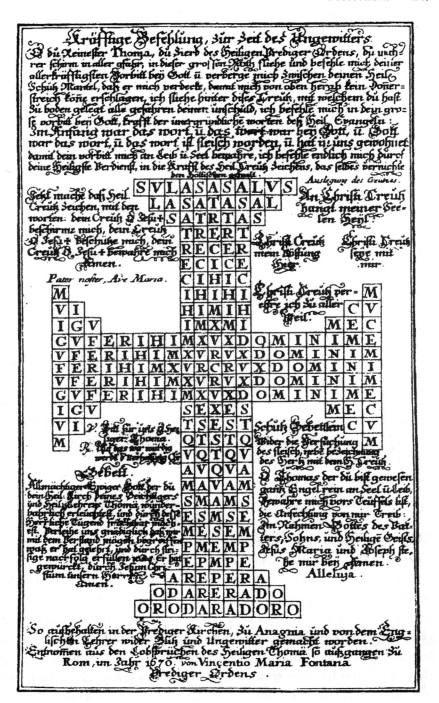

Recipe recommended for protection from meteors, Germany, 1670.

532 ◆ Protection against Hail and Storms

Three hailstones are thrown into the fire with an invocation of the holy Trinity; then the dominical orison and angelic salutation are added twice or thrice, then the Gospel of Saint John, "In the beginning was the Word," then the sign of the cross is made toward all sides, front, back, and toward the four cardinal points against the storm. Then, once one has repeated: "the Word was made flesh," and "by the words of the Gospel may this tempest be dispelled," three times, if the storm was caused by an evil spell, it will stop immediately.

 📖 Latin, late fifteenth century. *Malleus maleficarum*, 2.2.7, fol. 90v, b–91r, a.

533 ◆ Protection against the Tempest

It is said that the Lord's cross was made from four woods. The foot was of cedar, the trunk was cypress, the branches were palm, and the top was that of the olive tree. With this sign of the cross, may the storms vanish.

 📖 Spain, 1530, Franz, *Die kirchlichen Benediktionen*, 2:115.

534 ◆ Protection against Lightning

The night of Saint Lawence (August 10), mother and daughter should go outside; the daughter should lie down naked flat on her back on the ground while her mother draws a circle around her with ember, then steps over her three times while allowing three drops of blood to fall on her left palm.

 📖 Saxons of Transylvania, nineteenth century. Wlislocki, *Volksglaube*, 81.

535 ◆ Precious Orison for Protecting Us from Clouds

The following orison was found in the tomb of Our Lady, in the town of Josaphat, and has so many properties and virtues that one who reads or has it read once a day, or carries it on his person, in good intentions and devotion, cannot die by fire, nor by water, nor in battle, and will enjoy happiness and victory over his enemies, nor can they cause him harm or trouble him, and offers many advantages. For if a person has fallen into mortal sin, the Virgin Mary would come to his aid and comfort.

TRACTATVS

Quod dannabilis & igni tradendus

est quidem libellus coniuratorius:qui in
aliquibus Ecclesiis reperitur propter
verba suspecta & manifesta manda
cia quę in eo continetur
& apparet.

EX supradictis videtur etiam dannabilis & igni tradendus libellus quidam cóiuratorius contra tempestates cum suis similibus si reperiantur quem ego penes me habeo repertum in quadam parrochia visitationis meę qui icipit sic. In nomine domini nostri Iesu Christi ad saluādū fructᵒ terrę ✠ Christi ✠ Christi: sed fortiter descendisti ad terram &c. Nam re vera inter bonas in uocationes plurima continet verba suspecta & scandalosa: & ad inuocationem dęmonū expressam vel subintellectam pertinentia contra primam condi tionem superius positam per sanctū Tho mam: verba obsura suspecta & ignota

Martinus de Arles, *Tractatus de superstitionibus* (1559).
"Fragment of a prayer for protecting the fruits of the earth from meteors."

Orison to Protect All Things

O glorious Virgin Mary, mother of God, Lady of the benign Angels and pure hope and reassurance for all good creature, may it please you Lady and Mother of Angels, to protect body and soul, we pray your most precious son, that he seek to guard us from all perils and dangers, from the enemy, hell, and temptations for the merits of his beloved passion, bring an end to mortality, war, and protect the fruits of the earth, O Mother of God, full of mercy, have pity on the poor sinners, and spare us from eternal torment, and lead us to the kingdom of heaven, where we will find all before God, the important Father to whom on our knees we ask forgiveness, and may it please him to forgive us as he did Magdalene and the Good Thief when he asked for forgiveness on the tree of the Cross—May it be so.

Curiously, the tone of the text does not correspond to its heading. Its style and punctuation testify to the folk origin of this orison.

📖 France, eighteenth–nineteenth century. *Revue du clergé français* 89, no. 529 (1917), 247–48.

PROTECTIONS OF THE HOUSE

In 1496, the inquisitors Jacob Sprenger and Heinrich Kramer wrote this:

The surest protection for places, men, and beasts are the words of the glorious title of Our Savior inscribed at the four corners of the house in the shape of a cross: Jesus † Nazarene † King † of the Jews [= INRI]. One can add the name of the Virgin Mary to this or the words of John: "the Word made flesh."[2]

Here are some other practices, which of course have been Christianized, but whose pagan roots are clearly visible.

536 ◆ Protection of a New House

The person building a house should invite an enchanter to come and secretly bury a horse skull in the foundations and say:

> *Jesus entered Jerusalem alone on a horse,*
> *The Jews stoned him,*
> *The Lord said: "I am going to make you suffer*
> *For eternity!*
> *Your joy shall disappear,*
> *Your city shall be destroyed!"*
> *Lord Jesus, you who are in heaven,*
> *Good and sweet Christ,*
> *Do not destroy this home,*

Banish all evil folk,
This Satanic mob, beyond the sea of fire;
So that they cannot venture near!
May no enemy come near bearing fire or sword,
May no witch or minion of the devil come near;
May lightning bury itself in the ground,
May no illness or plague befall us,
May they bury themselves in the green forest
May they atone and amend their ways!
There flow the three springs of grace;
May they remain there until Last Judgment!
May the blood of Christ surround this house
So that it remains safe and solid
Like Christ rested in the arms of Mary!
May the Lord God grant this
For all eternity! Amen.

This must be said three times at each corner of the house.

A horse skull possesses apotropaic value. In the excavation of tenth-century buildings in Novgorod, horse skeletons were found. In Latvia, in the motte and bailey of the castle of Talsi, bones and skulls of horses were exhumed in 1936 that had been placed between the stones of the foundations of various buildings dating from the eleventh and twelfth centuries. Also found was a horse skull surrounded by ox bones, dating from the thirteenth century.

📖 Saxons of Transylvania, nineteenth century. Wlislocki, *Volksglaube,* 109.
📖 *HDA,* vol. 3, 1576–77, "Haussegen."

537 ◆ Protection for the Entire House

According to the magi, the bile of a male black dog is an amulet for the entire house: it is only necessary to perform suffumigations or purifications with this bile to obtain protection against all evil spells. The same is true of dog blood if it is sprinkled on the walls, or the genitals of this animal, if they are buried beneath the threshold of the door.

📖 Latin, first century. Pliny, *Historia naturalis,* XX, 82.

538 ◆ Protection against Enchantments

The right arm of a man with the head of a greyhound in a person's house posesses power against enchantments.

📖 Latin, Spain, thirteenth century. Ritter and Plessner, *Picatrix*, 3.11, 107.

539 ◆ Protection from Witches and Spirits

To protect houses from witches and spirits, this is written:

The deformed pentacle to the right of the magic square was called trolltecken (troll sign). It can be found in all the Germanic lands, where it is called "foot of the Drud" meaning of the "witch" or "nightmare." In 1872, in Norway, it takes the form of a double star of David and protects from nightmares. Oddly enough, this form of protection can also be found in Brittany (Morbihan), carved on a chimney (see illustration on page 255):

540 ◆ Protection for the Home

Repeat the following verse:

> *May come four holy virgins pious and pure;*
> *May they ward off from the four cardinal points*
> *Plague, misfortune, and fire!*
> *In the hand of the Almighty, this land*
> *Should remain for eternity.*
> *May the good Jesus Christ on the roof*
> *Protect this house both day and night!*
> *Even if the evil [spirits] come out from the green forests,*
> *The parched fields, the cold springs,*

> *The hot stones, we have no fear of them!*
> *Our God is a mighty fortress,*
> *Christ protects us!*
> *In the name of, and so on.*

📖 Saxons of Transylvania, nineteenth century. Wlislocki, *Volksglaube*, 108.

541 ◈ Protection for the House

When you have built a new house, spit at its four corners while saying this prayer at each of them and kissing them, then piss in front of the western gable:

> This house is built of green wood coming from the green forest, of white stone coming from the white rocks, of black dirt

coming from the black earth, and cold water coming from the cold water. Illness coming from the green forest, do not approach, you have enough wood! Women of the white rocks, do not approach, you have enough stones! Devil of the black earth, do not approach, you have enough dirt! Women of the springs, do not approach, you have enough water! Leave the dead in peace and avert from the living drowning, conflagration, famine, and lightning! Send them children who will continue to build, praise you, and raise their eyes toward Christ in heaven! In the name of, etc. Amen.

After pissing, say:

> Protect this building from thieves and enemies,
> Strike he who shits on me!*

Corners are an ambivalent site, the abode of either beneficial or malevolent forces. They are watered with certain liquids or this or that element will be placed near them. During construction, people would bury beneath one corner of the house one or more coins, a horseshoe, or even pour some mercury in the mortise of the beams in order to protect the house from lightning and all illnesses. Urine was reputed to send spirits fleeing, a belief also found in the Évangiles des quenouilles *[The Distaff Gospels] (late fifteenth century). In the first century, Pliny the Elder noted:*

> The magi expressly forbid people urinating from uncovering in the face of the sun or moon, or from urinating on the shadow of any object whatsoever. Hesiod recommends that people urinate on an object directly in front of them, so that no deity might be offended by their nakedness.³ Osthanes says that as protection against all noxious substances, one should drip some urine on his foot (*Historia naturalis*, XXVIII, 69).

Several warnings appear in the Évangiles des quenouilles, *such as "Pissing between two houses will earn you the affliction of the eyes called*

---

*The text uses the word *greinen*, "to snigger," but it refers in fact to *grumus merdae* and the belief that as long as thief's excrement remains warm, he can devote himself to his activity without hindrance.

a stye. . . . He who while pissing turns counter the sun, will have kidney stones all his life."

 📖 Saxons of Transylvania, nineteenth century. Wlislocki, *Volksglaube,* 110ff.

 📖 *HDA,* vol. 2, 438ff., "Harnen"; *Évangiles des quenouilles,* 127, 131; For more on corners, cf. Lecouteux, "Trois hypothèse sur nos voisins invisibles," in *Hugur: Mélanges offerts à Régis Boyer,* 289–97.

542 ◈ Protection against Fire

Write with a charcoal A.I.N.R.B. or *In te, Domine, speravi, non confundar in æternum.*[4]

 📖 France. *Les Œuvres magiques de Henri-Corneille Agrippa,* 81.

543 ◈ Conjuration of Rats

To get rid of rats, you must say: "*Erat verbum, apud deum nostrum:* I conjure you, rats and ratlings, by the Great God, to leave my house, all my dwellings, and make your way to [a place is named here] there to end your days." Then say these words in Latin three times: *Decretis, reversis et desembarassis virgo potens, Clemens, justitie.* Write these same words on three pieces of paper and fold them carefully, then place one under the door over which the rats being expelled will pass, and another on the path that should lead them to the spot where you sent them; this conjuration should be made at sunrise.

 📖 France (Ardennes), nineteenth century. Meyrac, *Traditions,* 176, no. 68.

544 ◈ Protection against a Thief

You must go to the place where you fear being robbed, and make a circle by walking from east to north while saying:

> *Three thieves arrived.*
> *Maria said: "Peterus, Peterus, Peterus!*
> *Bind, bind, bind!*
> *I have bound you with iron chains,*
> *No man, but one, can save you!*
> *All night, he should see and hear*
> *The stars in the sky and the sound of the bells.*
> *As insensitive as a log,*

> *Stiff as a staff!*
> *I leave you the problem of unbinding,*
> *I am taking away the key!*
> *Whether it blackens or stays white,*
> *Makes me neither hot nor cold!*
> *May this scoundrel*
> *Make no reproaches against me!"*

If the thief subsequently comes and steals something. The moment he takes it he will remain frozen in place until dawn. When the sun rises, he is freed but transformed into a black man and the one who banned him can never again speak this charm against thieves. That is why the property owner should return to the scene of the crime and free the malefactor while saying:

> *The key I hold*
> *And always carry on my person*
> *Opens the tomb of the Lord;*
> *I lend it to you gladly.*
> *The key is quite large*
> *The one with which I free you.*

After these words, the thief will drop the stolen goods and escape. He should not be retained or even scolded, otherwise you can never again ban a robber. Instead, you must call out to the fugitive, "Go, in the name of God!" He will never steal again.

📖 Pomerania, nineteenth century. Tettau and Temme, *Die Volkssagen*, 344ff.

545 ◆ Another Protection against a Thief

Declaim the following charm around the animal or object you wish to protect from theft:

> *Thief, remain stuck here,*
> *Advance no farther*
> *Your hands and feet will rot*
> *If you touch this animal.*

📖 Gypsies of Transylvania, nineteenth century. Wlislocki, *Volksdichtungen*, 148.

PROTECTION OF ANIMALS

In 1496, Jacob Sprenger and Heinrich Kramer mentioned women who on May 1 would pick branches, weave them into crowns, and hang them at the stable entrance to ensure the animals remained healthy and protected from all witchcraft (Malleus maleficarum, 2.2.7, fol. 90r).

546 ◈ To Break and Destroy All Evil Spells
Take a good amount of salt based more or less on the number of animals that have been cursed; speak over it the following:

Herego gomet hunc gueridans sesserant deliberant amei.

Walk around the animals three times beginning from the side of the rising sun and continuing by following the course of this body, the animals in front of you, while you are casting pinches of salt upon them, reciting the same words.

📖 France, 1670, Honorius, *Le livre des conjurations*, 83.

547 ◈ Pentacles for Guarding the Flock
Write above two pentacles made on virgin parchment the words that follow:

Aytheos † Anastos † Noxio † Bay † Gloy † Aper † Agia † Agios † Hischiros.

Deus Tetragrammaton misericors et pius, per ista sanctissima nomina et per tua sanctissima attributa da mihi fortunam et horm bonam in omnibus meis factis, at libera me omni male et perturbation. Amen. Three Credos, and so forth.

This pentacle should be made on parchment, as said; on it you will write the aforementioned orisons, then have a mass said over it, and ruffle the sheep with it, then place it between two boards at the exit of the sheepfold so that the flock passes over it; then pull said parchment out and conserve it properly.

📖 France. *Les Œuvres magiques de Henri-Corneille Agrippa*, 87.

548 ◈ Protection against the Evil Eye on Animals
Jesus and Mary were walking along the shore. There they spied the good valerian planted in the ground. Jesus pulled [it] up and

Saint Peter took [it]. The troll in the mountain stood up and shouted: "The root is no good for anything!" Saint Peter went forth and answered: "The root is good against numerous ills! It is good against exhaustion, anemia, the fangs of the wolf, the fangs of the bear, and the hand of sorcerers!"

In the Germanic countries, it was believed that valerian had the power to drive elves away. Anemia *here means the "presence of blood in the urine" (hemoglobinuria:* blodsot*), cf. R. Grambo,* Norske trolleformler og magiske . . ., 143.

📖 Norway, *Dovreboka, in Svartbok frå Gudbrandsdalen,* 70–77, no. 1, "For avind paa Kreaturene."

📖 Gubernatis, *La Mythologie des plantes,* 2:366.

549 ◈ To Allay Magic Arrows

The Virgin Mary said: What has happened to your beasts!—Sorcery and shots, you fly upon my animals! The Virgin Mary will take care of this.

> *Against the strikes (shots) of the mountain (trolls)*
> *Against the black strikes (shots)*
> *Against the strikes (shots) of the witch's children.*
> *And against all shot*
> *Against the magic shot*
> *And against the shots that fly in the wind and in the weather.*

📖 Norway, *Dovreboka,* no. 17: "At døve Ganskud."

550 ◈ Counter-Charm

Hostia sacra vera corrum, in putting down the great devil of hell, all words, enchantments, and characters that have been said, read, and celebrated over the bodies of my living horses, whether they may be broken or fractured behind me.

📖 France, 1670, Honorius, *Le livre des conjurations,* 118.

551 ◈ For Bewitched Livestock

Repeat the following spell:

In the name of God the Father, the Son, and the Holy Ghost, Amen.

I command not by myself, but with the assistance of Lord Jesus and the help of the holy Virgin.

Lord Jesus reached the Mount of Olives; the Lord Jesus took a small white staff in his most holy hand when rabid dogs assailed him; they tore apart his clothes but left his sacred body intact. Just as nothing happened to this lord nor to Saint John, may this livestock be protected from madness, not by my power but by that of Lord Jesus.

† And may the holy Virgin pray to her Son for nothing to happen—not by my power but by that of Lord Jesus. Saint John baptized the Lord Jesus in the Jordan and Mary Magdalene attended this baptism. The Jordan stopped flowing, and this madness will stop in the same way, not by my power but with the help of Lord Jesus, the Holy Trinity, the most holy Virgin, and all the saints. My words concern those gripped by madness, not by my power but by that of Lord Jesus, with the help of the most holy Virgin and all the saints. † I have put an end to these howls, neighs, and so on, with God the Father, the Son, and the Holy Ghost, Amen †††

All the saints appeared barefoot, and this is how the madness will appear, not by my power but with the help of Lord Jesus, and similar to this water falling will fall the frenzy of this animal, not by my power but by that of Lord Jesus and the aid of all the saints. Amen †

It is necessary to recite an Our Father at each cross and the Angelic Salutation, and repeat the entire spell three times.

📖 Eastern Prussia, nineteenth century. Tettau and Temme, *Die Volkssagen*, 269.

552 ❖ FOR ALL EVIL SPELLS

This amulet is called Gem of Jonas (*Gimsteinn Jónasar*); it wards off all evil spells in use north of the Equator. A certain Thorvald allegedly convoked the spirit of the sun this way and made it descend to 800 miles above the ground, thereby causing an earthquake.

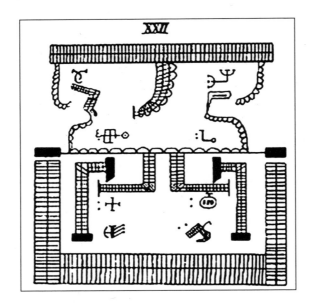

📖 Iceland, seventeenth century. Davidsson, "Isländische Zauberzeichen," 277.

553 ◆ Protection for Livestock from Curses and Magic

Write the following spell on a black tablet or paper and hang it anywhere in the stables:

SATOR
AREPO
TENET
OPERA
ROTAS

📖 Poland, nineteenth century. Vaitkevičienė, *Lietuvių užkalbėjimai*, no. 1533.

The spell of the magic square SATOR AREPO TENET OPERA ROTAS, *which was used to fight all manner of afflictions and evil spells.*

In France, the heart of an animal killed by witchcraft would be taken and pierced with nine hawthorn thorns, the first with one spell, the second with two spells, and so on (see illustration on page 263).

📖 For more on this spell, cf. Lecouteux, *Dictionary of Ancient Magic Words and Spells,* "Sator."

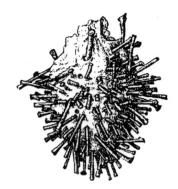

554 ◆ To Protect a Horse from Being Bewitched

To prevent a horse from being bewitched, a sour herring should be placed in its fodder.

📖 Pomerania, nineteenth century. Tettau and Temme, *Die Volkssagen,* 341.

555 ◆ To Protect Animals

Tie alyssum in a red cloth to the neck of a farm animal to ward off illnesses.

📖 Greek, first century. *Pedanii Dioscuridis Anazarbei De Materia Medica Libri quinque,* 3.87.

556 ◆ To Free Animals of All Ills

Read this over salt and malt, and give them to your animals:

> Jesus and the Virgin Mary were traveling along the shore when they saw the good valerian planted in the ground. Jesus began to dig up the root. The troll in the mountain began shouting about the uselessness of the root. Saint Peter arrived and answered the troll of the mountain this way: "It is good against many ills. It is good against exhaustion and anemia! It is good against the fang of the wolf and the claw of the bear and the tooth of Satan and the hand [the contact] of sorcerers and against all ill that flies between heaven and earth." By the three Names and [speak] the Our Father three times before and three times after.

📖 Norway, *Kvamsboka,* in *Svartbok frå Gudbrandsdalen,* 42–61, Norsk Folkeminnelags skrifter, 110 (Oslo, Bergen, Tromsø: Universiteforlaget, 1974), no. 4, "At fri sine Chreature fra alt ondt."

557 ◈ To Prevent Sheep from Taking the Gobes

Write the following verse on a piece of paper: *Super aspidem et basilicum ambulabis leonem et draconen.* Drive the sheep out of the sheepfold or the park, and *srouez* [?] them with this note, speaking the same words aloud.

A gobe is a hairball that is sometimes found in the digestive tracts of animals; the technical term is aegagropila.

📖 France. *Les Œuvres magiques de Henri-Corneille Agrippa,* 91–92.

558 ◈ Orison Pleading for Protection of Flocks

Repeat the following prayer:

> Saint Genevieve of Paris, you who guarded the lambs as once Joseph guarded the flocks of the pharaoh of Egypt, spread your holy grace over the shepherd's crook so that no wolf nor any wicked beast can come near.
>
> Saint Genevieve of Brabant, for whom Jesus and your good guardian angel guarded the doe from all peril and your person from the fury of Golo, pray for the lambs of this good pastor.
>
> Jesus, our sweet Savior, who was born in the manger of Bethlehem, do not suffer, we implore you, any evil to befall any of the animals that were the first witnesses of your coming into the world.
>
> *Saint Genevieve of Paris, intercede for us.*
> *Saint Genevieve of Brabant, pray for us.*
> *Jesus, answer our prayers.*

Among the references, we find the figure of Golo, which is part of the legend of Genevieve of Brabant. This legend forms the subject of many of the chapbooks that basically tell this story: before leaving to wage war at the side of Charles Martel, Comte Siffroy entrusted his wife, Genevieve, to his steward Golo. Golo declared his love and Genevieve pushed him away. He accused her of adultery and had her imprisoned. After many misfortunes, Genevieve reunited with her husband and Golo was drawn and quartered.

📖 France, eighteenth century. *Le Médecin des pauvres,* Troyes, 6ff.

📖 Leclerc, "Les mères douloureuses et les innocenses persécutées dans l'imaginaire populaire: Essai d'analyse iconographique," *Bulletin de la Société Archéologique* 328–31 (1993–94): 223–34, 260–73, 306–20, 458–72.

559 ❖ Protection against Wolves

To protect lost lambs against the wolf, you must say:

> Saint Peter and Saint John were strolling in these valleys,
> meeting there a she-wolf and pups,
> She-wolf and pups, what are you doing in these valleys?
> I am looking to see if there are any stray sheep.
> What will you do to them?
> I will rip out their throats and drink their blood.
> I conjure you to guard them until the sun rises.

Another spell quite similar to this one varies at the end: "I forbid you from piercing their skin and sucking their blood. Lockjaw, lockjaw, lockjaw!"

📖 France (Ardennes), nineteenth century. Meyrac, *Traditions,* 177, no. 74.

560 ❖ Protection for the Flock

To provide your flock protection from wolves, you must say when you find yourself at a crossroads:

> Saint Egarec,
> Who goes over mountains and valleys,
> On behalf of the great living God,
> I forbid you from touching flesh or blood
> [here the flock is named]
> Before the great guard [the sun] comes close.

📖 France (Ardennes), nineteenth century. Meyrac, *Traditions,* 179, no. 93.

561 ❖ To Protect Your Animals

Carve this sign on the horn of a goat, place it near your house, your animals will be protected.

📖 Iceland, Strandgaldur, Museum of Icelandic Sorcery and Witchcraft, Hólmavík.

562 ❖ To Protect Your Horse from the Devil

A circle is drawn around the left hoof of the horse with charcoal, and a cross on the right hoof, while saying:

> *Round, round, round,*
> *Stay health!*
> *May the devil forever avoid you*
> *May God always be with you!*
> *Gentle God drive*
> *Out of the body of this horse*
> *The father of Evil!*
> *Follow no person,*
> *I have just bought you*
> *Be handsome, be good*
> *Be of good humor!*
> *Listen you seven wives of Phuvush*
> *There are seven chains*
> *That protect and save*
> *This animal from you.*

📖 Gypsies of Transylvania, nineteenth century. Wlislocki, *Volksdichtungen*, 147.

563 ❖ Protection against the Death of Pigs

To protect your pigs from death, write these characters on as many notes as there are pigs and place them in their mash. Here are the words: *Futus, Eiortus ful, kout, Erfratus.*

📖 Norway, 1750, Bang, *Norske hexeformularer*, no. 1148, "For Svin Død."

564 ❖ Protection for Your Animals

Have three drops of blood from a child dripped on a piece of bread to be given to the animal you wish to protect, and say:

> *I give you three drops of blood,*
> *It is young and good!*
> *May the blood and flesh wither*
> *Of he who steals you!*

> *When the blood, when the blood*
> *Rests in your body,*
> *May the fire, may the fire*
> *Devour any man*
> *Who tries to approach you!*

📖 Gypsies of Transylvania, nineteenth century. Wlislocki, *Volksdichtungen,* 150.

565 ◆ To Preserve the Good Health of Horses

If you wish to keep your horses fat and active, you must smear their back with garlic during the waning of the moon and say:

> *May the devil quickly devour*
> *The sickness that is in you!*
> *May the good in you*
> *Grow and remain in you!*

📖 Gypsies of Transylvania, nineteenth century. Wlislocki, *Volksdichtungen,* 153.

566 ◆ Protection against Fox Bite

Carve this on the forehead of one of the castrated billy goats and the fox will not kill.

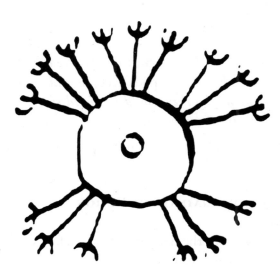

📖 Iceland, Strandgaldur, Museum of Icelandic Sorcery and Witchcraft, Hólmavik.

567 ❖ Another Protection against Fox Bite

Carve this on the forehead of one of the castrated billy goats and the fox will not kill; keep these runes in the sheepfold and you will have no fear of the bite of the fox.

📖 Iceland, Strandgaldur, Museum of Icelandic Sorcery and Witchcraft, Hólmavik.

568 ❖ Protection against the *Hospodařiče*

During the moon's first quarter and before the sun rises, pick some clumps of cherries, make from them a small repelling arrow and a doll, and hang this on the stable door. The kobold will amuse himself with this and leave the animals alone.

From at least the tenth century, it was believed that a spirit called a dwarf, elf, or later, a kobold (hospodařiček), *would come at night to ride the horses, the reason why they would be found covered in sweat in the morning, or else their manes would be braided.*

📖 Czech, Bohemia, seventeenth century. Eis, *Altdeutsche Zaubersprüche*, 235.
📖 Lecouteux, *Les Nains et les Elfes,* 179–82.

569 ❖ Protection against the Demon Called Grief

To protect a horse from the demon called Grief, it should be tied to a stake that has previously been rubbed with garlic. Then a circle is made on the ground with a red thread some distance from the horse, so he cannot touch it, and while doing this, one says:

> *May all evil remain caught*
> *In this thread, in this length!*
> *Grief, leave your water*
> *In the first brooklet*
> *And jump behind it!*

The urine of the Grief often causes abscesses on the animal's body. It would be covered the following day with a red rag that was placed that night in the hole of a tree; while this hole was being plugged up, one said:

> *Stay here*
> *Until the rag becomes animal,*
> *The animal, tree,*
> *The tree, a man**
> *Who will kill you.*

The Grief (Hágrin) is a demon that tortures animals at night. It was said to resemble a yellowish porcupine, around twenty inches long and a span in width. Because of its odor, garlic was reputed to send spirits fleeing, and a red thread has always possessed an apotropaic value. The circle made with it forms an impassable closure.

📖 Gypsies of Transylvania, nineteenth century. Wlislocki, *Volksdichtungen*, 151–52.

570 ◆ Protection for Pigs

To ensure that pigs remain with their new owner and thrive, a little garlic is mixed in with their first mash and one says:

> *You must prevent the Nivashi*
> *From eating your mash!*
> *Eyes that falsely gaze upon you*
> *Must perish here*
> *Must be eaten by you!*

On the Nivashi, see no. 409.

📖 Gypsies of Transylvania, nineteenth century. Wlislocki, *Volksdichtungen*, 148ff.

---

*According to a gypsy myth, the first men were born from the leaves of trees.

571 ◆ To Protect an Animal or an Object

Go to a crossroad at midnight with the animal or object you wish to protect and draw a circle around it. Then, taking a few hairs from the animal or a small pice of the object, toss it onto the ground outside the circle while saying:

> *Here is your part,*
> *Never spend any time at our home.*
> *I am giving you what I can.*
> *Listen, Phuvush,*
> *Block the thieves*
> *For we have three chains,*
> *Three good Urmen.*
> *They will save us.*

📖 Gypsies of Transylvania, nineteenth century. Wlislocki, *Volksdichtungen*, 149.

572 ◆ To Protect One's Horse

Dig a small hole in which you place nine kinds of herbs and hairs, then draw the left hoof in the dirt, cut out the imprint and, while saying the following, plug up the hole:

> *A sprig of herb, a hair,*
> *Never lack for fodder!*
> *May die whoever shall steal you,*
> *Die like this sprig and hair*
> *Rotting, planted in the earth.*
> *Phuvush, here is your part,*
> *Leave my horse safe and sound!*

A fine example of a reducing diagram; this operatory style survived into the twentieth century.

📖 Gypsies of Transylvania, nineteenth century. Wlislocki, *Volksdichtungen*, 148.

573 ◈ Protection from Spirits above the Highest Winds

This amulet is called "Signet of the Queen" (Drottningar Signet); it protects from all the spirits that are "above the highest winds."

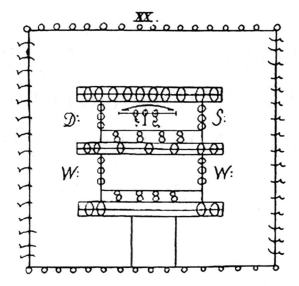

📖 Iceland, seventeenth century. Davidsson, "Isländische Zauberzeichen," 277.

APPENDIX I
MEDICAL MAGIC IN ITALY DURING THE FOURTEENTH–FIFTEENTH CENTURIES

Saint Bernardine of Siena (1380–1444), nicknamed the Star of Tuscany, never halted in his battle against the magical practices of healing, but, in so doing, left us a small overview of the recipes used in his time. In his tenth sermon (*De idolatria cultu,* 3.2), he lists twenty-five practices, some examples of which follow[1]:

1. First they do not eat the heads of animal so as to not have headaches and do other stupidities [*et alias stultitias operantur*].
4. There are many other errors of this kind inspired by the devil, such as this one. Against the falling or royal sickness,* on the day† of Assumption[2] and thereby offending the Virgin, they spend the night dancing[3] and at various follies, taking special pains not to fall on the ground, thinking themselves to be protected from this ill for the entire year.
*†‡§††‡‡§§

Morbus regius customarily means "jaundice."
†In another sermon, Bernadine provides another date: "They dance on the eve of Saint Bartholomew until the evening of the saint's feast day, to the sound of bells, trumpets, cymbals, and all kinds of racket."

5. Against dental pains, they touch their teeth with the tooth of a hanged man or the bone of those who died in other ways, or stick a sword in the ground with certain words, or else place a blade between their teeth when the bells ring on holy Saturday, and do many other like things.
6. To be cured of a sore throat or inflammation of the throat, some take a knife to the black sleeve and recite an incantation [*incantant*].
7. Against the ill of cramps, wear a ring made during the Passion of Our Lord, while observing the day and hour of the apostle.
8. Against dislocated bones or limbs they use two reeds and a young hazel shoot,* joining them end to end whereupon the devil unites them, and thinking this is a miracle, they hang them around their necks like holy relics [*quasi sanctus reliquias ad collum suspendunt*].
9. To heal kidney disease, they have the patient lie down with his face against the ground, as if he worshiped the devil, then a woman who has had twins treads on his kidneys [*calcando lumbo ejus*] while holding two frogs in her hands, then walks over him three times while speaking laughable idiocies. . . .
11. Against worms, especially in children, they write on their stomach, on lead, or on parchment, attaching the text with the thread of a virgin girl [*cum filo puellae virginis*] and throwing melted lead or garlic into the water. . . .
15. For healing daily, tertian, or quartan fever, they give the fasting patient leaves of trees, or apples, or sacred hosts with writing to eat for three days.
16. Against certain illnesses of children, they pass them into [*faciunt illos transire*] the roots of hollow oaks or the like, or through a recent hole.
19. Against the falling sickness [epilepsy], or the royal illness, they light twelve candles for the twelve apostles and, when the patient has been baptized in the name of Jesus Christ, they rebaptize him in the name of the devil, changing the name given him at baptism by giving him that of the apostle whose candle remained the last one alight.

---

*A kind of hazelnut also called synocha.

APPENDIX II
THE ACTIVITIES OF SORCERERS

The *Manual of the Inquisitor* Bernard Gui (circa 1321) contains a model of the interrogation of sorcerers that gives a good glimpse of the actions attributed to them[1]:

> To the accused sorcerer, fortune-teller or invoker of demons, one will ask . . .
>
> What does he know of enchantments or conjurations by means of incantations, fruits, plants, ropes, and so forth. . . .
>
> What does he know of the healing of illnesses by means of conjurations or incantations.
>
> What does he know of this way of harvesting plants, on his knees, facing the east, and while reciting the dominical orison, . . .
>
> One should inquire about this practice that consists of baptizing images of wax or others; one will ask the way they are baptized, what use is made of them, and what advantages one draws from them.
>
> One will interrogate the accused on the leaden images crafted by sorcerers.

The powers of sorcerers and witches was so feared, the Inquisition recommended to the judges of the ecclesiastical tribunals to wear "around the neck [*colligates collo eius*] consecrated salt and various other things, tied with the seven words of Christ on the cross written on a schedule. [The judge] should also wear, if this can be conveniently achieved on his naked body, a blessed candle the length of Christ's body and surround himself with other holy things (*Malleus maleficarum*, 3.16, fol. 108v).

Jean-Baptiste Thiers points out this belief: "Pluck certain herbs on Saint John's Day to prevent sorcerers from working evil" (*Traité des superstitions* [1777], 3:268).

An astounding text can be found in the works of Cyrano de Bergerac,[2] the *Letter on Behalf of Sorcerers* (1654), which lists everything sorcerers know how to do. This text throws a vivid light on the beliefs of an earlier age and explains the reason behind many prescriptions, It is a discourse by the magician Agrippa, that is to say, Cornelius Agrippa von Nettesheim (1486–1535), the author of *The Occult Philosophy*. On reading this text, it is easy to grasp how people could feel threatened and have the desire to protect themselves:

> It is through my charms, that are sent when it pleases me, sterility or abundance. I spark off wars by kindling them between the Spirits that govern the Kings. I teach shepherds the Paternoster of the wolf. I teacher diviners the way to turn the sieve and shears.*
>
> I cause the Ardans [will-o'-the-wisps] to race over the Marshes and Rivers to drown Travelers. I excite the Fairies to dance in the Moonlight. I compel the Gamblers to hunt for the four-leaf Clover under the Gallows. At midnight, I send Spirits from the cemeteries, wrapped in a sheet, to ask their heirs to fulfill the oath they made to the dead. I order Demons to inhabit the abandoned Castles, to slit the throats of the passers-by finding lodging there, until one with resolve compels them to reveal the treasure. I help the wretched I seek to enrich find the Hands of Glory.† I cause to burn

---

*Description of a divination procedure.
†Mains de Gloire ("hands of glory") is a corruption of the French word for mandrake, *mandragore*. It permits one to steal with complete impunity.

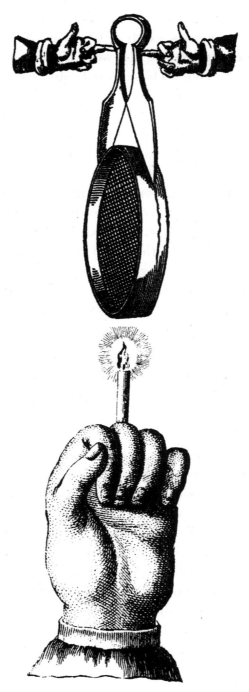

Turning the sieve and shears (*top*); Hand of glory (*bottom*).

for Thieves the Candles of Hanged Man fat, that keep the Homeowners sleeping while they perform their theft. I provide the flying Pistol that leaps back into the pocket after it has been used. I give to Lackeys those rings that allow them to go from Paris to Orleans and back again in one day. I cause everything to be turned topsy-turvy in a House by the Spirits, who will knock over the bottles, glassware, plates, although nothing breaks, nothing spills, and no one sees anyone.³ I reveal myself to the Old to heal fevers with words. I awaken the Villagers on St. John's Eve to gather his herb while fasting and without talking. I teach sorcerers how to become Werewolves. I force them to eat children on the paths and then abandon them when some cavalier cuts off a paw*⁴ [which proves to be a human hand] and they are recognized and put into the hands of Justice. I send to the woebegone a large black man that promises to make them rich, if they but give themselves to him. I blind those who take promissory notes, so that when they demand 30-year terms, I make them see the 3 before the 0, which I have put after. I twist the necks of those who read in the Grimoire without the knowledge to make me appear, and who give me nothing. I peacefully turn back with those who having called me give me only an old slipper, a hair, or a straw. I carry off from the Churches being consecrated any stones that have not been paid for. I let those about at night who encounter the Sorcerers going to Sabbat only see a troop of Cats, whose prince is Marcou.† I send all the *Confederez*‡ to the offering, and present them to kiss the ass of the Goat, seated atop a stool. I treat them splendidly, but with meats without salt. I cause all to faint, if some Foreigner ignorant of the customs, makes the blessing; and I leave him in a wild place, in the middle of thorns, three hundred leagues from his Country. I cause the finding in the

---

*The wound restores the human form.
†In the sixteenth century, Marcou designated a fat male cat. It is also the name give to the seventh son of the same mother, reputedly born to be a sorcerer.
‡The members of the Sabbat.

beds of the debauched, Incubi for Women and Succubi for Men. I send the Cochemard [nightmare] to sleep in the form of a long piece of marble with those who forgot to sign themselves before going to bed. I teach Nigromancers how to bring about the undoing of their enemies, making a waxen image of their enemy and sticking it or throwing it in the fire to make the original feel, what the copy is suffering.[5] I remove on the Sorcerers the feeling in parts, or the Ram marks them with his Seal. I imprinted a secret virtue into *Nollite fieri*,* when it is recited backward, which prevents butter from being made. I instructed the Peasants to place beneath the threshold of the Sheepfold whose ruin they sought, a tuft of hair, or a Toad, with three *maudissions* [curses], to cause the sheep passing over it to become emaciated and die. I showed Shepherd how to knot the breeches closed on the Wedding Day,[6] when the Preacher says *Conjungo eos*.† I give the money that later turns into Chestnut leaves. I lend to Magicians a Demon familiar,‡ who accompanies them and prevents them from undertaking anything without the leave of Master Martinet [Satan].

I teach that to break the curse that has charmed someone, the triangular bread of Saint Wolf must be kneaded and given as alms to the first poor person you meet. I heal the patients of the Werewolf, striking them with a fork, right between their eyes. I make felt the blows dealt to sorcerers, provided they are beaten with a club of Elder. I unbind the *Moine borru*[7]§ on the Christmas Advents, I command him to roll like a barrel, or at midnight drag chains through the streets, in order to wring the necks of those that stick their heads out the window. I teach

---

*"Let it not be done." The phrase is from Psalm 31.
†"I join you together," the ritual phrase of marriage.
‡The famous *spiritus familiaris*.
§The *moine-borru* [monk wearing a thick woolen habit] is a ghost feared by the people. They believe it to be a tormented soul that races through the streets during the Christmas Advents and mistreats passersby, or who wrings the necks of people whose curiosity drives them to stick their nose out the window. Molière alludes to this figure in *Don Juan* (3.1).

the composition of Magical Notes, Curses, Charms, Sigils, Talismans, Magic Mirrors, and constellated Figures. I teach them to find the Mistletoe on New Year's,* the herb of misdirection,† the magnetic poultice. I send the Goblin, the hobnailed mule,‡ the Filourdy,[8]§ King Hugon,‖ the Connestable, the Black Men, the White Ladies, the Lemurs, the Will-o'-the-Wisps, the Larva, the Lamia, the Shades, the Manes, the Specters, the Ghosts: finally, I am the Damned Far Devil, the Wandering Jew, and the Great Huntsman[9]# of the Forest of Fontainebleau.

In his comedy, *Le Pedant joué* [The Pedant Imitated] (1654), Cyrano adds to "the herb of misdirection" fern seed, virgin parchment, cameos, and *caracteres*.

---

*Supposed to provide good luck the entire year. The name became *aguillanneuf*. [Gui is French for mistletoe. —*Trans.*]

†Still called *herbe d'engaire*, the herb that sends astray. [In English this is known as fairy grass or the herb of distraction. —*Trans.*]

‡A ghost mule who forms the subject of folk beliefs.

§Word composed of *fil ourdy* [warp thread], which designates a bogeyman.

‖He rides at night, striking down those who cross his path.

#The Connétable and the Great Huntsman are leaders of the fantastic hunts.

341 Opusculum I. De Incant. seu Ensalmis.

pro Concilio Trident. congregatis anno 1546. tradidisse quendam sanctæ vitæ Græcum Archiepiscopum ad idem Concilium concurrentem: qui constat ex literis, & versibus, seu significationibus subsequentibus, quemque testabatur, inuentum in Antiocheno Benedictinorum monasterio in quadam menbrana conscriptum, & à Zacharia Hierosolimitano Episcopo relictum: quemque rursus idem Archiepiscopus ad brachium sinistrum in quadam itidem membrana literis exaratum circumferebat. Hac vero lege operari prædictum beneficium; si nempe portetur ad brachium in membrana scriptum, tum literis, tum versibus, seu significationibus statim referendis: si vero portans fuerit sacerdos; dicat orationem infra ponendam finita Missa.

✠ *Crux Christi libera me.*

I *Iesus domus Dei libera me.*

D *Deus Deus meus expelle pestem à loco isto, & libera me.*

I *In manus tuas Domine comendo spiritum meum, & corpus meum.*

A *Ante cælum, & terram Deus erat & potens ab ista peste me liberare.*

✠ *Crux Christi potens est ad expellendam pestem à loco isto, & corpore meo.*

B *Bonum est postulare auxilium Dei cum silentio, vt expellat pestem.*

I *Inclinabo cor meum ad faciendas iustificationes tuas, vt non confundar, quoniam inuocaui te.*

Z *Zelaui super iniquos, pacem peccatorum videns, & speraui in te.*

✠ *Crux Christi fugat dæmones, & aerem corruptum, & pestem expellit.*

S *Salus tua ego sum, dixit Dominus, clama ad me, voca me patrē, & ego exaudiam te, & liberabo ab ista peste.*

A *Abyssus abyssum inuocat, & in voce tua expulisti dæmones, & liberasti me.*

B *Beatus qui sperat in Domino, & non respexit in vanitates, & insanias falsas.*

✠ *Crux, quæ antea fuit in opprobriū, nunc & in gloriam, & in nobilitatē, sit mihi in salutem, & expellat à loco isto diabolum, & aerem corruptum, & pestem à corpore meo.*

Z *Zelus honoris tui comedat me, antequam moriar votū offerā Deo, & sacrificium laudis, & fidei illi, qui potes est istum locum, & me à peste liberare, quia qui non confidunt in illo, confundentur.*

G *Gutturi meo, & faucibus meis adhæreat lingua mea, si nō benedixero tibi, & laudauero nomē tuū, quia sanctum est, & liberas sperātes in te, in te cōfido, libera me Deus meus ab ista peste, & locū istum, vbi nomē tuū inuocatū est.*

F *Facta sunt tenebræ super vniuersam terram in morte tua Domine. Deus Deus meus fiat lubrica, & tenebrosa diaboli potestas, & quia ad hoc venisti Fili Dei Viui, vt dissoluas opera diaboli, expelle tua potentia à loco isto, & à me seruo tuo peste istā, & aerē corruptum in tenebras exteriores. Amen.*

✠ *Crux Christi defende nos, expelle à loco isto pestem, & seruum tuū libera à peste ista, quia bonus es Domine, & misericors, & multa misericordia, & verax.*

B *Beatus qui sperat in Domino, & nō respexit in vanitates, & insanias falsas, & in nocte mala liberabit eum Dominus. Domine in te speraui libera me ab hac peste.*

F *Factus es Domine adiutorium mihi, quia in te speraui, libera me ab hac peste.*

R *Respice in me, & miserere mei, & libera me ab hac peste.*

S *Salus mea es tu, sana me Domine, & sanabor, saluum me fac, & saluum &c.*

Ore-

APPENDIX III
THE USE OF ENCRYPTED SPELLS

Zachariah (d. 614), Bishop of Jerusalem wore around his left arm, this spell:

✠ I D A ✠ B I Z ✠ S A B ✠ Z G F ✠ B F R S. Oremus

Thanks to Manuel do Valle de Moura (1620) we know what this means. The spells of the text (facing page) refer to the Scriptures in this order;

I: Luke 23:46	B: Jer. 3:26	I: Ps. 119:112	Z: Ps. 72:3
A: Ps. 41:8	B: Ps. 39:5	G: Ps. 136:6	F: Luke 23:44
B: Ps. 39:5	F: Ps. 93:22	R: Ps. 21:1	S: Jer. 17:14

The text enjoyed great success and can be seen again, for example, in the *De inconstantia in ivre admittenda vel non* by Francisco Albito (Amstelædami, 1683, 449ff.), in Gelasius de Cilia's *Locupletissimus Thesaurus* (Augusta Vindel. & Ratisbone, 1744, 125–27), in the *Collectivo sive apparatus absolutionum, benedictionum, coniurationum, exorcismorum, rituum . . .* , Bassani (Joseph Remondini & Son, 1815, 193ff.), in the *Antidoti spiritali contra del cholera morbus, e di ogni altra pubblica calamitá* by Danielo Maria Zigarelli, archbishop of Salerno (Avellino, 1837, 42–44).

The examples of encrypted abbreviations of the following Latin grimoires are taken from Gian Baptista Porta's *De occultis literarum notis* (Argentorati: Impensis Lazari Zetzneri, 1606). They were reprinted by Johannes Trithemius in his *Libri Polygraphiae* (Argentorati: Sumptibus Lazari Zetzneri, 1613).

Encrypted abbreviations of Latin grimoires.

Secret alphabet of Honorius of Thebes.

The Use of Encrypted Spells

603

Hoc fuit alphabetum Laimielis magni zophi Arti-
corum cognomento Megalopÿ viri sapientissimi, quo
vtebatur in arcanis, quod & ipsum pluraliter potest
mutari. Cui & nos amore principis nostrum subieci-
mus istud, in quo crebrius per tempora vsitatus faci-
lior scriba fiet.

a b c d e f g h I K L m n
⊃ ⚡ ɣ ʋ L I ⊬ ⌐ c T ⋏ ⚔
o p q r s ſh ch ʋ r ʒ w
t l ɣ 8 a m Œ ꝫ ꝫ ꝫ ꝫ ꝫ

Alphabet of Laimielis the Great, a geomancer.

APPENDIX IV
SUPERSTITIOUS HEALING METHODS ACCORDING TO FERNEL

The illustration on the facing page is a list that contains several healing methods for toothaches, epilepsy, the bite of a rabid dog, a method to help pregnant women, and other remedies for scrofula and fevers. The list is from *De abditis rerum causis libri dvo* [On the Hidden Cause of Things] by Johannis Fernelii Ambiani, who was more commonly known as Jean Fernel.

Employer quelqu'un des remedes exterieurs dont Fernel parle en cette sorte a : Se scarifier les gencives avec une des dents d'une personne morte d'une mort violente, pour guerir le mal de dents. Boire la nuit de l'eau de fontaine dans le test d'un homme mort & brusté, pour se délivrer du mal caduc. Se faire des pilules du test d'un pendu pour se guerir des morsures d'un chien enragé. Percer le toit de la maison d'une femme qui est en travail d'enfant, avec une pierre, ou avec une fleche, dont on aura tué trois animaux, sçavoir un homme, un Sanglier & une ourse, de trois divers coups, pour la faire aussi-tost accoucher : ce qui arrive encore plus asseurément quand on perce la maison avec la hache ou le sabre d'un Soldat arraché du corps d'un homme, avant qu'il soit tombé par terre. Manger de la chair d'une beste tuée du mesme fer dont on a tué une personne, pour guerir l'epilepsie. Avec les mains de quelques personnes mortes d'une mort avancée guerir les écroüelles, les glandes qui viennent autour des oreilles & les maux de gorge, en les touchant seulement. Dans l'accés de la fiévre tierce boire trois fois dans un pot neuf, autant à une fois qu'à l'autre, de l'eau de trois puits differens, meslée ensemble, & jetter le reste ensuite. Pour guerir la fievre quarte, envelopper dans la laine, & noüer autour du cou quelque morceau d'un clou de Croix. Boire du vin dans lequel on aura trempé une épée dont on aura coupé la teste d'une personne ; ou envelo,er dans un linceüil les rogneures de ses ongles, puis attacher ce linceüil au ou d'une anguille vive, & la laisser aller aussi tost dans l'eau. Cracher dans la gueule d'une

a Lib. 2. de abditis rerum causis. c. 18.

Johannis Fernelii Ambiani, *De abditis rerum causis libri dvo*

APPENDIX V

KNOTTING THE BREECHES LACES*

The canon *Si per sortiarias atque maleficias*[1] by Hincmar (d. 882), bishop of Reims, often reprinted, mainly in *Gratian's Decretum*,[2] states that the consummation of a marriage can be prevented by magic and witchcraft. Those who use these evil spells should be excommunicated, we are told by the synodal statutes of Eudes of Sully (d. 1208), bishop of Paris, those of Pierre of Colmieu, archbishop of Rouen in 1245, and many others. In the *Statuts et ordonnances de l'Église métropolitaine et primatiale de Lyon* (1577), we read:

> Let us forbid all evil spells, such as knotted breeches laces, charms, drinks, prolation of illicit and non-used words, all diabolical superstition and invention, in marriage, on pain of anathema and excommunication.

Those who practice them are called "magicians, sorcerers, and charmers [*charmador* for men and *charmaressas* for women]," and "should be excommunicated along with all those who resorted to them," the *Ritual du diocèse* of Beauvais in 1637 tells us.

In the sixteenth century, in his *Traicté enseignant en bref les causes des maléfices, sortilèges en enchanteries tant des ligatures et*

---

*The knotting of a man's pants causes impotence.

*noeuds desguillettes,*³ René Benoît (1521–1608), priest of Saint-Eustache of Paris, condemns those who unknot the breeches laces with the help of orisons that he describes as an "abominable and diabolical method." And in 1702, the Oratorian Pierre Lebrun (1661–1729) gives us a little glimpse of how the breeches laces were knotted in his time:⁴

> It is nonetheless this damnable wickedness [the impotence spell], this diabolical action in which fall those who . . . recite one of the verses of the Psalm Miserere mei Deus backward, who next say aloud the name and first name of the two newlyweds, while forming the knot the first time, slightly tightening it the second, and knotting it completely the third, and while saying how long they want it to remain knotted, which is observed for those who have not yet been married. But for those who have already been, the groom's breeches laces are knotted during the church service when the priest blesses the ring, and the first and last names of the new couple are spoken aloud when he places the ring on the ring finger of the new wife.
>
> Those who turn their hands around and entwine their fingers together starting with the little finger of the left hand, and continuing this way until both thumbs are touching, and do this when the groom presents the ring to his bride in the church. . . .
>
> . . . Those who tie the penis of a wolf⁵* to the names of a newlywed man and woman; those who attach certain notes, or certain small pieces of cloth or fabric to the clothing of the new husband or wife; those who strike certain parts of their bodies with their hands in a certain way; those who speak certain words, which I do not wish to record, when they take each by the hand in the church; those who touch them with certain clubs or wands of a certain kind of wood; those on their wedding day

---

Le Petit Albert says in this regard: "Have the prick of a freshly killed wolf and being close to the door of the person you seek to bind, call him by his proper name, and as soon as he responds, you will bind said wolf prick with a white string, and he will be rendered so impotent to the Venus act, that he could not be more so if he had been castrated."

make them drink certain liquors or eat certain cooked pasta; those who make with either the left or right hand certain figures in the air or on the ground, when the priest approaches to begin the wedding...

Lebrun next repeats all that Jean-Baptiste Thiers (1636–1703) had written on the unknotting of the breeches' laces in his *Traité des superstitions* (1679). Johann Weyer cites other means of recovering sexual potency, such as this one: "He who has been bewitched and cannot have intercourse with his wife should urinate in his wedding ring (4.8), which Martin Delrio reused in 1611 when he criticized those who "piss through their betrothal ring, for fear that someone is knotting their breeches' laces, or that they are being bewitched" (3.2, 472).

APPENDIX VI

SEVERAL POPULAR SAINTS INVOKED IN FRANCE AND BELGIUM FOR ILLNESSES AND PROTECTION

It is noticeable how the comparisons work, often based on the homophony that justified the relationship between the saint's name and the affliction he or she cures.

> Acaire: to mellow cantankerous [*acariâtre*] individuals.
> Agapet: against the windy colics [*pet* is French for "fart" —*Trans.*]
> Agrafà: for stomach aches.
> Amant: for rheumatisms.
> Aignan (Sain Taignan): against ringworm [*teigne*].
> Aiguebaut: against those who knot the laces of the breeches.
> Atourni: for dizzy spells [*étourdissements*]
> Bernard: for cramps
> Blaise: for neck problems (cf. the verbs *bléser, zézayer,* "to lisp").
> Boniface: for achieving embonpoint.
> Clair: for eye ailments.
> Cloud: against pimples, zits.
> Corneille: falling sickness (epilepsy).

Étanche: for hemorrhoids.
Fiacre: for eye ailments, colic.
Flaminie de Clermont: for eye problems.
Fort: against weaknesses [fort in French means "strong" —*Trans.*]
François de Sales: for cankers and ulcers.
Fulcrand: for blindness and sterility.
Genès: for stomach aches.
Genou [knee]: against gout.
Gertrude: against rats and mice.
Guignolet: against sterility.
Guiral: for the protection of flocks.
Hadelin: aginst rheumatic pains.
Jean: falling sickness.
Job: against scabies and shameful diseases.
Ladre: against leprosy (the adjective "*ladre*" means "leprous").
Léger [light]: against embonpoint.
Liénard: against the languishing diseases because "Saint Liénard lie et délie" [Saint Liénard ties and unties].
Loup: for leg problems.
Luce: for eye problems.
Mammard: for breast problems ["breasts" are *mamelles* in French].
Mein: for scabies of the hands.
Marcoul: against scrofulous sores.
Ouen: to recover hearing.
Paterne: against sterility.
Pierre: for shivering.
Raphael: against ringworm.
Reine: against bad moods.
Roch de Soiron: for contagious diseases.

APPENDIX VII
THE PROTECTIVE TALISMANS OF BALINAS (APOLLONIUS DE TYANE)

One of the curious features of Hamadan is the stone lion at the gates of the city. It is said to be a talisman against the cold and one of the works of the Greek Balinas, the creator of the talisman. It was sent by Qubâd the Great when he sought to dispel by enchantment the calamities affecting his land. In earlier times, the horsemen perished in the snows of Hamadan because they were so abundant. Balinas therefore crafted the talisman—the statue of a large lion in stone—and set it facing Mount Arwand, which overlooks Hamadan, and the snow and cold diminished.

Next Balinas made a talisman to the right of the lion that worked against snakes, another against scorpions, and the numbers of these animals diminished.

He also made a talisman against floods, and the inhabitants thus found themselves spared of these afflictions; another against fleas, and another against fever, which became rare.

 Ibn al-Faquîh al-Hamadâni, *Abrégé du Livre des pays,* trans. Henri Massé (Damascus: Institut français de Damas, 1973), 290.

AGAINST HEMORRHAGE

You shall write this seal on the end of the shell of an ostrich egg; the woman shall hang it from the right leg and the blood will disappear from her with the permission of God:

F	Q	Ğ	M	Ḥ	M	T
Ḥ	M	T	F	Q	Ğ	M
Q	Ğ	M	Ḥ	M	T	F
M	T	F	Q	Ğ	M	Ḥ
Ğ	M	Ḥ	M	T	F	Q
T	F	Q	Ğ	M	Ḥ	M
M	Ḥ	M	T	F	Q	Ğ

📖 Al-Suyûtû, fifteenth century. *Kitâb al-Rahma*, cited by Jean-Charles Coulon, *La magie islamique et le corpus burianum au Moyen Âge*, thesis for Paris-Sorbonne, 2013, 596ff.

FOR EPILEPSY

Section in which I shall mention the names of the mother of the Koran* and the benefits and defenses that it holds. The eighth name is "she who heals" as was reported from a companion: he recited it into the ear of an epileptic and this latter was healed. . . . Abû Sa'id al-Hudri created a prophylactic incantation (with this sura) on someone stung by a scorpion and he was healed.

📖 Pseudo-al-Bûnî, sixteenth century. *Ourte Šams al-ma'ārif al-suġrā* [*The Little Sun of the Understandings*], cited by Coulon, *La magie islamique*, 1273.

TO BE IN SAFETY

He who after having fasted for two weeks while maintaining the state of ritual purity, writes this square on a virgin page on Thursday on the hour of Jupiter, the moon being in conjunction with the sun and Jupiter and the ascendant in Gemini . . . and bears it on the stitching of his

---

*Al-Fatiha (Arabic), opening sura of the Koran.

The Protective Talismans of Balinas (Apollonius de Tyane) 293

garment, he will be in safety with God's power against thieves and all detestable things. Make certain to never carry it in impurity and never place it in a dirty place.

A	Ḥ	Y.Â	Y.D
Y.B	Y.Ǧ	B	Ḍ
W	Ǧ	Y.W	Ṭ
Y.H	Y	H	D

📖 Al-Bûnî, *Latâ'if al-išârât* [*The Subtleties of the Clues*], as cited by Coulon, *La magie islamique*, 963.

NOTES

INTRODUCTION. THE MANNER OF THE CURE

1. Hesiod, *Works and Days,* ll. 90–105 (trans. Evelyn-White).
2. Josephus, *Antiquities of the Jews,* bk. 8 (trans. Whiston).
3. Migne, *Patrologia graeca,* vol. 122, col. 1316ff.
4. Gaster, *Les plus anciens contes de l'humanité,* 182.
5. Delatte, *Herbarius,* 157–58.
6. St. Gallen, Stiftsbibliothek, MS 1395.
7. Lecouteux, *Dictionary of Ancient Magic Words and Spells,* 358.
8. *Jam noli peccare, ne deterius tibi aliquid contingat.*
9. Ecclesiasticus = Sirach, 38:1–2, 9.
   Honora medicum propter necessitate;
   Etenim illum creavit Altissimus.
   A Deo est enim omnis medela [...]
   Fili, in tua infirmitate ne despicias te ipsum ;
   sed ora Dominum, et ipse curabit te.
10. Matthew 9:8–9, 9:20–22, 9:27–30; Luke 4:39, 5:12–13, 5:18–25, 9:37–43.
11. Augustine, *On Christian Doctrine,* bk. 2, chap. 30 (trans. Shaw).
12. *Capitula ex orientalium Patrum synodis,* canon 74, in *Martini episcopi Bracarensis opera omnia.*
13. Cf. the *Lex Visigothorum,* XI, 2, 2, in Zeumer, ed., *Leges Visigothorum* (*MGH, LL nat. Germ.* 1), 403.
14. *Concilium Turonense,* Canon 42, in *MGH Conc.* 2, 1, 292.
15. Caspari, *Eine Augustin fälschlich beigelegte Homila de sacrilegiis,* 39–40.
16. *Admonitio generalis,* in *MGH LL Capit.* 1, 55.
17. Cf. especially Paulus Grillandus, *Tractatus de hereticis et sortiliegijs,* fol. 60r ff.

18. Cf. the list of healing saints provided in Haver, *Nederlanse Incantatie-literatuur*, 485–86.
19. Lévi-Strauss, *The Savage Mind*, 221.
20. Merceron, "Une démarche médico-magique de la religion populaire," 70.
21. *Decretum*, fol. 193v.
22. Thomas is referring to the *Decretum Gratiani* (twelfth century), II, causa 26, quaestio 5, c 3: *Nec in collectionibus herbarum, que medicinales sunt, aliquas obseruationes aut incantationes liceat attendere, nisi tantum cum symbolo diuino, aut oratione dominica, ut tantum Deus creator omnium et Dominus honoretur.*
23. Aquinas, *Summa Theologica*, II, II, 96, 4 (trans. from Benziger Brothers edition).
24. Ibid., II, II, 96, 2 (trans. from Benziger Brothers edition).
25. *Malleus maleficarum*, II, 2, 6 (edition of 1496), fol. 86r, 87r.
26. Grillandus, *Tractatus*, fol. 57r–v.
27. Ibid., fol. 15r.
28. Book printed in the *Theatrum Diabolorum*, chap. 29, §5, 57r, and chap. 37, 83v–84r.
29. Luke 9:42.
30. Luke 4:39.
31. "*Quando Christus natus est, / omnis dolor passus est,*" in *Theodori Prisciani Euporiston libri III*, 303.
32. Vair, *Trois livres des charmes, sorcelages, ov enchantemens*, I, 5, p. 53.
33. Weyer, *De praestigiis daemonum et incantationibus ac ueneficijs libri sex*, V, 2, pp. 448–49.
34. Ibid., V, 4, pp. 454, 457 (trans. Shea)
35. Ibid., V, 8, p. 474 (trans. Shea).
36. Vair, *Trois livres des charmes*, p. 314.
37. Grillandus, *Tractatus de hereticis*, fol. 27r–v.
38. Weyer, *De praestigiis daemonum*, V, 7, p. 472 (trans. Shea from *Witches, Devils, and Doctors in the Renaissance*, 386–87).
39. Delrio, *Disquisitionum magicarum libri sex*, VI, 3.
40. Ibid., I, 3, q. 4.
41. Cf. Wickersheimer, "Figures médico-astrologiques des IXe, Xe et XIe siècles," 164–65.
42. Bouché-Leclercq, *L'Astrologie grecque*, 319.
43. Bernard de Gordon, *Lilium medicinae*, V, 6; Vair, *Trois livres des charmes*, I, 6, p. 60.
44. Cited in Cabanès and Barraud, *Remèdes de bonne femme*, 137–38.

45. Wickersheimer, *La médecine et les médecins en France a l'époque de la Renaissance*, 535.
46. Vair, *Trois livres des charmes*, I, 6, pp. 59–60.
47. Porta, *Phytognomonica*, chap. 2.
48. Fernel, *De abditis rerum causis libri dvo*, 244ff. Partially included in Thiers, *Traité des superstitions selon l'Écriture sainte*, 332–33.
49. Mizauld, *Memorabilium, utilium ac iucundorum centuriae novem*, VI, 38.
50. Bernardino of Siena, *Sermo* 1; cited in Thiers, *Traité des superstitions qui regardent les sacrements selon l'Écriture sainte*, xiii.
51. Thiers, *Traité des superstitions*, 332.
52. "Maleficium cum ligaturis," *Lex Salica*, emendata 24, in *MGH, LL nat. Germ*. 4, 2, 66.
53. Mansi, *Sacrorum conciliorum nova et amplissima collectio*, vol. 10, col. 1200.
54. Cf. Lecouteux, "Les maîtres du temps: Tempestaires, obligateurs, défenseurs et autres."
55. Agobard of Lyon, *De grandine et tonitruis*.
56. Vair, *Trois livres des charmes*, I, 11, pp. 97–98.
57. Cf. Lecouteux, *The High Magic of Talismans and Amulets*.
58. The verbs *adpendere, impendere, suspendere* are all variants of "to hang" or "to suspend," while *ligare* and *portare ad/circa collum* refer to "tying" or "wearing at/around the neck."
59. Cf. Delatte, *Herbarius*, 3rd ed., vol. 4, fasc. 4.
60. Cf. the treatise *De radiis* by Al-Kindi (ca. 800–866), translated into Latin at the end of the twelfth century, in which it is said: "It is celestial harmony that carries out the diversity possessed by the figures as both virtues and effects, attributing to each, thanks to the rays it emits, its own ability to produce a movement on which the diversity of forms and figures depends" (chap. 7). For an edition of the text, see d'Alverny and Hudry, "Al-Kindi, *De radiis*"; French translation in Matton, *La magie arabe traditionnelle*, 77–128.
61. Cf. Baader, "Handschrift und Inkunabel in der Überlieferung der medizinischen Literatur."
62. Howald and Sigerist, eds., *Antonii Musae de Herba Vettonica Liber*. See also Singer, "The Herbal in Antiquity and Its Transmission to Later Ages."
63. Cf. Lecouteux, *A Lapidary of Sacred Stones*.
64. *Marcelli De medicamentis liber*, ed. Niedermann and Liechtenhan.
65. Claude Lecouteux, *The Book of Grimoires*.
66. These include: Schmitt, *Liber ordinis rerum*; Schnell et al., *Vocabularius ex quo*; and Kirchert and Klein, *Die Vokabulare von Fritsche Closener und Jakob Twinger von Königshausen*.

CHAPTER 2. THE ILLNESSES OF HUMANS AND THEIR CURE

1. Klapper, *Erzählungen des Mittelaters*, 268 (*et donavit et hanc virtutem, ut quecumque herba crescens, que fimbriam eius attigit, a tactu superne virtutis erat, ut ab illa infirmi sanarentur*).
2. Psalm 8:3 (Vulgate).
3. Afanassiev, *Poetičeskije vozzrenija slavjan na prirodu* [The Slavs' Poetic Concepts of Nature], vol. 2, 69–70.
4. Afanassiev, *Poetičeskije vozzrenija slavjan na prirodu*, vol. 2, 16.
5. This is a fragment taken from the Roman Missal. The complete text reads: *Communicantes, et memoriam venerantes, in primis gloriosae semper Virginis Mariae, Genetricis Dei et Domini nostri Iesu Christi: sed et beati Ioseph, eiusdem Virginis Sponsi, et beatorum Apostolorum ac Martyrum tuorum, Petri et Pauli, Andreae, Iacobi, Ioannis, Thomae, Iacobi, Philippi, Bartholomaei, Matthaei, Simonis et Thaddaei: Lini, Cleti, Clementis, Xysti, Cornelii, Cypriani, Laurentii, Chrysogoni, Ioannis et Pauli, Cosmae et Damiani) et omnium Sanctorum tuorum; quorum meritis precibusque concedas, ut in omnibus protectionis tuae muniamur auxilio. Per Christum Dominum nostrum. Amen.*
6. Brouzet, *Essai sur l'éducation médecinale des enfants, et sur leurs maladies*, vol. 2, 43.
7. In the Latin MS 7056 of the Bibliothèque nationale, these names are in a different order and show variations: "Eugenius, Stephanus, Porcatius, Sanbutius, Dyonisius, Gelasius, Blasius, and Quyriacus."
8. Martino, *La terre des remords*.
9. Cf. Lecouteux, *Elle courait le garou*, 44–45.
10. British Library, Harley 585, fol. 184r–v. The Dutch spell gives us: *ka † ay † vinga † adonay † satheos † o theos † emanuel † ineffabile † ominigan † onaan † iman † misane † dias † modo † undi † nemar † gamasten † orcamin † signimie † berusor † irritas † venas † causidulis † fervor † fixantis † sangnens † siccatur † fla † fla † graza † frigula † mugon † et sidon † benedicite dominus †*. Ghent, Universiteitsbibliotheek, MS 1317, fol. 396r–v.
11. Cf. Wipf, *Althochdeutsche poetische Texte*, 64–66.
12. Cf. Gaster, *Les plus anciens contes de l'humanité*, 88–89.
13. See the study by Saintyves, *La Guérison des verrues*.

CHAPTER 7. PROTECTIONS

1. This is reminiscent of the phrase *Jesus autem transiens per medium illorum ibat* ("But Jesus passing through their midst went His way"; Luke 4:30), which was much used by travelers during the Middle Ages.

2. Kramer and Sprenger, *Malleus maleficarum*, 1496 edition.
3. *Works and Days*, v. 727.
4. Psalm 70:1 (Vulgate).

APPENDIX I. MEDICAL MAGIC IN ITALY DURING THE FOURTEENTH–FIFTEENTH CENTURIES

1. Zachariae, "Abergläubische Meinungen und Gebräuche des Mittelalters in den Predigten Bernardinos von Siena."
2. On "religious" dances with therapeutic aims, cf. Backman, *Den religiösa dansen inom kristen kyrka och folkmedicin*.
3. For dance as therapy, cf. Höfler, *Deutsches Krankheitsnamenbuch*, 727–29.

APPENDIX II. THE ACTIVITIES OF SORCERERS

1. Gui, *Manuel de l'Inquisiteur*, 24–25.
2. Cyrano de Bergerac, *Les Œuvres diverse de Monsieur Cyrano de Bergerac*, 86–91.
3. Description of the activity of poltergeists; cf. Claude Lecouteux, *The Secret History of Poltergeists and Haunted Houses*.
4. Cf. Lecouteux, *Elle courait le garou*.
5. For more on these voults, cf. no. 500.
6. Cf. recipe no. 398.
7. According to Sébillot, *Le Folklore de France* (1907), vol. 4, 219.
8. Cf. Oudin, *Curiositez françoises pour supplément aux dictionnaires*, 174.
9. Cf. Lecouteux, *Phantom Armies of the Night*.

APPENDIX V. KNOTTING THE BREECHES LACES

1. *Gratian, Decretum magistri Gratiani*, ed. Aemilius Friedberg, Corpus Iuris Canonici, vol. 1 (Leipzig, 1879), causa 33, quaestio 1, chap. 4, col. 1149ff.
2. Gratian, *Decretum*, 33, quaestio 1.
3. Paris: Jean Poupy, 1579.
4. Lebrun, *Histoire critique des pratiques superstitieuses qui ont séduit les Peuples & embarrassé les Savans*, vol. I, chap. 7, 320–23.
5. *Le Petit Albert*, 21–22.

BIBLIOGRAPHY

MANUSCRIPTS

Bamberg, Staatsbibliothek, Codex medicinalis 1.
Berlin, Staatsbibliothek Codex mgf 817.
Bruges, Episcopal Archives, Reckening Kapelnij St. Agnes, 1490–95.
Bucharest, Biblioteca Academiei Române din Bucureşti, MSS Romanian BAR 1517; BAR 2183; BAR 4458; BAR 4743; BAR 4917; BAR 5706.
Cambrai, Municipal Library, MS 351.
Cambridge, St. John's College D.4.
Cambridge, Trinity College, MS O 1.20; MS R 14.30.
Dresden, Sächsische Landesbibliothek, MS C 326.
Erfurt, Wissenschaftliche Allgemeinbibliothek, MS Ampl. D 17.
Gand, Universiteitsbibliotheek, MSS 697; 1021A; 1317.
Gelinden, Parochiaal Archief, no. a, 1597.
Heidelberg, Universitätsbibliothek, Cpg 244; 265; 267; 268.
Kalocsa, Hungary, Főzékesegyházi Könyvatár, MS 629.
Karlsruhe, Badische Landesbibliothek, MS Donaueschingen 792.
Leiden, MS Mij. Ned. Letterk. 960.
London, British Library, Additional 15236; 28170; 39638; Additional 17527 in folio.
London, British Library, Landsdowne 1202 4to.
London, British Library, Sloane 146; 692; 962; 963; 2584; 3002; 9550; Harley 273; 585; 1684.
Marburg, Universitätsbibliothek, MS B 20.
Munich, Bayerische Staatsbibliothek, MSS Cgm 92; Clm 100.
Oxford, Bodleian Library, Digby 69; Ashmole 1444.
Paris, Bibliothèque de l'Arsenal, MS 2872.
Paris, Bibliothèque nationale, MS français 14788.

Paris, Bibliothèque nationale, MS Lat. 8654 B; Lat. 6838 A; Lat. 13246.
Paris, Bibliothèque nationale, MS nouvelle acquisition française 10034.
St. Gallen, Stiftsbibliothek, Codex 751.
St. Gallen, Stiftsbibliothek, Codex 1395.
Stockholm, Royal Library, MS X, 114.
Utrecht, Library of the Royal University, MS 1355, no. 16.
Vienna, Österreichische Nationalbibliothek, Codex 751; Codex 2817 [med. 9], Codex 2999.
Wroclaw, University Library, MS III, F 10.
Zurich, Zentralbibliothek, C. 58.

BOOKS, STUDIES, AND REFERENCE WORKS

Addabbo, Anna Maria. "Stupidus in monte ibat: un caso di interdizione verbale?" *Civiltà classica e cristiana* 12 (1991): 331–41.
Afanassiev, A. N. *Poetičeskije vozzrenija slavjan na prirodu*. 3 vols. Moscow: Sovremennyj pisatel', 1995.
Agobard of Lyon. *De grandine et tonitruis*. In *Agobardi Lugdunensis Opera Omnia*. Edited by L. Van Acker. Turnhout: Brepols, 1981.
Al-Hamadâni, Ibn al-Faquîh. *Abrégé du Livre des pays*. Damas: Institut français de Damas, 1973.
Amilien, Virginie. *Le Troll et autres créatures surnaturelles dans les contes populaires norvégiens*. Paris: Berg International, 1996.
Antidotarium Bruxellense. Edited by Valentin Rose. In *Theodori Prisciani Euporiston libri III*, Leipzig: Teubner, 1894.
Antonius Musa. *De herba vettonica*. In *Antonii Musae De herba vettonica liber, Pseudoapulei Herbarius, Anonymi De taxone liber, Sexti Placiti liber Medicinae ex animalibus*. Edited by Ernest Howald and Henry E. Sigerist. Leipzig and Berlin: Deutscher Verein fur Kunstwissenschaft, 1927.
Aquinas, St. Thomas. *Summa Theologica*. Translated by Fathers of the English Dominican Province. Cincinnati: Benziger Brothers, 1947.
Arbatel. *Libro de segreto della magia divina*. Rome: Ediziono Brancato, 2012.
Arnaud, Louis. "La baskania ou le mauvais œil chez les Grecs modernes." *Échos d'Orient* 15 (1912): 385–94, 510–24.
Arnold of Villanova. *Opera*. Lyon: Fradin, 1509.
Artelt, Walter. *Kosmas und Damian, die Schutzpatrone des Ärzte und Apotheker: Eine Bildfolge* Darmstadt: E. Merck Chemische Fabrik, 1949–1954.

Auchet, Marc, ed. *Le Secret d'Odin: Mélanges offerts à Régis Boyer.* Nancy: PUN, 2001.
Augustine. *On Christian Doctrine.* Translated by J. F. Shaw. Mineola, N.Y.: Dover, 2009.
Baader, Gerhard. "Handschrift und Inkunabel in der Überlieferung der medizinischen Literatur." In *Buch und Wissenschaft: Beispiele für die Rolle des Buches in der Geschichte der Medizin, Naturwissenschaft und Technik.* Edited by Eberhard Schmauderer, 15–47. Düsseldorf: VDI-Verlag, 1969.
Backman, Eugène Louis. *Den religiösa dansen inom kristen kyrka och folkmedicin.* Stockholm: Norstedt, 1945.
Bajburin, A. "Quelques aspects de la mythologie de l'île." *Cahiers slaves* 7, (2004).
Bang, Anton Christian. *Norske hexeformularer og magiske opskrifter.* Christiania [Oslo]: Dybwad, 1901–02.
Bartels, Max. "Über Krankheits-Beschworungen." *Zeitschrift für Volkskunde* 5 (1895): 1–40.
Bartholin, Thomas. *De Transplantatione morborum dissertation epistolica.* Copenhagen: Paulli, 1673.
Baufeld, Christa. *Kleines frühneuhochdeutsches Wörterbuch.* Tübingen: Niemeyer, 1996.
Belin, Dom Jean-Albert. *Traité des talismans ou figures astrales.* Paris: De Bresche, 1658.
Benoit, René. *Traicté enseignant en bref les causes des maléfices, sortilèges et enchanteries tant des ligatures et nœuds desguillettes, etc.* Paris: Poupy, 1579.
Bernard de Gordon. *Lilium medicinae.* Frankfurt: Jenni, 1617.
Berthoin-Matthieu, Anne. *Prescriptions anglaises du Xe au XIIe siècle: Étude structurale.* Paris: AMAES, 1996.
Biedermann, Hans. *Handlexikon der magischen Künste: Von der Spätantike bis zum 19. Jahrhundert.* Graz: Akademische Druck- und Verlagsanstalt, 1968.
———. *Medicina magica: Metaphysische Heilmethoden in spätantiken und mittelalterlichen Handschriften.* Graz: Akademische Druck- und Verlagsanstalt, 1978.
Biraben, Jean-Noël, and Jacques Le Goff. "La Peste dans le Haut Moyen Âge." *Annales E.S.C.* 24 (1969): 1484–1510.
Birlinger, Anton. "Aus einem elsässischen *Arzneibuche* des XIV. Jahrhunderts." *Alemannia* 10 (1882): 219–32.
Blocquel, Simon. *La Magie rouge: Crème des sciences occultism naturelles ou divinatoires, par l'helléniste Aaron.* Lille: Blocquel Castiaux, 1844.
Boers, Hedda. *Folketro om taender, tandmidler og tandbehandling hos almuen i*

Danmark: Et studium i dansk folkemedicin. Copenhagen: Dansk Videnskabs Forlag, 1954.

Bonser, Wilfrid. "The Seven Sleepers of Ephesus in Anglo-Saxon and Later Recipes." *Folklore* 56 (1945): 254–56.

Bouché-Leclercq, Auguste. *L'Astrologie grecque.* Paris: Leroux, 1899.

Bremer, Ernst, and Klaus Ridder, eds. *Vocabularius optimus.* 2 vols. Tübingen: Niemeyer, 1990.

Bridier, Sophie. *Le Cauchemar: Étude d'une figure mythique.* Paris: P.U.P.S., 2002.

Brillet, Pascale, and Alain Moreau. *Bibliographie générale, vol. 4 of La Magie, Actes due colloque international de Montpellier (25–27 mars 1999).* Edited by A. Moreau and Jean-Claude Turpin. Montpellier: Université de Montpellier III, 2000.

Brouzet, N. *Essai sur l'éducation médecinale des enfants, et sur leurs maladies.* 2 vols. Paris: Cavelier & Fils, 1754.

Browe, Peter. "Die Eucharistie als Zaubermittel im Mittelalter." *Archiv für Kulturgeschichte* 20 (1930): 134–54.

Buckland, Raymond. *Buckland's Book of Gypsy Magic: Travelers' Stories, Spells, and Healings.* San Francisco: Red Wheel Weiser, 2010.

Bulk, Wilhelm. *St. Apollonia, Patronin der Zahnkranken: Ihr Kult und Bild im Wandel der Zeiten.* Munich and Bielefeld: Zahn-Haus Wilhelm Bulk, 1967.

Burchard of Worms. *Decretum.* Cologne, 1548. Facsimile: *Decretorum libri XX.* Edited by Gérard Fransen and Theo Kölzer. Aalen: Scientia, 1992.

Cabanès, Augustin, and Dr. Barraud. *Remèdes de bonne femme.* Paris: Maloine, 1907.

Campbell, Sheila, Bert Hall, and David Klausner, eds. *Health, Disease, and Healing in Medieval Culture.* New York: St. Martin's, 1992.

Camus, Dominique. *Le livre des secrets: Les mots et les paroles qui guérissent.* Paris: Dervy, 2001.

———. *Paroles magiques, secrets de guérison: Les leveurs de maux aujourd'hui.* Paris: Imago, 1990.

———. *La Sorcellerie en France aujourd'hui.* Rennes: Ouest-France, 2001.

Camus, Giulio. *L'Opera salernitana "Circa instans" ed il testo primitivo del "Grant herbier en francoys."* Modena: Società Tipografica, 1886.

Caspari, Carl Paul. *Eine Augustin fälschlich beigelegte Homilia de sacrilegiis.* Christiania [Oslo]: Dybwad/Brügger, 1886.

Cato the Elder. *Les Agronomes Latins, Caton, Varron, Columelle, Palladius.* Paris: Dubochet, 1844.

Cockayne, Oswald. *Leechdoms, Wortcunning, and Starcraft of Early England.* 3 vols. London: Longman, Green, Longman, Roberts, and Green, 1864–66.

Coppin, Brigitte, and Michaël Welply. *La Peste: Histoire d'une épidémie*. Paris: Gallimard, 2006.

Compilatio Singularis Exemplorum. Edited by A. Hilka in *Jahresbericht der Schleisischen Gesellschaft für vaterländische Cultur* 90 (1913): 1–24.

Coulon, Hyacinthe. *Curiosités de l'histoire des remèdes comprenant des Recettes employées au Moyen âge dans le Cambrésis*. Cambrai: Régnier Frères, 1892.

CSB = *Corpus der deutschen Segen und Beschwörungsformeln* at the Institut für Sächsische Geschichte und Volkskunde, Dresden.

Cyrano de Bergerac. *Les Œuvres diverse de Monsieur Cyrano de Bergerac*. Paris: Antoine de Sommaville, 1661.

D'Alverny, Marie-Thérèse, and Françoise Hudry. "*Al-Kindi, De Radiis.*" *Archives d'Histoire doctrinale et littéraire du Moyen Âge* 41 (1974): 139–260.

Daems, Willem F. "Edelsteine in der Medizin." *Die Drei: Zeitschrift für Wissenschaft, Kunst und soziales Leben* 51 (1981): 504–18.

Davidson, Gustav. *A Dictionary of Angels, Including the Fallen Angels*. New York and London: The Free Press, 1967.

Daviðsson, Ólafur. "Isländische Zauberzeichen und Zauberbücher." *Zeitschrift des Vereins für Volkskunde* 13 (1903): *150–167, 267–279*.

Daxelmüller, Christoph. *Zauberpraktiken: Eine Ideengeschichte der Magie*. Düsseldorf: Artemis & Winkler, 1993.

Delatte, Armand. *Herbarius: Recherches sur le cérémonial usité chez les anciens pour la cueillette des simples et des plantes magiques*. 2nd ed. Paris and Liège: Droz, 1938.

———. *Herbarius: Recherches sur le cérémonial usité chez les anciens pour la cueillette des simples et des plantes magiques*. 3rd ed. Brussels: Palais des Académies, 1961.

———. "Le Traité des Plantes Planétaires d'un manuscrit de Léningrad." *Annuaire de l'Institute de Philologie et d'Histoire Orientales et Slaves* 9 (1949): 145–77.

Delrio, Martin. *Les Controverses et Recherches magiques*. Paris: Petit-Pas, 1611.

———. *Disquisitionum Magicarum Libri Sex: Quibus continetur accurata curiosarum artium, & vanarum superstitionum confutatio, utilis theologis, iurisconsultis, medicis, philologis*. Cologne: N.p., 1679.

Deroux, C., ed. *Maladie et Maladies dans les textes latines et médiévaux*. Brussels: Latomus, 1998.

Descombes, René. *Les Carrés magique: Histoire, théorie et technique de carré magique, de l'Antiquité aux recherches actuelles*. Paris: Vuibert, 2000.

De Vinck, Pascale. "La *guérison magique*: Entre médecine et sorcellerie; Une enquête en Puisaye (France)." *Civilisations* 36, no. 1–2 (1968): 365–87.

Dovreboka. In Velle Espeland, ed. *Svartbok frå Gudbrandsdalen,* 70–77. Oslo, Bergen, Tromsø: Universitetsforlaget, 1974.

Du Cange, Charles du Fresne. *Glossarium mediae et infimae latinitatis.* 10 vols. Niort: Favre, 1883–87.

Du Laurens, André. *De mirabili strumas sanandi, solis Galliae regibus christianis divinitus concessa.* Paris: Apud Marcum Orry, 1609.

Ebermann, Oskar. *Blut- und Wundsegen in ihrer Entwicklung dargestellt.* Berlin: Mayer & Müller, 1921.

Edsman, Carl-Martin. "Folklig sed med rot I heden tid." *Arv* (1946): 145–76.

Eis, Gerhard. *Altdeutsche Zaubersprüche.* Berlin: de Gruyter, 1964.

Eliade, Mircea. *Images and Symbols.* London: Harvill Press, 1961.

Elworthy, Frederick Thomas. *The Evil Eye: An Account of This Ancient and Widespread Superstition.* London: John Murray, 1895.

Evans, Joan. *Magical Jewels of the Middle Ages and Renaissance, Particularly in England.* Oxford: Clarendon Press, 1922.

Les Évangiles des Quenouilles [The Distaff Gospels]. Edited by Madeleine Jeay. Montreal: Vrin, 1985.

Fehringer, Barbara. *Das Speyerer Kraüterbuch mit den Heilpflanzen Hildegards von Bingen: Eine Studie zur mittelhochdeutschen Physica-Rezeption mit kritischer Ausgabe des Textes.* Würzburg: Königshausen & Neumann, 1993.

Fernel, Jean [Johannis Fernelii Ambiani]. *De abditis rerum causis libri dvo.* Paris: Weche, 1548.

Fiedler, Wilhelm. *Antiker Wetterzauber.* Stuttgart: Kohlhammer, 1931.

Fischer, Heinrich Ludwig. *Das Buch vom Aberglauben, Mißbrauch, und falschen Wahn.* Oberdeutschland: Verlag des Unterricht- Noth- und Hülfsbüchlein, 1790.

Franz, Adolf. *Die kirchlichen Benediktionen in Mittelalter.* 2 vols. Graz: Herder, 1960 [1909].

Fühner, Hermann. *Lithotherapie: Historische Studien über die medizinische Verwendung der Edelsteine.* Ulm: Haug Verlag, 1956.

Gaidoz, Henri. *Un vieux rite medical.* Paris: Rolland, 1892.

Gaster, Théodore H. *Les plus anciens contes de l'humanité.* Paris: Payot, 1953.

Ghāyat al-hakīm. Ritter, Hellmut Ritter and Martin Plessner, trans. *"Picatrix": Das Ziel des Weisen von Pseudo-Magrītī.* London: Warburg Institute, 1962.

Grabner, Elfriede. "'Ein Arzt hat dreierlei Gesicht. . .': Zur Entstehung, Darstellung und Verbreitung des Bildgedankens 'Christus coelestis medicus.'" *Materia Medica Nordmark* 24 (1972): 297–317.

———. "Die 'Transplantatio morborum' als Heilmethode in der Volksmedizin." *Österreichische Zeitschrift für Volkskunde* XXI/70 (1967): 178–96.

―――. "Der *'Wurm'* als Krankheitsvorstellung: Süddeutsche und südosteuropäische Beiträge zur allgemeinen Volksmedizin." *Zeitschrift für deutsche Philologie* 81 (1962): 224–40.

Graesse, Johann Georg Theodor. *Bibliotheca magica et pneumatica*. Leipzig: Engelmann, 1843.

Graff, Eberhard. *Althochdeutscher Sprachschatz oder Wörterbuch der althochdeutschen Sprache*. 7 vols. Berlin: Nikolai, 1834.

Grambo, Ronald. "A Catalogue of Nordic Charms—Some Reflections." *NIF Newsletter* 2, no. 19 (1977): 12–16.

―――. "Gamle norske folkebønner. Ein motivanalyse." *Maal og minne* (1977): 103–14.

―――. "Norske kjærestevarsler." *Maal og minne* (1966): 122–34.

―――. *Norske tannbønner*. Oslo: NEG/Norsk folkemuseum, 1974.

―――. *Norske trollformler og magiske ritualer*. Oslo, Bergen, and Tromsø: Universitetsforlaget, 1984.

―――. "Vernebønner mot ulv og bjørn. Ein motivanalyse." *Maal og minne* (1965): 153–60.

Gratian, Decretum Magistri Gratiani. Edited by Emil Friedberg. Leipzig: Tauchnitz, 1879. Reprint, Graz: Akademische Druck- und Verlagsanstalt, 1959.

Greenfield, Richard P. H. "Saint Sisinnios, the Archangel Michael, and the Female Demon Gylou: The Typology of the Greek Literary Stories." *Byzantina* 15 (1989): 83–142.

Greeven, Heinrich. *Krankheit und Heilung nach dem Neuen Testament*. Stuttgart: Kreuz Verlag, 1948.

Grillandus, Paulus. *Tractatus de hereticis et sortiliegijs*. Lyon: Jacob Giuncti, 1545 [1st ed. 1536].

Grimm, Jacob. *Deutsche Mythologie*. 4th edition. 3 vols. Graz: Akademische Druck- u. Verlagsanstalt, 1968 [1875–1878].

―――. *Deutsche Mythologie,* 3 vol. Darmstadt: Wissenschaftliche Buchgesellschaft, 1965.

Gruel-Apert, Lise. *La Tradition orale russe*. Paris: P.U.F., 1995.

Gubernatis, Angelo de. *La Mythologie des plantes: Ou les Légendes du règne végétal*. 2 vols. Paris: Reinwald, 1878–82.

Gui, Bernard. *Manuel de l'Inquisiteur*. Edited and translated by G. Mollat. Paris: Les Belles Lettres, 1964.

Hamès, Constant. "Entre recette magique d'Al-Bûnî et prière islamique d'al-Ghazali: textes talismaniques d'Afrique occidentale." *Systèmes de pensée en Afrique noire* 12 (1993): 187–223.

Hampp, Irmgard. *Beschwörung, Segen, Gebet: Untersuchungen zum Zauberspruch aus dem Bereich der Volksheilkunde.* Stuttgart: Silberburg, 1961.

Harmening, Dieter. "Das magische Wort." *Perspektiven der Philosophie. Neues Jahrbuch* 23 (1997): 365–85.

Hauck, Karl. "Gott als Arzt: Eine exemplarische Skizze mit Text und Bildzeugnissen aus drei verschiedenen Religionen zu Phänomenen und Gebärden der Heilung." In *Text und Bild.* Edited by Christel Meier and Uwe Ruberg, 19–63. Wiesbaden: Ludwig Reichert, 1980.

Haver, Jozef van. *Nederlanse Incantatieliteratuur: Een gecommentarieerd compendium van Nederlandse Bezweringsformules.* Ghent: Koninklijke Vlaamse Academie voor Taal- en Letterkunde, 1964.

HDA = Bächtold-Stäubli, Hans, and Eduard Hoffmann-Krayer. *Handwörterbuch des deutschen Aberglaubens.* With a foreword by Christoph Daxelmüller. 10 vols. Berlin and New York: De Gruyter, 1987.

Heim, R. "Incantamenta magica graeca latina." *Jahrbücher für classische Philologie,* Supplementband 19 (1892): 463–576.

Hengel, Rudolf, and Martin Hengel. *"Die Heilungen Jesu und medizinisches Denken."* In *Medicus viator: Festschrift Richard Siebeck,* 332–61. Tübingen: Mohr, 1959.

Herr, Michael. *Das neue Tier- und Arzneibuch des Doktor Michael Herr A.D. 1546.* Edited by Gerhard E. Sollbach. Würzburg: Königshausen & Neumann, 1994.

Hervé, Georges. "Superstitions populaires suisses concernant les armes, le tir, la guerre, les blessures." *Revue anthropologique* 26 (1916): 350–65.

Hesbert, Dome René-Jean. *Corpus Antiphonalium Officii.* 6 vols. Rome: Herder, 1963–79.

Hesiod. *Homeric Hymns, Epic Cycle, Homerica.* Translated by Hugh G. Evelyn-White. London: William Heinemann, 1914.

Hildegard von Bingen. *Physica: Elementorum, Fluminum aliquot Germaniae, Metallorum, Leguminum, Fructuum, & Herbarum, etc.* Argentorati [Strassburg]: Scottus, 1533.

Hock, Auguste. *Croyances et Remèdes populaires du pays de Liège.* Vol. 4 of *Oeuvres complètes.* Liège: Vaillant-Carmane, 1872–74.

Höfler, Max. *Deutsches Krankheitsnamenbuch.* Munich: Piloty & Loehle, 1899.

Hole, Christina. "Some Instances of Image-Magic in Great Britain." In *The Witch Figure: Folklore Essays by a Group of Scholars in England Honoring the 75th Birthday of Katherine M. Briggs.* Edited by Venetia Newall, 80–94. London & Boston: Routledge & Kegan Paul, 1973.

Hollen, Godescalcus *[Gottschalk]. Preceptorium divinae legis.* Nuremberg: Koberger, 1499.

Holthausen, Ferdinand. "Rezepte, Segen und Zaubersprüche aus zwei Stockholmer Handschriften." *Anglia* 19 (1897): 74–88.

Honko, Lauri. *Krankheitsprojektile: Untersuchungen über eine urtümliche Krankheitserklärung.* Helsinki: Academia Scientiarum Fennica, 1959.

Honorius. *Le livre des conjurations du Pape Honorius.* Rome: Trajectoire, 1670. Reprint, Paris: Éditions Magnard, 2001.

Howald, Ernst, and Heinrich E. Sigerist, eds. *Antonii Musae de Herba Vettonica Liber. Pseudo-Apulei Herbarius. Anonymi de taxone liber. Sexti Placiti Liber medicinae ex animalibus, etc.* Leipzig and Berlin: Teubner, 1927.

Jacquart, Danielle, and Agostino Paravicini Bagliani, eds. *La Scuola medica salernitana: Gli autori e i testi.* Salerno and Florence: SISMEL, 2004.

Jacquart, Danielle, and Claude Thomasset, et al. *Lexique de la langue scientifique (Astrologie, Mathématiques, Médicine): Matériaux pour le Dictionnaire du Moyen Français.* Paris: Klincksieck, 1997.

Johannes de Cuba. *Hortus Sanitatus.* Strassburg: Prüss, 1497.

Joret, Charles. "Les Incantations botaniques des manuscrits F. 277 de la Bibliothèque de l'École de médecine de Montpellier et F. 19 de la Bibliothèque académique de Breslau." *Romania* 17 (1888): 337–54.

Josephus, Flavius. *The Works of Flavius Josephus.* Translated by William Whiston. Philadelphia: David McKay, n.d.

Joubert, Laurent. *La Première et Seconde partie des erreurs populaires, touchant la Médecine et le régime de santé.* Rouen: Du Petit Val, 1601.

Julliard, André. "Gestes et paroles populaires du malheur: Pratiques médicales magiques et sorcellerie dans les sociétés rurales contemporaines de la Bresse et du Bugey (Ain)." Thesis, Paris Descartes University (Paris V), 1985.

Kieckhefer, Richard. *Magic in the Middle Ages.* Cambridge: Cambridge University Press, 1989.

Kirchert, Klaus, and Dorothea Klein. *Die Vokabulare von Fritsche Closener und Jakob Twinger von Königshofen, Überlieferungsgeschichtliche Ausgabe.* 3 vols. Tübingen: Niemeyer, 1995.

Klapper, Joseph. *Erzählungen des Mittelaters.* Breslau: M. & H. Marcus, 1914.

———. "Das Gebet im Zauberglauben des Mittelalters, aus schlesischen Quellen." *Mitteilungen der schlesischen Gesellschaft für Volkskunde* 9 (1907): 5–41.

Klintberg, Bengt af. *Svenska trollformler.* Stockholm: Wahlström and Widstrand, 1965.

Kropej, Monika. "Charms in the Context of Magic Practice: The Case of Slovenia." *Folklore* 24 (2003): 62–77.

Kuhlen, Franz-Josef. *Zur Geschichte der Schmerz-, Schlaf-, und Betäubungsmittel in Mittelalter und früher Neuzeit.* Stuttgart: Deutscher Apotheker Verlag, 1983.

Kornreuther, Johann. *Magia ordinis atrium et scientiarum abstrusarum. Anno 1515.* Wellcome Library, MS. 3130.

Kramer, Heinrich. *Malleus maleficarum 1487 von Heinrich Kramer (Institoris).* Edited by Günter Jerouschek. Hildesheim: Olms, 1992.

Kramer, Heinrich [Institoris], and Jacob Sprenger. *Malleus meleficarum.* Nuremburg: Koberger, 1496.

Kvamsboka. In Velle Espeland, ed., *Svartbok frå Gudbrandsdalen,* 42–61. Oslo, Bergen, Tromsø: Universitetsforlaget, 1974.

ΚΥΡΑΝΙΣ: Mély, Ferdinand de. *Les Lapidaires de l'Antiquité au Moyen Âge.* Vol. 2, pts. 1 and 2: Les lapidaires grecs. Paris: Leroux, 1898.

Laisnel de la Salle, Germain. *Croyances et légendes du centre de la France.* Paris: A. Chaix et Cie, 1875–1881.

Laissez dire et faites le bien: Le Médecin des pauvres. Troyes: Baudot, n.d. (circa 1840).

Laubach, Fritz. *Krankheit und Heilung in biblischer Sicht.* Wuppertal: Brockhaus, 1976.

Laurens, André du. *De mirabili strumas sanandi, solis Galliae regibus christianis divinitus concessa.* Paris : N.p., 1609.

Le Blevec, Daniel. "Pharmocopée populaire en Comtat Venaissin: Les recettes du notaire Jean Vital (1395)." *Razo* 4 (1984): 127–31.

Lebrun, Pierre. *Histoire critique des pratiques superstitieuses qui ont séduit les Peuples & embarraffé les Savans.* Vol. I. Paris: Desprez and Cavelier, 1750.

———. *Superstitions anciennes et modernes, préjugés vulgaires qui ont induit les Peuples à des usages & à des Pratiques contraires à la Religion.* Amsterdam: Bernard, 1733.

Leclerc, Marie-Dominique. "Les maladies des femmes dans la Bibliothèque bleue." *La Vie en Champagne* 340 (1984): 16–21.

———. "Les mères douloureuses et les innocences persécutées dans l'imaginaire populaire: Essai d'analyse iconographique." *Bulletin de la Société Archéologique, Historique et Artistique* 328–31 (1993–94): 223–34, 260–73, 306–20, 458–72.

Lecouteux, Claude. "Agla: Remarques sur un mot magique." In *Le Secret d'Odin: Mélanges pour Régis Boyer.* Edited by Marc Auchet, 19–34. Nancy: P.U.N., 2001.

———. "Agla, Sator: Quelques remarques sur les *charmes* médicaux au Moyen Âge." *Nouvelle Plume: Revue d'Études mythologiques et symboliques* 2 (2001): 19–34.

———. *The Book of Grimoires: The Secret Grammar of Magic.* Rochester, Vt.: Inner Traditions, 2013.

———. "Le *cauchemar* dans les croyances populaires européennes." In *Le Cauchemar: mythologie, folklore, arts et littérature*. edited by Bernard Terramorsi, 75–86. Paris: SEDES, 2004.

———. "Un démon des croyances populaires: L'esprit-amant." *Mythes, Symboles, Littératures* 2 (2002): 21–32.

———. *Demons and Spirits of the Land: Ancestral Lore and Practices*. Rochester, Vt.: Inner Traditions, 2015.

———. *Dictionary of Ancient Magic Words and Spells: From Abraxas to Zoar*. Rochester, Vt.: Inner Traditions, 2015.

———. "Le double, le cauchemar, la sorcière." *Études germaniques* 43 (1988): 395–405.

———. *Eine Welt im Abseits: Studien zur niederen Mythologie und Glaubenswelt des Mittelalters*. Dettelbach: Röll, 2001.

———. *Elle courait le garou: Lycanthropes, hommes-ours, hommes-tigres*. Paris: Corti, 2008.

———. *The High Magic of Talismans and Amulets: Tradition and Craft*. Rochester, Vt.: Inner Traditions, 2014.

———. *A Lapidary of Sacred Stones: Their Magical and Medicinal Powers Based on the Earliest Sources*. Rochester, Vt.: Inner Traditions, 2012.

———. "Les maîtres du temps: Tempestaires, obligateurs, défenseurs." In *Le Temps qu'il fait au Moyen Âge: Phénomènes atmosphériques dans la littérature, la pensée scientifique et religieuse*. Edited by Joëlle Ducos and Claude Thomasset, 151–69. Paris: P.U.P.S., 1998.

———. "Mara–Ephialtes–Incubus: Le cauchemar." *Études germaniques* 42 (1987): 1–24.

———. "La médecine magique au Moyen Âge." In *Guérir l'âme et le corps: Au-delà des médecines habituelles*. Edited by Phillipe Wallon, 176–87. Paris: Albin Michel, 2000.

———. *Les Nains et les Elfes au Moyen Âge*. Paris: Imago, 2013.

———. "Les pierres magiques et le merveilleux." In *Deutsch-französische Germanistik: Mélanges pour Émile Georges Zink*. Edited by Sieglinde Hartmann and Claude Lecouteux, 53–67. Goppingen: Kümmerle, 1984.

———. *Phantom Armies of the Night: The Wild Hunt and the Ghostly Processions of the Undead*. Rochester, Vt.: Inner Traditions, 2011.

———. "Romanisch-germanische Kulturberührungen am Beispiel des Mahls der Feen." *Mediävistik* 1 (1988): 87–99.

———. *The Secret History of Poltergeists and Haunted Houses: From Pagan Folklore to Modern Manifestations*. Rochester, Vt.: Inner Traditions, 2012.

———. "Trois hypothèses sur nos voisins invisibles." In *Hugur: Mélanges offerts à Régis Boyer pour son 65e anniversaire*. Edited by Claude Lecouteux and Olivier Gouchet, 289–97. Paris: P.U.P.S., 1997.

———. *Witches, Werewolves, and Fairies: Shapeshifters and Astral Doubles in the Middle Ages*. Rochester, Vt.: Inner Traditions, 2003.

Lecouteux, Corrine, and Claude Lecouteux. *Contes, Diableries et Autres Merveilles au Moyen Âge*. Paris: Imago, 2013.

Le Mesnagier de Paris. Edited by G. E. Brereton and J. M. Ferrier. Paris: Le Livre de Poche, 1994, coll. "Lettres gothiques."

Leonardi, Camillo. *Les Pierres talismaniques (Speculum lapidum, livre III)*. Edited and translated with commentary by Claude Lecouteux and Anne Monfort. Paris: P.U.P.S., 2003.

Le Pesant, M. "Prières superstitieuses du pays d'Ouche." *Annales de Normandie* 3, nos. 3–4 (1953): 327–36.

Le Roy Ladurie, Emmanuel. "L'aiguillette." *Europe* (March, 1974): 134–46.

Les Agronomes Latins, Caton, Varron, Columelle, Palladius. Paris: Dubochet, 1844.

Lévi-Strauss, Claude. *The Savage Mind*. Chicago: University of Chicago Press, 1966.

Lexa, François. *La Magie dans l'Égypte antique*. Paris: Geuthner, 1925.

Liber Kyranidorum. Textes latins et vieux français relatifs aux Cyranides. Edited by Louis Delatte. Liège and Paris: Droz, 1942.

Livre des simples médecines, codex Bruxellensis IV 1024: A 15th-century French Herbal. Edited by Carmélia Opsomer and William Thomas Stearn. 2 vols. Antwerp: De Schutter, 1984.

Lüthi, Max. *Volksliteratur und Hochliteratur: Menschenbild—Thematik—Formstreben*. Bern and Munich: Francke, 1970.

Macer Floridus. *De viribus herbarum una cum Walafridi Strabonis, Othonis Cremonensis et Ioannis Folcz carminibus similis argumenti, etc*. Edited by Johann Ludwig Choulant. Leipzig: Voss, 1832.

Mackenzie, D. A. "Colour Symbolism." *Folk-lore* 33, no. 2 (1922): 136–69.

Malzew, Alexei P. *Bitt-, Dank- und Weihe-Gottesdienste der Orthodox-Katholischen Kirche des Morgenlandes*. Berlin: Siegismund, 1897.

Mansi, Giovanni. *Sacrorum conciliorum nova et amplissima collectio*. 31 vols. Florence and Venice, 1758–98.

Manuel do Vale de Moura. *De incantationibus seu ensalmis opusculum primum*. Évora: Crasbeeck, 1620.

Marbode. *Marbode of Rennes' "De lapidibus."* Edited by John M. Riddle. Translated by C. W. King. Wiesbaden: Steiner, 1977.

Marcellus of Bordeaux. *Marcelli De medicamentis liber*. Edited by Max Niedermann and Eduard Liechtenhan. 2 vols. Berlin: Akademie-Verlag, 1968.
Martin of Braga. *Martini episcopi Bracarensis opera omnia*. Edited by Claude W. Barlow. New Haven: Yale University Press, 1950.
Martino, Ernesto de. *La Terre des remords*. Translated by Claude Poncet. Paris: Gallimard, 1966.
Martinus de Arles. *Tractatus de superstitionibus, contra maleficia seu sortilegia quae hodie vigent in orbe terrarum*. Rome: Vincentium Luchinum, 1559.
Marzell, Heinrich. *Geschichte und Volkskunde der deutschen Heilpflanzen*. Stuttgart: Hippocrates Marquardt, 1938.
Masing, Oskar, ed. *Volksmedizin*. Dresden: Ehlermann, 1938.
Maspero, Gaston. *Recueil de travaux relatifs à la philologie et à l'archéologie égyptiennes et assyriennes*. 40 vols. Paris: Honoré Champion, 1870–1923.
Matton, Sylvain. *La magie arabe traditionnelle*. Paris: Retz, 1976.
Mazalova, Natalia E. "La médecine populaire dans les villages de la Russie du Nord." *Ethnologie française* 26:4 (1996): 666–76.
Le Médecin des pauvres. Châlons-sur-Saône: Montalan, 1857.
Le Médecin des pauvres. Troyes: Baudot, n.d.
Merceron, Jacques E. "Une démarche médico-magique de la religion populaire: Tirer les saints, déterminer la maîtresse place et voyager (XVIe–XXIe siècles)." *Mythologie française* 256 (2014): 70–86.
Mesmin, Claude. "Un objet thérapeutique: La prière." *Nouvelle Revue d'Ethnopsychiatrie* 33 (1997): 109–46.
Le Mesnagier de Paris. Edited by G. E. Brereton and J. M. Ferrier. Paris: Le Livre de Poche, 1994. Coll. "Lettres gothiques."
Meyer, Paul. "Recettes médicales en français publiées d'après le ms. B. N. lat. 8654 B." *Romania* 37 (1908): 358–77.
Meyrac, Albert. *Traditions, Coutumes, Légendes et Contes des Ardennes*. Charleville: Le Petit Ardennais, 1890. Reprint, Avallon: Éditions F.E.R.N., 1966.
MGH = *Monumenta Germaniae Historica*. Digitized versions online at: www.dmgh.de
Migne, J.-P. *Patrologia graeca*. 161 vols. Paris: Migne Imprimerie Catholique, 1857–66.
Mizauld, Antoine. *Memorabilium, utilium ac iucundorum centuriae novem*. Lutetia [Paris]: Morelle, 1584.
Moulinier, Laurence. "La science des urines de Maurus de Salerne et les Sinthomata magistri Mauri inédits." In *La Scuola medica salernitana: Gli autori e i testi*. Edited by Danielle Jacquart and Agostino Paravicini Bagliani, 261–81. Salerno and Florence: Sismel, 2004.

———. *L'Uroscopie au Moyen Âge: "Lire dans une verre la nature de l'homme."* Paris: Champion, 2012.

Mozzani, Éloïse. *Le Livre des superstitions: Mythes, croyances et légendes.* Paris: Laffont, 1995.

Müller, Gottfried. *Aus mittelenglischen Medizintexten: Die Prosarezepte des Stockholmer Miszellankodex X.90.* Leipzig: Tauchnitz, 1929.

Müller, Irmgard. *Die pflanzlichen Heilmittel bei Hildegard von Bingen.* Salzburg: Müller, 1982.

———. "Krankheit und Heilmittel im Werk Hildegards von Bingen." In *Hildegard von Bingen, 1179–1979, Festschrift zum 800. Todestag der Heiligen.* Edited by Anton P. Brück, 311–49. Mainz: Selbstverlag der Gesellschaft für Mittelrheinische Kirchengeschichte, 1979.

Naphy, William, and Andrew Spicer. *The Black Death and the History of Plagues, 1345–1730.* Stroud, UK: Tempus, 2000.

Nasturel, Petre. "Autour du phylactère slavo-roumain de Budaneşti." *Études et documents balkaniques et méditerranéens* 4 (1887): 52–55.

Nelson, Nicolas. *Charmes et bénédictions. Reflets de l'univers mental du monde médiéval, étude d'un corpus germanique.* Ph.D. thesis. Paris-Sorbonne, 2005.

Nergaard, Sigurd. *Skikk og bruk: Folkeminne fraa Østerdalen, V.* Oslo: Norsk folkeminnelag, 1927.

Newall, Venetia, ed. *The Witch Figure: Folklore Essays by a Group of Scholars in England Honoring the 75th Birthday of Katherine M. Briggs.* London and Boston: Routledge & Kegan Paul, 1973.

Nisard, Charles. *Histoire des livres populaires.* 2nd ed. 2 vols. Paris: Dentu, 1864.

Oeconomidès, Démétrès. "Yello dans les traditions des peuples Hellénique et roumain." Λαογραφία 22 (1965): 328–34.

Les Œuvres magiques de Henri-Corneille Agrippa, mises en français par Pierre d'Aban; avec des secrets occultes, notamment celui de la Reine des Mouches velues. Rome: N.p., 1744.

Ohrt, Ferdinand. *Die ältesten Segen über Christi Taufe und Christi Tod in religionsgeschichtlichem Lichte.* Copenhagen: Levin & Munksgaard, Ejnar Munksgaard, 1938.

———. *Danmarks trylleformler.* 2 vols. Copenhagen and Christiania [Oslo]: Gyldendal / Nordisk forlag, 1917–1921.

———. *De danske Besvaergelser mod Vrid og Blod: Tolkning og Forhistorie.* Copenhagen: Høst & Søn, 1922.

———. *Fluchtafel und Wettersegen.* Helsinki: Academia scientiarum fennica, 1929.

———. *Herba, gratiâ plena; die legenden der älteren segensprüche über den göttlichen ursprung der heil- und zauberkräute*. Helsinki: Academia scientiarum fennica, 1929.

———. "Über Alter und Ursprung der Begegnungssegen." *Hessische Blätter für Volkskunde* 35 (1936): 49–58.

———. "Zu den Jordansegen." *Zeitschrift für Volkskunde, Neue Folge* 1 (1930): 269–74.

Olsan, Lea. "The Three Good Brothers Charms: Some Historical Points." *Incantatio* 1 (2011).

Önnerfors, Alf. "Iatromagische Beschwörungen in der *Physica Plinii Sangallensis*." New § 83 (1985): 235–52.

Oudin, Antoine. *Curiositez françoises pour supplément aux dictionnaires*. Rouen: de Sommaville, 1656.

Paré, Ambroise. *La Méthode de traicter les playes faictes par hacquebutes et aultres bastons à feu et de celles qui sont faictes par flèches, dardz, et semblables, aussi des combustions spécialement faictes par la pouldre à canon*. Paris: Gaulterot, 1545.

Peterson, E. "Engel- und Dämonennamen, nomina barbara." *Rheinisches Museum für Philologie, Neue Folge* 75:4 (1926): 393–421.

Patera, Marie. "Les rites *d'extraction* des *plantes* dans l'Antiquité: Magie, botanique et religion; L'exemple de la mandragore." *Revue des Archéologues et des Historiens d'Art de Louvain* 27 (1994): 21–34.

Pelagonius. *Artis veterinariae quae extant*. Edited by Maximilian Ihm. Leipzig: Teubner, 1892.

Pedanii Dioscuridis Anazarbei De Materia Medica Libri quinque. Edited by Max Wellmann. Berlin: Weidmann, 1906–1914.

Petit Albert: Secrets merveilleux de la magie naturelle et cabalistique du Petit Albert. Lyon: Beringos Fratres, 1764.

Petzold, Leander, ed. *Magie und Religion*. Darmstadt: Wissenschaftliche Buchgesellschaft, 1978.

Peuckert, Will-Erich. "Die Egyptischen Geheimnisse." *Arv* 10 (1954): 40–96.

Picatrix [the *Ghāyat al-hakīm*]. Bibliothèque nationale, France, 14788.

Phaneg, G. [Georges Descormiers]. "L'Écho du merveilleux" 219 (February 15, 1906): 74–79.

Pinon, Roger. "Une très vielle prière à sainte Apolline." *Enquêtes du Musée de la Vie Wallonne* 169–72 (1980–1981): 1–47.

Platearius, Matthaeus. *Livre des simples médecines*. French translation of *Liber de simplici medicina dictus Circa instans de Platearius tirée d'un manuscript du XIIIe siècle* (MS 31113 of the St. Geneviève Library of Paris). Paris: Société française d'histoire de la médecine, 1913.

Pliny [the Elder]. C. *Plini Secundi Naturalis historiae libri XXXVII*. 6 vols. Edited by Ludwig von Jan. Leipzig: Teubner, 1865–1870.

———. *The Natural History*. Translated by John Bostock and H. T. Riley. London: Bohn, 1857. Perseus Digital Library, http://www.perseus.tufts.edu/hopper.

Pócs, Éva. "Evil Eye in Hungary: Belief, Ritual, Incantation." In *Charms and Charming in Europe*. Edited by Jonathan Roper. New York: Palgrave Macmillan, 2004.

Porta, Giambattista della. *Phytognomonica*. Frankfurt: Wechel & Fischer, 1591.

Pradel, Fritz. *Griechische und süditalienische Gebete, Beschwörungen und Rezepte des Mittelalters*. Giessen: Toppelmann, 1907.

Pseudo-al-Bûnî. *Ourte Šams al-maʿārif al-ṣuġrā* [*The Little Sun of the Understandings*]. Cited by Coulon. *La magie islamique*, 1273.

Pseudo-Apuleius. *Herbarius*. In *Antonii Musae de Herba Vettonica Liber. Pseudo-Apulei Herbarius. Anonymi de taxone liber. Sexti Placiti Liber medicinae ex animalibus, etc.* Edited by Ernst Howald and Heinrich E. Sigerist. Leipzig and Berlin: Teubner, 1927.

Pseudo-Theodore. See *Theodori Prisciani Euporiston*.

Puhlmann, Theodor. "Die lateinische medizinische Literatur des frühen Mittelalters: Ein bibliographischer Vesuch." *Kyklos* 3 (1930): 395–416.

Rätsch, Christian. *Lexikon der Zauberpflanzen aus ethnologischer Sicht*. Graz: Akademische Druck- und Verlagsanstalt, 1988.

Reichborn-Kjennerud, Ingjald. "Krankheit und Heilung in der Frühgeschichte Norwegens." *Niederdeutsche Zeitschrift für Volkskunde* 14 (1936): 1–17.

———. *Vår gamle trolldomsmedisin*. 5 vols. Oslo: Dybwad, 1927–47.

Reier, Herbert. *Leben, Krankheiten und Heilungen im Mittelalter (800–1400)*. Kiel: Reier, 1987.

Rituale Romanum Pauli V Pontificus Maximi. Rome: N.p., 1955.

Rochholtz, Ernst Ludwig. "Aargauer Besegnungen." *Zeitschrift für deutsche Mythologie und Sittenkunde* 4 (1859): 103–40.

Röhrich, Lutz. "Krankheitsdämonen." In *Volksmedizin: Probleme und Forschungsgeschichte*. Edited by Elfriede Grabner, 283–88. Darmstadt: Wissenschaftliche Buchgesellschaft, 1987.

Roper, Jonathan, ed. *Charms and Charming in Europe*. New York: Palgrave Macmillan, 2004.

Roscher, Wilhelm Heinrich. *Ausführliches Lexikon der griechischen und römischen Mythologie*. Leipzig: Teubner, 1884.

Rothschuh, Karl E. *Iatromagie: Begriff, Merkmale, Motive, Systematik*. Opladen: Westdeutscher Verlag, 1978.

Rybakov, Boris. *Le paganisme des anciens Slaves*. Paris: Puf, 1994.
Saintyves, Pierre. *Les Grimoires à oraisons magiques*. Paris: Nourry, 1926.
———. *La Guérison des verrues: De la magie médicale à la psychothérapie*. Paris: Nourry, 1913.
———. "Le transfert des maladies aux arbres et aux buissons." *Bulletin de la Société préhistorique française* 15:6 (1918): 296–300.
Sauvé, Léopold-François. *Lavarou Koz / Proverbes et dictons de la Basse-Bretagne*. Paris: Champion, 1878.
Schipperges, Heinrich. *Hildegard von Bingen: Heilkunde. Das Buch von dem Grund und Wesen und der Heilung der Krankheiten*. Salzburg: Müller, 1957.
Schmitt, Peter. *Liber ordinis rerum (Esse-Essencia-Glossar)*. 2 vols. Tübingen: Niemeyer, 1983.
Schneegans, Heinrich. "Sizilianische Gebete, Beschwörungen und Rezepte in griechischer Umschrift." *Zeitschrift für romanische Philologie* 32:5 (1908): 571–94.
Schnell, Bernhard, Klaus Grubmüller, Hans-Jürgen Stahl, Erltraud Auer, and Reinhard Pawis. *Vocabularius ex quo: Überlieferungsgeschichtliche Ausgabe*. 6 vols. Tübingen: Niemeyer, 1988–89.
Schöpf, Hans. *Zauberkräuter*. Graz: Akademische Druck- und Verlagsanstalt, 1986.
Schullerus, Pauline. *Rumänische Volksmärchen aus dem mittleren Harbachtal*. Edited by Rolf W. Brednich and Ion Taloş. Bucharest: Kriterion, 1977.
Schuster, Friedrich Wilhelm. *Siebenbürgisch-sächsische Volkslieder, Sprichwörter, Räthsel, Zauberformeln, und Kinder-Dichtungen*. Hermannstadt: Steinhaussen, 1865.
Scot, Reginald. *The discoverie of witchcraft, Wherein the lewde dealing of witches and witchmongers is notablie detected, the knaverie of coniurors, the impietie of inchantors, the follie of soothsaiers, the impudent falsehood of cousenors, the infidelitie of atheists, the pestilent practices of Pythonists, the curiositie of figure-casters, the vanitie of dreamers, the beggerlie art of Alcumystrie, The abhomination of idolatrie, the horrible art of poisoning, the vertue and power of naturall magike and all the conveiances of Legierdemaine and iuggling are deciphered: and many other things opened, which have long lien hidden, howbeit very necessarie to be knowne*. London: Brome, 1584.
Sébillot, Paul. *Le Folklore de France*. 4 vols. Paris: Maisonneuve & Larose, 1904–1907.
Seligman, Siegfried. *Der böse Blick und Verwandtes: Ein Beitrag zur Geschichte des Aberglaubens aller Zeiten und Völker*. Berlin: Barsdorf, 1910.

Sethe, Kurt. *Die Altaegyptischen Pyramidentexte Pyramidentexte nach den Papierabdrucken und Photographien des Berliner Museums.* 3 vols. Leipzig: Hinrichs, 1908–12.

Seyfarth, Carly. *Aberglaube und Zauberei in der Volksmedizin Sachsens: Ein Beitrag zur Volkskunde des Königreichs Sachsen.* Leipzig: Heims, 1913.

Sigerist, Henry E. *Studien und Texte zur frühmittelalterlichen Rezeptliteratur.* Leipzig: Barth, 1923.

Singer, Charles. "The Herbal in Antiquity and Its Transmission to Later Ages." *Journal of Hellenic Studies* 47:1 (1927): 1–52.

Stahl, Paul-Henri. "L'organisation magique du territoire villageois roumain." *L'Homme* XIII/3 (1973).

Staricius, Johannes. *Grimoire ou la Magie naturelle.* The Hague, n.d. (circa 1750).

Storms, Gotfrid. *Anglo-Saxon Magic.* The Hague: Nijhoff, 1948.

Svartebok in Ål. Norwegian Folklore Archives (NFS), University of Oslo, Blindern.

Taylor, Archer. "*Vogel federlos* Once More." *Hessische Blätter für Volkskunde* 49–50 (1958): 277–94.

Terramorsi, Bernard, ed. *Le Cauchemar: Mythologie, folklore, arts et littérature.* Paris: SEDES, 2004.

Tettau, Wilhelm A. J., and Jodocus Deodatus Hubertus Temme. *Die Volkssagen Ostpreussens, Litthauens und Westpreussens.* Berlin: Nicolai, 1837.

Theatrum Diabolorum, Das ist: Ein sehr nützliches verstenndiges Buch, etc. Frankfurt: Schmid, 1569.

Theodori Prisciani Euporiston libri III, cum physicorum fragmento et additamentis pseudo-Theodoreis. Edited by Valentino Rose. Leipzig: Teubner, 1894.

Thiers, Jean-Baptiste. *Traité des superstitions selon l'Écriture sainte.* Paris: Dezallier, 1679.

———. *Traité des superstitions qui regardent les sacrements selon l'Écriture sainte, les décrets des conciles et les sentiments des saints pères et des théologiens.* 4 vols. Avignon: Chambeau, 1777.

———. *Traité des superstitions: Croyances populaires et rationalité à l'Âge classique.* Edited by J. M. Goulemot. Paris: Le Sycomore, 1984.

Tillhagen, Carl-Herman. "The Conception of the Nightmare in Sweden." In *Humaniora: Essays in Literature, Folklore, Bibliography; Honoring Archer Taylor on His Seventieth Birthday.* Edited by Wayland Hand and Gustave Arlt, 317–39. New York: Augustin, 1960.

———. *Folklig läkekonst.* Stockholm: LTs Förlag, 1962.

Timotin, Emanuela. "Un aspect méconnu des fées roumaines: Observation sur un texte magique manuscrit." *Revue des Études sud-est Européennes* 45 (2007): 433–43.

———. *Les Charmes roumains manuscrits: Évolution et transmission d'un savoir traditionnel aux XVIIIe–XIXe siècles*. Thesis, Grenoble III, 2009.

———. *Descântecele manuscrise românești (secolele al XVII-lea–al XIX-lea)*. Bucharest: Academiei Române, 2010.

———. "Irodia, doamna zânelor: Notes sur les fées roumaines et leur cohorte fantastique." In *Les entre-mondes: Les vivants, les morts*. Edited by Karin Ueltschi and Myriam White-Lee Goff, 179–94. Paris: Klincksieck, 2009.

———. *Limba descântecelor românești*. Thesis, Bucharest University, 2007.

———. "The *Năjit* between Prayers and Charms: A Study of the Romanian Manuscript Tradition." In *The Power of Words: Studies on Charms and Charming in Europe*. Edited by James A. Kapaló, Éva Pócs, and William Francis Ryan, 239–56. Budapest and New York: CEU Press, 2013.

———. *Paroles protectrices, paroles guérisseuses. La tradition manuscrite des charmes roumains (XVIIe-XIXe siècle)*, Paris : P.U.P.S., 2015.

Trüb, Carl Ludwig Paul. *Heilige und Krankheit*. Stuttgart: Klett-Cotta, 1978.

Trümpy, Hans. "Similia similibus." *Schweizerisches Archiv für Volkskunde* 62 (1966).

Vair, Leonard. *De fascino libri tres*. Venice: Apud Aldum, 1589.

———. *Trois livres des charmes, sorcelages, ov enchantemens*. Paris: Chesneau, 1583.

Vaisbrot, Marc. "Édition critique de la *Compilatio singularis exemplorum* (seconde partie) d'apres les mss. d'Upsal, de Tours, et de Berne." Thesis, l'École des Chartes, Paris, 1968.

Vaitkevičienė, Daiva. *Lietuvių užkalbėjimai: Gydymo formulės*. Vilnius: Lietuvių literatūros ir tautosakos institutas, 2008.

Vegetius. *P. Vegeti Renati Digestorum artis mulomedicinae libri*. Edited by Ernst Lommatzsch. Leipzig: Teubner, 1903.

Villeneuve, Roland. *L'Envoûtement*. Geneva and Paris: La Palatine, 1963.

Vinagradova, L. N. "Les croyances slaves concernant l'esprit-amant." *Cahiers slaves* 1 (1997): 237–53.

Vinjeboka: Den eldste svartebok fra norsk middelalter. Edited by Oskar Garstein. Oslo: Solum, 1993.

Wackernagel, Hans Georg. "Ein schweizerischer *Waffensegen* aus dem 16. Jahrhundert." *Schweizerisches Archiv für Volkskunde* 40 (1942–44): 121–23.

Weyer, Johann. *De praestigiis daemonum et incantationibus ac ueneficiis libri sex*. Basel: Oporinus, 1568.

———. *Medicarum observationum libri II*. Amsterdam: van den Berge, 1660.

———. *Witches, Devils, and Doctors in the Renaissance: Johann Weyer, De praestigiis daemonum*. Translated by John Shea. Binghamton, N.Y.: Medieval and Renaissance Texts and Studies, 1991.

Whipple, A. D. *The Story of Wound Healing and Wound Repair*. Springfield, Ill.: Charles C. Thomas, 1963.

Wickersheimer, Ernest. "Figures médico-astrologiques des IXe, Xe et XIe siècles." *Janus* 19 (1914): 157–77.

———. *La médecine et les médecins en France a l'époque de la Renaissance*. Paris: Maloine, 1905.

William of Alvernus. *De universo*. In *Opera omnia*. Vol. 1. Frankfurt : Minerva, 1963.

Wipf, Karl A. *Althochdeutsche poetische Texte*. Stuttgart: Reclam, 1992.

Wittich, Engelbert. "Zauber und Aberglauben *der Zigeuner*." *Schweizerisches Archiv für Volkskunde* 15 (1911): 147–51.

Wlislocki, Heinrich von. *Volksdichtungen der siebenbürgischen und südungarischen Zigeuner*. Vienna: Graeser, 1890.

———. *Volksglaube und Volksbrauch der Siebenbürger Sachsen*. Berlin: Felber, 1893.

Wolters, Paul. *"Faden und Knoten als Amulett." Archiv für Religionswissenschaft* 8 (1905): 1–22.

Wuttke, Adolf. *Der deutsche Volksaberglaube der Gegenwart*. Berlin: Wiegandt & Grieben, 1900.

Zachariae, Theodor. "Abergläubische Meinungen und Gebräuche des Mittelalters in den Predigten Bernardinos von Siena." *Zeitschrift des Vereins für Volkskunde* 22 (1912): 113–34, 225–44.

Ziegler, Konrat, and Walther Sontheimer. *Der Kleine Pauly. Lexikon der Antike*. 5 vols. Munich: DTV, 1979.

Zingerle, Oswald von. "Segen und Heilmittel aus einer Wolfsthurner Handschrift des XV. Jahrhunderts." *Zeitschrift für Volkskunde* 1 (1891): 172–77; 315–24.

Zoega, Georg. *Catalogus codicum copticorum manuscriptorum qui in museo Borgiano Velitris adservantur*. Rome, 1810. Reprint, Leipzig: Hinrichs, 1903.

Zupanič Slavec, Zvonka, and Marija Makarovič, eds. *Zagovori v slovenski ljudski medicini ter zarotitve in apokrifne molitve*. Ljubljana: Inštitut za zgodovino medicine Medicinske fakultete, 1999.

INDEX

abscess, 34–35
affliction, 36
airy spirits, 204
Allatius, Leo, 201
amulets, 6–7, 8
angina, of the throat, 36–37
animals, healing of
    blood flow, 212
    bouquet (sheep scab), 212–13
    charbon (anthrax), 213–14
    to cleanse a cow's milk, 220
    to cure a cow of disease, 220–21
    farcy, 214
    fertility, 214–15
    ganglia, 215
    horses, 219–20
    laminitis, 215
    livestock diseases, 219
    nail wound, 216
    paralysis of horses, 216–17
    against sickness, 220
    sprain, 217
    trenches of horses, 217–19
animals, protection of
    to allay magic arrows, 260
    for all evil spells, 261–62
    for bewitching livestock, 260–61
    to break and destroy all evil spells, 259
    counter-charm, 260
    against demon called Grief, 268–69
    against the evil eye, 259–60
    for the flock, 259, 264–65
    against fox bite, 267–68
    to free of all ills, 263
    general, 263, 265–67, 270
    for horses, 263, 266, 267, 270
    against hospodarice, 268
    for livestock, 262
    for pigs, 266, 269
    for sheep, 263, 264
    from spirits above the highest winds, 271
    against wolves, 265
anthrax, 37–38, 56–57
apotropaic spell, 233–34
Arles, Martinus de. *See* Martinus de Arles
arrowheads, to remove, 144
astrology, 15–17
Apollonia, Saint, 163
Augustine, Saint, 4–5

Balinas, protective talismans of, 291–93
Bergerac, Cyrano de. *See* Cyrano de Bergerac
Bernard de Gordon, 20
Bernardine of Siena, Saint, 22, 272

birth
  to accelerate, 40
  to compel to give, 39
  to deliver a child, 40–43
  difficult, 42–43
  illustration, 41
  late in giving, 38–39
  more quickly, 41
  overview, 38
  pains following, 43
  quick, 42
  without danger, 40
  woman cannot give, 42
  woman in long labor and, 42
birthmarks, to cure, 114
bites
  dog, 44
  ferocious beasts and, 45
  fox, 267–68
  scorpion, 45
  serpent and, 44
  snakebites, 43, 44–45, 46
  troll, 207, 208
  wolf, 46
bladder pain, 118
bleeding
  blood loss, 4
  against the gush of blood, 47–48
  hemorrhage, 49
  hemorrhage of the uterus, 50–51
  nosebleeds, 116–18
  spell against, 46
  to stop, 47, 48–50, 51–53
  of a vein, 48
blindness, 53
blood loss, 49
boils, 54, 55–56, 167–68
bolts, to extract, 144
Book of Grimoires, 26

breeches laces, knotting, 286–88
burns, 54

calander, 27
cankers, 55–56, 213
carreau, 133–34
catarrhs, 56
charbon, 56–57, 213–14
charms, 3, 6
children
  bewitched, to cure, 187–88
  catarrhs of, 56
  curses on, 184–85
  exposed, prayer against, 210–11
  to have, 148–49
  to heal of carreau, 134
  to know if cursed by the evil eye, 186–87
  protection from curses and illnesses, 230
cholera, orison in case of, 113–14
Christianity, 4–9
Circle of Petosiris, 14, 16
colic
  animal, 57
  to be cured of, 57–58
  protection from, 57
conjunctivitis, 112
constipation, 58
consumption, 68–69, 166
contagious diseases, 37–38
cough, 58
cow's milk, to cleanse, 220
cramps, 59
crops, protection of, 248
crying, to stop, 146
curses. *See also* evil spells
  against, 187
  cast on children, 184–85
  charm for lifting, 189

incantation against, 188
to lift, 183–84
lifting, 188–89
protection for children from, 230
against, so God may aid you, 189
cuts, 59–60
Cyrano de Bergerac, 275, 279

dark mood, against, 36
deafness, 60–61
delirium, to cure, 109
Delrio, Martin, 13, 25, 180, 288
demons
   charm against, 185–86, 191
   to drive away, 194, 195
   to expel from the body, 195
   to make flee, 193–94
   possession, 196
   prayer against, 205–6
   protection against attacks of, 204
   protection from, 231
   remedy for, 193
   spell against, 199–200
the devil
   against, 197
   against all temptations of, 203–4
   to chase away, 197
   incantation to Christ for driving away, 198–99
   malice, to eclipse, 194
   to protect horses from, 266
   protection against, 196
   those that copulate with, 203
diagnosis
   healers and, 14–15
   know how a patient is feeling, 29–30
   know if a patient is promised to death, 29–30
   know if a patient will live or die, 27–30, 32
   know if a patient will survive, 29–30
   know if a wounded man will recover, 31
   know when a patient will heal, 31
   learn if patient will be healed or not, 28
   prognosis of typhoid fever, 32
Dian Cecht, 3
dislocation, 108
doctors, medieval and sixteenth-century, 15–21
dog bite, 44
dropsy, to heal, 95
dry patch, 61

earaches, prayer for healing, 112
ear glands, swollen, 167
edema, to heal, 95
elves, 203–4
enchantment, to break, 184
encrypted spells, 281–83
enemies, protection against, 231, 237–38
envy, 180, 185–86
epilepsy
   against, 67
   to cure, 62, 65
   falling sickness and, 64–65, 66–67
   medicine against, 63–64
   memorization, 62
   spasms, to stop, 62
   spitting up of blood, to stop, 62
   succor an epileptic and, 65
   talismans of Balinas, 292
epistaxis, 116–18
erysipelas
   against, 67
   to get rid of, 68
   to treat, 68
Étisie, 68–69
evil, to send away, 192

evil eye, the
  against, 186
  to know if child has been cursed by, 186–87
  phylactery for children against, 229–30
  protection from, 229–30
  protection in animals, 259–60
  to thwart, 196–97
evil spells
  against, 184, 187
  bewitched children, to cure, 187–88
  to break and enchantment, 184
  charm against demons and envy, 185–86
  charm for lifting, 188–89
  to cure the bewitched, 183
  against curses so that God may aid you, 189
  to destroy, 192
  from the devil, against, 183
  against the evil eyes, 186
  fear of, 180
  to get rid of, 181
  of impotence, 181–83
  incantation against cast curses, 188
  to lift curses, 183–84
  to lift from a husband or wife, 183
  lifting, 188–89
  for no magic to harm you, 190
  protection from, 231
  protection of animals from, 261–62
evil spirits
  against all, 205
  to dispel, 211
  to drive away, 194
  protection against, 236–37
  to ward off, 205
eyes
  to clean, 69
  to cure, 104–6
  to expel ailments, 69
  to heal, 69
  leucoma and, 102–4
  ophthalmia and headaches, 70
  orison for a problem, 106
  pain, to relieve, 69–71
  protection of, 243
  sharpening sight and, 70
  styes, 152–53
  white spots, to cure, 69, 70, 104

falling sickness
  against, 64
  for, 65, 67
  mysterious ring for, 66
  requesting the healing of, 66
farcy, 214
fatigue, 71
fear, 71, 96
Fernel, Jean, 21, 284–85
ferocious beasts, driving away, 45
fertility, animal, 214–15
fever(s)
  against, 78, 79, 80
  for all, 72, 73, 74–75
  against all manner of, 112–13
  to cause to vanish, 75
  conjuration of, 75–77
  to cure, 71–72, 77
  defined, 71
  demi-tertian, 83–84
  to get rid of, 81
  to heal, 75, 77–78
  malaria treatment and, 81–82
  prayer for, 78–79
  quartan, 82–83
  to reduce, 72
  remedy for, 73–74
  spell for repelling, 73

tertian, 83–85
tertian and quartan, 84–85
for three types of, 79
finger/toenail abscess, 172
fire, protection against, 257
fistulas, 37–38, 55–56
Flavius Josephus, 1–2
flux, 85
foot
    abscess, 35
    sprained, 147
    varicose veins in, 169
fox bite, protection against, 267–68
fracture, 108
fruits, protection of, 247–48

ganglia, animal, 215
garden
    pests, benediction to kill, 244–47
    protection of, 243–44
ghosts, 197, 236–37
Gordon, Bernard de. *See* Bernard de Gordon
gout
    against, 87–88
    charm for relieving, 89
    conjuration of, 86–87
    to cure, 88
    defined, 85
    for, 85–86
    to heal, 86, 88
    to provide relief to the foot, 87
    to relieve pain of, 87
Grillandus, Paulus, 8, 12, 13
groin pain, 118
Gylou, spell against, 200

hail and storms, protection against, 248–50
hate and jealousy, protection against, 238

headaches
    against, 91
    to cure, 89, 90
    to dispel, 89
    to find relief from pain, 90
    for, 92
    to heal, 70, 90, 169
    migraines, 89, 91
    prayer for healing, 112
healers
    diagnosis and, 14–15
    duties of, 13
    European Union regulation and, 14
healing
    of animals, 212–21
    heterodox methods, condemnation of, 13–14
    plants, 20–21
    practices, curiosities in, 21–22
    practices, transmission of, 25–26
    several disorders, 121
    superstitious methods according to Fernel, 284–85
hearing, 60–61
heatstroke, 92–93
hemorrhages
    against, 49
    talisman of Balinas, 292
    of the uterus, 50–51
hemorrhoids, 93–94
herbs, 21
herpes, 61
hiccups, to stop, 94
Hildegard of Bingen, Saint, 25
hip problems, 138
holy fire, 136–37
horses
    to heal, 219–20
    paralysis of, 216–17
    to preserve good health of, 267

324   Index

protection of, 263, 266, 268–69, 270
trenches of, 217–19
house protection
   conjuration of rats, 257
   against enchantments, 254
   entire house, 253
   against fire, 257
   general, 254–57
   new house, 252–53
   against a thief, 257–58
   from witches and spirits, 254
hysteria, 95–96

Iele, against, 206
illnesses. *See also specific illnesses*
   against all, 96–97
   to expel, 110
   in general, 96–97
   invoking saints for, 289–90
   to make, take flight, 96
   protection for children from, 230
imbalance, 71
impetigo, 97–98
incantations
   against cast curses, 188
   for driving the devil away, 198–99
   early use of, 5
   as forbidden, 5
   against the serpent, 44
   for sore throats, 37
   against wolf bites, 46
inflammation
   of the joints, clipping, 98
   to lose, 61, 85
injury, prayer against, 113
insanity, 109
insomnia, 98–100, 115

jaundice, to cure, 100–101
joint pain, 118

journeys, protection on, 223–25

kidney pain, 119–20
kidney stones, talisman against, 120
Kircher, Athanasius, 17
knotting the breeches laces, 286–88

labor, long, 42
lactation, to increase, 101
laminitis, 215
Lebrun, Pierre, 18, 287
lethargy, 101
leucoma, 102–4
Lévi-Strauss, Claude, 6
lightning, protection against, 228, 250
livestock
   bewitched, 260–61
   to heal diseases, 219
   protection for, 260–61, 262
Longinus, charm of, 242
loss of speech, 106
lumbago, 138
lumps, 106–7
lunacy, 107–8
luxation, 108

madness, to cure, 108, 109
magic therapy, 8–9
malaria treatment, 81–82
malemort (tragic or sudden death), 109–10
malignant pustules, 56–57
Martinus de Arles, 39, 180, 245, 251
medical magic in Italy (14th–15th centuries), 272–73
memorization, 63
migraines, 89, 91. *See also* headaches
misfortune, to banish, 96
Mizauld, Antoine, 22
mouth, for ailments of, 155–56, 157

multiple-purpose recipes, 110–14

nail wounds, animals', 216
najit, against, 197–98
nasty bite, against, 208
neck pain, 122
von Nettesheim, Agrippa, 18, 275
nevus, 114
nightmares, 115–16, 197
night spirits, 203
night terrors, protection against, 193
nosebleeds, to stop, 116–18
nursing, 209

overheating, 92

pain
  against, 120–21
  amulet to relieve, 27
  bladder, 118
  to expel, 110
  eye, 69–71
  following birth, 43
  gout, 87
  groin, 118
  holy fire, to relieve, 136
  joint, 118–19
  kidney, 119–20
  neck, 122
  to remove, 121
  spleen, 146
  sprain, 147
  throat, 36–37
  tooth, 160
paishe, 123
palpitations, 122
Pandora, 1
Paracelsus, 20
parotides, 122
pestilences, 55–56

pigs
  protection of, 266, 269
  to rid of worms, 176
plague
  to get rid of, 123
  patients, blessing, 123–25
plants
  healing, 20–21
  in protection spells, 23
pleurisy, 125
poison
  against, 125, 126
  to drive away, 126–27
  protection against sudden death, 127
  to stop effects of, 126
Porta, Giambattista della, 20
possession
  demon, 196
  potion for, 193
pox, orison in case of, 113–14
property, protection of, 243–52
protection
  against airy spirits, 204
  against all damage, 235
  against all magic, 234
  of all things, 251–52
  of animals, 259–71
  bref, 225–26
  from charms and curses, 234, 238–40
  from colic, 57
  from cramps, 59
  of crops, 248
  from cuts, 59–60
  from danger on land or sea, 224
  for the dangers of the road, 223
  against dangers of water, 228
  against demons and enemies, 231
  against demons and spirits, 204
  against the devil, 196
  against diabolical glamors, 236

326   Index

against elves and night spirits, 203
against enemies, 237–38
from the evil eye, 229–30
from evil spells, 231
against evil spirits, 236–37
of the eyes, 243
of fruits, 247–48
of the garden, 243–47
against ghosts, 236–37
against hail, 248–50
against hate and jealousy, 238
of the house, 252–58
if you meet a bear, 229
importance of, 23
of the individual, 222–43
from insomnia and nightmares, 115
invoking saints for, 289–90
on a journey, 223–25
from lightning, 228
against lightning, 250
magical, 22–25
against miasms of earth and air, 241–42
from the night gods and fauns, 202
from nightmare demons, 115–16
from night terrors, 193
against nosebleeds, 116
from peril and sickness, 241
against phantoms, 236
practices, transmission of, 25–26
of property, 243–52
from rabid dogs, 44
recipes and rituals of, 23
second pentacle of the moon for, 227
from the shakes, 142
sixth pentacle of Jupiter for, 226–27
from snakebites, 43
from sore throats, 155
so that none may bewitch you, 235
against sudden death, 127
against the tempest, 248–50
while traveling, 222
against voults, 231–33
against weapons, 240–41
against witches, 234–35
for woman in labor, 209
pustules, 127–28

quartan fever, 82–83

rabid dogs, 44, 129
rabies, 128–29
rash, to get rid of, 129–31
rats, conjuration of, 257
revenants, charm against, 235
rheum, to cure, 131
rheumatism, 133
rickets, 133–34
ringworm, 134–35

safety, 71, 292–93
Saint Anthony's Fire, 136–37
saints, invoking for illnesses and protection, 289–90
Saint Vitus' dance, 66
scabies, 137
scarlet fever, 137
scarlet fever, orison in case of, 113–14
sciatica, 137–38
scorpion stings, 45
scrofula
    chasing away, 141
    defined, 138
    to heal, 140–41
    healing illustration, 139
    orison for requesting the healing of, 140
    overview, 138–39
scurvy, 142
second pentacle of the moon, 227

serpent, incantations against, 44
shakes, the, 142
sheep, protection of, 263
shingles, 143
shots
    arrowheads, to remove, 144
    charm against, 145
    for healing from arquebuses, 145–46
    types of, 144
sixth pentacle of Jupiter, 226–27
sleep
    to fall asleep, 99
    to induce, 99
    to make someone, 98–99
    to return to, 99–100
snakebites, 43, 44–45, 46
Solomon's seal, 1–2
sorcerers
    activities of, 274
    fear of, 274–75
    interrogation of, 274
sore throat
    against, 36
    charm against, 155
    for, 156
    to heal, 37
    incantation for, 37
    protection from, 155
spasmodic sob, 146
spasms, 59
speech, loss of, 106
Sphere of Bians, 16
spirit lover, against, 206–7
spirits. *See also* evil spirits
    conjuration of, 204
    house protection from, 254
    protection against, 204
    protection against attacks of, 204
spleen pain, 146

sprains
    against, 148
    animal, 217
    to heal, 147
    prayer for fixing, 147–48
    to relieve pain of, 147
squinancy, 158
sterility, 148–49
stings, 149
stomachaches
    charm for, 150
    great recipe against the pains of, 149–50
    orison for requesting the healing of, 66
    spell against, 151–52
stomach growls, 152
stomach worms, 173
styes, 152–53
sudden death, 109–10
sunstroke, 92–93
sweating sickness, orison in case of, 113–14
swollen glands, 153
syphilis, 153–54

talismans
    of Balinas, 291–93
    against scorpion stings, 45
tertian fever, 83–85
Testament of Solomon, The, 2–3
Thiers, Jean-Baptiste, 22, 275, 288
thieves, house protection against, 258–59
Thomas Aquinas, Saint, 6–8
thorns, 154–55
throat
    for ailments of, 156–57
    to dislodge bone from, 156
    for mouth and, 155–56
    problems, 155–57
    sore, 36–37, 155, 156

tongue, pustules on, 127–28
tongue bumps, 157–58
tonsillitis, 158
toothaches
   against, 162, 164–65
   to avoid, 165
   charm for, 159
   charm for Saint Apollonia, 163
   to cure, 158, 162, 165
   for, 160, 162–63
   to heal, 158, 165–66
   pain, to get rid of, 160
   prayer for healing, 112
   violent, 164
tooth worms, 172–73
torment, delivery from, 111
transplantatio morborum, 129, 130
travel fatigue, 71
traveling, protection while, 222
trembling, 74
trolls
   against the bite of, 207, 208–9
   prayer against, 205–6
tuberculosis, 166
tuberculosis of the bone, 166–67
tumors
   to dissolve, 168
   to heal, 167
   to rid, 25–26
typhus, orison in case of, 113–14

ulcers, 167–68
uterus
   to bind, 95–96
   hemorrhages of, 50–51
uveitis, 168

vacillating mind, 109
Vair, Leonard, 9, 11, 20, 26, 246, 248
varicose veins, 168–69
vein spasm, 169

venom, 125–27
vermin, charm against, 111–12
vertigo, 169
Villa Nova, Arnaldus de, 15–17, 19
voults, protection against, 231–33

warts
   to drive away, 170
   to get rid of, 170
   to heal yourself, 172
   to make disappear, 170, 172
   to make fall off, 170
   to make go away, 170
   to remove, 171
water dangers, protection against, 228
weapons, protection against, 240–41
weeping abscess, 34
Weyer, Johann, 9, 10, 12–13, 288
white spots, to cure, 69, 70, 104
whitlow, 172
witches
   protection from, 234–35
   protection of the house from, 254
wolf bites, 45
wolves, protection against, 228–29, 265
woman
   in labor, to protect, 209
   for nursing, 210
the word, power of, 8–9
worms
   against, 174–75
   charm against, 173–74
   to dry up, 174
   to rid an animal of, 175
   to rid a pig of, 176
   stomach, 173
   tooth, 172–73
wounds, benediction for, 176–78

zodiac man, 15–17